The Monocle Guide to Building Better Cities

For more information, please visit
gestalten.com

———

Bibliographic information
published by the Deutsche
Nationalbibliothek. The Deutsche
Nationalbibliothek lists this
publication in the Deutsche
Nationalbibliografie; detailed
bibliographic data is available
online at *dnb.d-nb.de*

MIX
Paper from
responsible sources
FSC
www.fsc.org FSC® C011712

This book was printed on paper certified
according to the standards of the FSC®

Edited by *Andrew Tuck*

Monocle editor in chief
and chairman: *Tyler Brûlé*
Monocle editor: *Andrew Tuck*
Books editor: *Joe Pickard*

———

Designed by *Monocle*
Proofreading by *Monocle*
Typeset in *Plantin & Helvetica*

———

Printed by *Offsetdruckerei Grammlich,
Pliezhausen*

Made in Germany

Published by *Gestalten*, Berlin 2018
ISBN 978-3-89955-503-5

© Die Gestalten Verlag GmbH & Co.
KG, Berlin 2018

Cover image:
Badi Oberer Letten, Zürich
by *Marvin Zilm*

CONTENTS

Introduction
What makes a city?

How we make better cities – places that deliver quality of life for all – is one of the most important issues of our times. Yet the debate can all too often get wrapped up in jargon or be made to sound like something that big business and powerful players should be left alone to tackle. That's not the way forward.

So how can we all feel part of our city's story – whether as a campaigner, architect, entrepreneur, rooftop urban farmer or simply someone who needs a good park for their children to play in? How can we ensure that the argument is less about projections into an unknown future and more about the here and now? And how can we show that, in the end, what makes us truly love a city is something complex, layered and gritty? Something that means that many supposedly state-of-the-art new cities, despite all the headlines they grab, will never win out over a historied Lisbon or Hong Kong.

Well, one way of pulling the focus back is by bringing together examples of best practice, inspiring stories and clever ideas from around the globe in one book: *The Monocle Guide to Building Better Cities*.

Since launching in 2007, MONOCLE as a magazine has kept a close eye on what makes cities tick: there's our annual Quality of Life ranking of the best cities to call home, as well as hundreds of interviews with mayors and urban visionaries. When we started Monocle 24 radio, one of the first shows we created was *The Urbanist* ("The show about the cities we live in"). Then there's our collection of more than 30 city guidebooks, each of which takes

time to look at the urban story. This, you can see, is important territory for us.

And after all these years we have come to some simple conclusions: that we can all make an impact on where we live; that we benefit from seeing what others have achieved; that small ideas often deliver more than grand plans; and that a lot of what's written about cities often fails to connect with most people.

While acknowledging that there are countless challenges, we want this book to be a celebration of what we can do – of the possibility for change. There are many stories that didn't make it onto the page but we hope the ones that did may get you to open your window, look across your city and think, "I can make a difference."

Thank you for reading, city lovers.

Andrew Tuck, editor

Manifesto
Make better cities

It's not always about the big idea, the tech solution or the grand plan. Sometimes all you need to make a better city is some humanity, a sense of scale and keen citizens.

Be wise, not smart:

The term "smart cities" is abused. What's the alternative – a dumb city? Advocates are often linked to a salesman at a Silicon Valley tech company. City halls have always collected information (or "big data") and tried to glean truths from it. Just because techies can now crunch the data quicker doesn't make it a change that should invoke evangelical tones. The wisest cities also focus on "small data" – the incidentals that actually make our lives better.

Buy a pot, some soil and a seed:

If you walk the streets of London or Kyoto you'll see houses where people have chosen to ignore the risk of vandalism and theft, and placed plants outside their homes, offices and shops. A small act of faith and a belief in investing in where they live. These acts soon multiply and deliver change.

Branch out:

Too many cities put saplings in the ground that struggle to take hold. Trees with handsome canopies provide places to rest under on sunny days and add a splash of colour to the concrete. Trees also act as living city branding: the gingko is Tokyo (especially when it dazzles yellow come autumn) and the London plane is the UK capital with its bristling summer flutter.

Fix up, look sharp:

One of the most exciting shifts of the past decade has been to see the bulldozer retired and replaced by teams of fixer-uppers. People are starting to understand that we should embrace what we have; that today's ugly is often tomorrow's beautiful; that in every city there is a potential High Line. This shift is also propelled forward by the understanding that the young and creative need cheaper, unreformed spaces for work and play. Squeaky clean can be seriously dull.

Fight for diversity:

Cities are the shelters and promoters of difference. Their vibrancy and security are built on a sense of being welcoming and we have to do more to protect that.

Join the dark side:

The past few years have seen lots of cities appoint night mayors; champions charged with protecting the night-time economy. Too many cities see bars and clubs as dens of sin (what's wrong with that?) and clamp down on licences. But the night is a generator of money – and taxes – and cities need to let their hair down. Plus jobs in bars and restaurants are often entry points to the world of work for new arrivals.

Make good maps:

We need to get people walking – it saves space on packed public transport and helps us stay lean. But folk often feel lost above ground not following a subway line. Make great maps, display sharp wayfinding and we'll take a hike.

Talk more:

From laptop-glued nomadic workers to seniors sent into a world of self-checkout and autopay, city-dwellers are feeling more and more isolated. Urbanism can help. Look at how a great Italian piazza works, throwing everyone together. The essence of the square can be used to engineer living rooms for the city with the aid of plants, seating, a news kiosk and an outdoor gym.

Say yes:

Cities need rules but most also get carried away with admonishing people for all sorts of modest rebellions against their regulations. How about letting people lock their bikes to the railings, walk on the grass and skateboard where they like?

Be tentative with tall living:

The solution to rising populations and a scarcity of land in many cities is to build ever taller towers – and we're only just beginning to grasp the consequences. Less-considered projects can lead to people feeling disconnected, detached and depressed. There are many for whom high living will never be the solution, so don't push them in the lift.

See the light:

Good lighting can work miracles. Illumination helps make cities feel safe and encourages a night-time economy. But it also, like trees, acts as city branding. The rooftop neon signs for banks and watch brands in Geneva are bright sparks of creativity, while the light show that is a Hong Kong tower come dusk is a flashy display of trading might.

Pass the pooch test:

Individuals are getting hitched later and later in life – or not at all – and living longer, often alone after a partner has passed away. That's why we see the rise of the pampered pet. Don't be sniffy about the trend or laugh at those who spend money on dog clothes. These animals are trusted companions who help owners navigate the stresses of city life. And cities need to embrace this fact. Dog runs, parks that make space for hounds and bars that say "yes, dogs welcome" are to be encouraged. A pooch-positive city is a potent force for wellbeing.

Be kinky:

There's something about the curve of a lane and the twists of a street that simply adds appeal. The grid is efficient; the tangle enchanting. We build straight to allow for traffic flow but as we embrace a more walkable city, we should enjoy being kinky. These snaking routes also deliver serendipity and surprise.

14

Account for all ages:

City-planners must cater for toddlers, seniors and everyone in between. As we look at housing and care solutions, we need to mix people where it's wise but also leave places of sanctuary for all too.

15

Respect your rivers:

In many cities, the connection with a river – the very reason that these metropolises were often established there – has been downplayed. Since the chugging, barging, boating glory of the 19th century, we've allowed our rivers to become cleaner but also underused. They're potential highways, places for leisure, pop-up beaches and spots for seeing life float by. Hats off to the likes of Seoul and Paris which have re-embraced their waterways.

16

Press for benches:

Cities often see public seating as an unnecessary cost, which speaks ill of their humanity. Benches allow a city to operate at a slower pace and provide homeless people with a place to rest. But we need more than neat rows of seats. Invest in deckchairs for parks come summer and chairs that can be moved to meet our needs.

17

Bust a move:

Many think of cycling as the panacea for all our ills and the private car as the devil's work. But there are plenty of parents with kids and older couples unable to saddle up who would disagree. And just because someone is on a bike, it doesn't mean that they're a hero – lots of our biker pals jump lights, smack into the unsuspecting and scream obscenities at anyone who gets in their way. As we rightly shift towards cleaner transport solutions, including the bike, we need a harmonious mix of mobility ideas.

18

Have faith in the crowd:

Many cities are experimenting with a crowdsourcing model to determine how some of their budget is spent. In places such as Paris and Madrid, the experience seems to have been mostly successful (Madrid says that when its citizens decide where the cash should go they are progressive, wise and sensible about budgets). We like these experiments but be wary – sometimes the mood of a crowd can be mean or reflect narrow concerns. But, in the end, it's important that we trust people and bring them into the process of governing.

19

But know when to say 'no' to the crowd:

Sometimes people power – or "participatory" urbanism – drags everything down to a homespun level. Too many "people's parks", for example, lack any aesthetic appeal. And asking everyone what they want is a recipe for banality. Know when to have faith in an architect or urban-planner, to let the experts determine the route.

20

Make some noise:

In many cities there's a creeping sense that all noise is bad – people object to the hum of a happy crowd at a bar, the sound of a carpenter working in his shop. But the city is not the countryside – and noise is to be lived with and even enjoyed (because the alternative is a grim silence).

Don't build to speculate:

London, for one, is a city scarred by projects that are designed to be "investment tools" rather than someone's home. Investors from Beijing to Moscow buy apartments as places to stash their cash when what the city aches for is affordable housing. Yes, welcoming some foreign money is good but the process can become bloated and grubby.

Meet and greet:

City halls are vital but too often their design makes them feel a little dull and removed from the everyday life of a city. Reimagine these spaces to be open to the public – with meeting rooms for anyone to book, cafés to visit and places to catch up on the local news. Civic buildings need to be a part of a city's metabolism.

Do the business:

Cities need the veins of trade running through them – it's what keeps people employed and paying their taxes. So embrace the business world – don't push companies beyond the city limits – and make your zoning flexible.

Don't hate the suburbs:

The suburbs have been demonised. They're seen as the home of a mumsy, drab set of people who ignore their city cores and have an unhealthy passion for the automobile. The suburbs are also synonymous with urban sprawl. In fact the best suburbs work well, functioning more as mini towns with their own retail and cultural hearts and often some playful architecture too. But they fail when they're not connected to good transport links. So while no one likes a flabby city, much can be done to embrace these misunderstood zones.

Be prepared:

Unfortunately we have to enlist urban design to protect us from terror. And that's best done as a first thought when planning, not as an add-on. Done well, planters that would block the routes of a hijacked lorry, or curbs that cannot be mounted, go unnoticed – until they're needed.

Be wary of bright paint:

If you decorate a favela home pink, or make the exterior of a run-down apartment block yellow, you may be making it look prettier for passers-by but you're not changing the lives of the people who live there. Poverty needs addressing with more than a paintbrush.

Keep an eye on the spray can:

Not all graffiti is art and actually it doesn't make a city a better place to live. But there are some works that have helped lift the spirits of a neighbourhood. The key is a sense of community involvement, a coalition of ambitions to make a splash.

Press on:

Many cities have lost their dedicated magazine or daily paper – but not all. And numerous radio stations still give a voice to a city's concerns. We must be alert to what we lose when a metropolis's media scene crumbles – a sense of knowing your community, its interests and needs.

Cast your vote:

This is the age of the mayor. Through organisations such as C40, city leaders are setting the pace on sustainability, civil rights and innovative governance. A mayor can have a greater impact on your life than your PM or president. So quiz candidates, get involved. And vote wisely.

33

Get high:

It's surprising how many planners and property owners still fail to grasp what could be done with their rooftops. Whether a football pitch on the peak of a Tokyo tower or a nightclub on the crown of a Beirut high-rise, there's a whole layer of our cities that's under-utilised. There are pioneers – urban farmers included – but too often we neglect the potential above us.

30

Channel your inner Jane Jacobs:

The celebrated American-Canadian was perhaps the first urbanist to seep into the public's mind. Her fight against Robert Moses in New York and his plans to carve a highway across Manhattan is now the stuff of legend. But there are many nascent Jane Jacobs among us and we need to champion them. Ordinary citizens can change their cities for the better.

34

Corner the market:

The proverbial corner shop has been reinvented in many city neighbourhoods and we salute these owner-run outposts. The best provide good food and essentials all within walking distance of your front door, take in deliveries, know the names of all the nearby tradesfolk and generally act as a community talking shop.

31

Go places:

Mayors should be encouraged to travel long haul, take part in conferences, meet contemporaries and be fired up with new ideas. Voters – don't be mean, get them the ticket.

35

Trust the temporary:

Pop-up shops may have become a cliché but pop-up urbanist interventions ought to be embraced. If a plot of land is going to lie empty for years, turn it into a temporary park. If a rooftop is going to waste, use it for a sunny hangout every summer. Flexibility adds to the creative flavour.

32

Be flexible:

The rapid rise of co-working and co-living spaces is affecting the look and feel of many cities. It's urged on by the changing nature of work and the desire for our lives to be acted out in a series of "cool" neighbourhoods. Some of what's being erected is corporate and chain-y but cities are going to be increasingly impacted by this move and will need to adjust their planning accordingly. The city will need to become ever more flexible.

Spin the globe. Pick a city. Drop in. What you'll discover are citizens and city halls, campaigners and the simply concerned, all facing the same tangle of problems. How do we make our city cleaner and safer? How do we deliver a better quality of life for the people who call this place home? How can we provide more housing and get people around the city with greater ease? While many of the challenges are universal, the solutions are not – and, just as important, neither are the resources and skill sets needed to fix, soothe and push forward.

This book is mostly about the people and places getting it more right than wrong; the projects and ideas that we can all take as benchmarks for success. And in this chapter we want to take you to cities that have become star turns at the urbanist game. Copenhagen is one such pin-up for global city-makers; it's even spawned its own city-making term, "Copenhagenisation". Over the following few pages we'll show you how the Danish capital got its act together to become a seat of inspiration – and also how, even here, there are hurdles on the road to nirvana.

As well as wealth and an interesting social contract (Danes simply believe in sharing resources and opportunity; it's the Nordic vibe), Copenhagen has the benefit of scale. With a population of just over a million people, its civic leaders don't face the challenges of, say, São Paulo or New York. So how do you run a megacity? Well, there are lessons to be taken from Tokyo on that score – and we'll reveal those too.

While we want to focus on the way forward, we're also going to take you to places where the challenges are grittier and progress is clearly slower (but where there are often other urban compensations). So, from well-oiled to occasionally creaky, here are 20 cities reshaping their futures with plans, schemes and citizen-led projects that you should know about.

I.

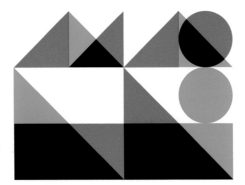

CITIES
IN FOCUS

1. Street life
Tokyo
Walkable neighbourhoods make this a liveable and vibrant megacity.

Hosting the 2020 Olympic Games has been Tokyo's excuse to embark on a citywide spruce up. Glass towers are appearing in place of old wooden homes and low-rise offices. New tunnels and rail lines are shortening travel times to the city's two international airports. Unsightly overhead utility lines are being moved underground and new bike lanes are being painted. Even taxi operators are revamping their fleets with a bulbous Toyota in a dark shade of indigo known as the JPN Taxi.

There's a strange dichotomy at work here. This is a city that operates on predictability. Trains run on time, packages get delivered when they're supposed to, blackouts rarely occur, crime is rare. But in Tokyo hardly anything stays the same for long. Everywhere you look giant cranes are altering the skyline. With so much in flux you might expect to find chaos but somehow order prevails.

The city has been in the midst of a tower-building spree since the early 2000s. It started in the Marunouchi business district and Roppongi and has spread to other areas. Toranomon, Ginza and Hibiya are the latest neighbourhoods to get state-of-the-art structures filled with shops and restaurants, spacious offices and upscale hotels and residences.

Commerce in Tokyo tends to be concentrated around railway stations, so it's big news that the city centre will have two new stations. But the scale of those projects pales in comparison to the 14-year makeover for Shibuya Station. When the rebuilding is finished in 2027, there will be new towers, rerouted tracks and a path along a resuscitated river.

There is hardly time to lament what's gone: the small, family-run rice sellers, tofu-makers and tatami mat shops that were once as common as convenience stores are now rare. There is, however, in pockets of the city, a backlash against disappearing street-level shops and the urge to build upwards. In the Togoshi neighbourhood, branding agency Owan, and Jo Nagasaka, of Schemata Architects have breathed new life into the traditional *shotengai* (commercial street) starting with Okomeya, a tiny shop selling rice balls.

Something similar is taking place in the Nezu area, to the east, where Soichiro Hirabayashi opened Vegeo Vegeco, a tiny *yaoya* (neighbourhood vegetable shop) with produce from organic farms and antique lamps and cedar display boxes dreamed up by Wonderwall designer Masamichi Katayama. Not far away, in Ueno, a developer has used a new mid-market hotel to highlight the metal, glass and kimono artisans who have been a mainstay of the neighbourhood for decades.

Tokyo officials would be wise to keep in mind this side of the city as they proceed with big urban projects. One scheme in particular springs to mind: the relocation of the much-loved Tsukiji fish market. The plan is to move the traders and wholesalers to the site of a former gas plant and redevelop the old property, with a new food theme park. What officials fail to grasp are the elements that made Tsukiji so popular and unique: the cramped wooden booths, the mind-boggling diversity of fish, the glimpse inside the inner workings of the world's biggest seafood market. In other words, the opposite of a sterile, hi-tech theme park.

Human scale:
The Daikanyama
neighbourhood is
home to Log Road,
a 220-metre-long
path along former
rail tracks, with shops
including a bakery

Make the moat of it: On early mornings and at weekends, the path around
the Tokyo Imperial Palace and its vast moat is a popular running route

25

2. Green light for change
Lisbon

From new parks to spruced-up squares, the city offers moments of escape.

Blue skies, sandy beaches, the crash of the surf. Lemon-yellow and pink houses on hillsides, intricately tiled palace façades and formidable ancient castles. Shoppers from Africa, China and Europe browsing boutiques on tree-lined avenues. The scent of grilled fish wafting on the breeze. Cold beers and caipirinhas. Welcome to Lisbon.

Blessed with a sunny climate and natural beauty (few European capitals have as many beaches on their doorstep), Lisbon also has the charm of a city that's individual. In a world where high streets barely vary from Brisbane to Berlin, Lisbon retains a unique streetscape. Thanks to a city council initiative protecting historic shops, tiny old spaces dedicated to everything from haberdashery to candles still exist. Small restaurants serve traditional dishes and wooden trams trundle up cobbled streets past fading palaces and grand theatres.

Lisbon also has remarkable social cohesion. To date there is no terrorist threat and anti-immigrant sentiments are few and far between, perhaps because until recently most immigrants came from former Portuguese colonies and shared a common language and cultural references. African, Indian and Asian music, food and dance play a large role in Lisbon's culture and its peoples add life and diversity to its streets.

Out to grass: Lisbon has more than doubled its green space since 2005 but it has also invested in restoring existing parks and gardens such as Alameda Dom Afonso Henriques Park. These verdant spots are being connected by a corridor that runs from the Monsanto Forest Park to the Tagus River, which in turn encourages cycling and walking. It's a good example of how multiple benefits can flow from one clever decision

Maat finish: The Museum of Art, Architecture and Technology (*see page 306*) has had a multitude of interesting urban impacts. It has helped to pull people back to the Belém neighbourhood, played its part in the reimagining of the river banks, become an icon overnight and triggered urban pride. Maat is a prime example of how a new cultural institution can change a city's global image (as, say, the Guggenheim did for Bilbao)

Lisbon is having its moment. Money is pouring in and the energy of the start-up culture has arrived. Young foreigners, particularly those whose jobs are freelance and don't necessitate a specific home base, are colonising the city. Shared workspaces such as Second Home – with its SelgasCano-designed interiors, featuring more than 1,000 plants and a client base ranging from hopeful tech entrepreneurs to established brands – are buzzing. Entrepreneurial locals are also cashing in with new restaurants and bars.

The Lisbon bank of the Tagus, ignored and a little desolate in the first decade of the century, is now a draw for locals and visitors alike. The Maat museum development has spearheaded a focus on the riverside. Access ways and bike paths are being installed and improved, food trucks are popping up alongside smart bars and there's a riverside rooftop swimming pool that you can access for a fee.

The linear silhouettes of cranes are a common sight in the city as property developers, many of them international, buy up and renovate old buildings. The city council's rules on maintaining historical façades keep the street view intact but behind the faded fascias everything is changing. Developers are gutting buildings to install modern necessities such as parking spaces and lifts; buyers are coming from abroad with cash in hand and property prices in the city are skyrocketing.

This gentrification of the historic city centre is bringing with it changes, some welcome, others less so. Dilapidated neighbourhoods are being refreshed but local residents are being pushed out as developers seek the rental returns that the short-term tourism market offers. The city's new cruise port welcomes two ships a day in the summer, disgorging more than 5,000 passengers. And the city is in danger of becoming overwhelmed by the swarm.

Grocery shops are turning into souvenir outlets and hardware shops into tequila bars. Locals no longer use the trams, as tourists queue for 40 minutes or more to ride one, relegating public transport to a Disney-style experience. Trains to the beach have become standing-room only as the council and government desperately play catch up, unable to match supply to demand. Lunchtime at the food market resembles half-time at a football match: queues snake from each stand; arguments break out over seating. Finding a table on a sunny terrace has become a distant dream, rubbish litters the plazas and bemused locals are choosing to live, shop and socialise outside the city centre.

Despite these issues, on the whole Lisbon is benefiting from tourism and gentrification. Unemployment in Portugal, at 8 per cent, is at its lowest in 13 years. The council coffers are healthy thanks to a flood of property sales tax; the economy is booming. No one doubts that there are issues that need to be addressed but, in the meantime, Lisbon's growing cosmopolitanism, wealth and energy is to be celebrated: preferably at a street party on a warm summer night with a sardine snack and red wine in hand.

3. Uncovering its secrets
Seoul

Lost rivers revealed, flyovers turned into parks, old buildings saved – and a soul rediscovered.

Seoul lost a few key parts of its identity during the 20th century and now the city is looking back in order to find what went missing. The South Korean capital is plagued by a bad pun: "Seoul has no soul". This wordplay was contrived as the city was rebuilt at breakneck speed in the decades following the Korean War (1950 to 1953). During these boom years, known as the "Miracle on the Han", Seoul transformed itself from a war-torn backwater into one of Northeast Asia's most vibrant and wealthy metropolises. The city's population rose to 10 million, it became home to world-class enterprises and is now an epicentre of pop-culture power.

But it somehow felt empty. Following the war, Seoul "lost its identity" says Seung H-Sang, who heads the firm IROJE and served as the local government's first city architect from 2014 to 2016. He explains that this "tragedy" occurred when Seoul attempted to emulate western, or rather US, ideals of urban development that focused on growth and expansion (and cars).

Well before Seoul became the capital of cosmetic surgery, it underwent a makeover of its own. Concrete apartment blocks and steel office towers obscured views of Seoul's surrounding mountains. Many of its streams and creeks, once the lifeblood of the city, were relegated to drainage canals or covered with asphalt. And thanks to the prowess of conglomerates such as Hyundai, cars and elevated highways became signifiers of South Korea's emergence as a modern nation. According to Seung, it was this inharmonious development that changed the city's natural

characteristics. To find what was lost during the years of rapid urbanisation and fill that void, Seoul is re-examining its recent history.

In the first two decades of the 21st century, Seoul has not only removed but also remodelled and repurposed artefacts of its industrial era to give residents of this densely populated city some much needed space in which to walk, relax and ride. One of the first relics of Seoul's gritty past to come down was an overpass that covered the Cheonggyecheon, a stream that once flowed through the ancient city. While no longer fed by natural springs, the 11km waterway now stretches from central Gwanghwamun to the Han River and is flanked by stone walkways.

The rebirth of the stream and its success as a reclaimed semi-natural space inspired the rehabilitation of several other forsaken waterways, including the Seongbuk Cheon and the Dorimcheon. It also led to a rethinking of how traffic flows throughout the city. No matter how aesthetically unpleasant they are, elevated highways were regarded as a means to reduce gridlock. But coupled with an increasing number of dedicated bus lanes and the city's continuously expanding surface and underground transportation systems, Seoul found that it could do away with some of these eyesores without creating havoc.

The Seoullo 7017, an overpass erected in 1970 to channel cars from one side of Seoul Station's adjacent railway yard to the other, was spared. Dutch design firm MVRDV led the renovation project that turned this dilapidated structure into a sky garden that features thousands of

plants, fauna and trees. The 1km-long Seoullo 7017 reaches 17 metres at its highest point and, via several off-ramps, connects to the train station, local businesses and Mount Namsan before sloping down into Namdaemun Market.

For Kim Young-joon, who served as Seoul's second city architect, the restoration of Seoullo 7017 in 2017 signalled a turning point for the capital's urban planning. "It's a new symbol that we are living in a different time," he says. A time that's greener and less dependent on cars.

Seoul now maintains 115 sq km of public parks and continues to purchase private property or acquire former industrial zones, which are converted into recreational spaces. A notable example is the Gyeongui Line Forest Park, a 6.3km stretch of formerly abandoned train tracks that by 2016 had become a tree-lined path that winds its way through residential neighbourhoods. Another is the Oil Tank Culture Park in Mapo, a hillside exhibition centre that consists of six vast tanks that once brimmed with crude oil when it was an oil depot decades ago.

But the largest addition of public land will come when Seoul officially acquires the Yongsan Garrison, a military base that for more than a century was home to both Japanese and then US forces. Spanning from the southern slope of Namsan to the Han River, swathes of this former base will be transformed into an urban park. Central Seoul is in need of more green space and integrating this land into the surrounding communities could help the city reclaim much of its lost nature – and assist with creating a new identity altogether.

Ups and downs: The city looked up to repurpose a 1km-long highway overpass into a sky garden called Seoullo 7017, overseen by Dutch practice MVRDV; it also dug deep to uncover the Cheonggyecheon waterway, paved over in the 1950s, that now provides an 11km-long pedestrian route (*bottom*)

4. Living life on the grid
Barcelona
This revolutionary hotspot is also nicely square when it comes to urbanism.

Barcelona has fire in its belly. Rebellious, revolutionary and reeling for a fight, revolt is such a regular feature of the city's history that a contrarian spirit has signed itself into the urban credo.

In 1909, when a royal decree imposed conscription on the working class, the masses responded with a wave of arson attacks against churches and convents, earning the city the nickname *La Rosa de Foc* (The Rose of Fire). More than a century later, this fiery epithet is still worn as a badge of pride. Barcelona doesn't like being told what to do.

The legacy of the 1992 Olympics is lauded as one of the world's best examples of transformative urbanism but Barcelona was re-imagining its cityscape well before the Games. In the mid-1800s, when industrial growth spurred on by the textile sector saw a surge in both prosperity and population, engineer Ildefons Cerdà was enlisted to rework the city grid. Cerdà's plan to improve quality of life was realised with the construction of the ambitious Eixample district (literally "expansion").

The 520 new city blocks erected radically altered the city. By the end of the century, seven peripheral villages had been absorbed into the metropolis. Guided by his own studies on the living habits of the working class, Cerdà considered the social benefits of public parks and ensured that access to food shops and markets, education and health services were evenly distributed on his blueprints. Cerdà published his own findings in two books, pioneering a new discipline and coining the term "urbanisation" as far back as 1867.

The city has a timeworn tendency for experimentation. In the 19th century, proletariat passions saw factories razed and ad-hoc barricades burnt with such frequency that authorities started to widen streets as a cautionary measure (making it harder to build barricades). At the turn of the century, the resurgent identity politics of *Catalanisme* spurred architects such as Antoni Gaudí and Lluís Domènech i Montaner to embellish the streetscape with the whimsical extravagance of *modernisme*. Not to mention the infamous two-year period in the 1930s of anarchist rule.

This deep-seated inclination to go against the grain has also nurtured the city's desire to impress. When international tourism began taking off in the early 20th century, a city-led initiative recycled fixtures from edifices demolished elsewhere in the city into the so-called Gothic Quarter, a stylised ode to an earlier era. Nearly a century later, the Olympics seemed to round out the vision. Not only did the bold works reconnect the city to its waterfront, they also attracted legions of visitors.

One of the symbols of the city's constant quest for urban improvement is the Plaça de les Glòries Catalanes – first envisaged as the heart of Cerdà's city expansion plan. The intersection of important roads, often referred to as just Glòries, has long suffered from the oscillating priorities of politicians. A new design museum resembling a stapler was erected on its edge; the age-old open-air flea market was crowned with a futuristic stainless-steel awning; and a network of traffic tunnels will, hopefully, turn the car-clogged roundabout into a park.

Paradoxically, the pursuit of improvement has become a source of friction: with millions of tourists flooding the city each year, residents have rallied together to reclaim their food markets from gentrification and fight rising rents. This same incendiary spirit has shaped and shaken Barcelona's streets for centuries. Here, the city's success has long rested on its residents' flair for making themselves heard.

Square deal: The grid network prevalent in much of Barcelona served its citizens well by delivering a considered mix of greenery and well-proportioned housing. But the city is now investing in new parks and gardens and replanting courtyards as it attempts to deliver leafy corridors and take back street space from car traffic

5. Breaking the rules
Beirut
Out of chaos comes a city that has both urban thrills and lessons in resilience.

Like all great cities, there's something intangible about Beirut that makes it so addictive. Yes, the food is fantastic – from the hole-in-the-wall za'atar-crusted *manouche* pastry to the extravagant multicourse mezze dinners. The balmy Mediterranean climate doesn't hurt either, nor does the extensive coastline that hosts sun-worshippers by day and clubbers by night (and also serves as a major source of public space in the city). The art scene is more vibrant than ever, with new galleries popping up every month, and the international success of Beirut Design Week has given a boost to the creative industries.

But at the base of all this are the people. It's the individuals who make life liveable in a city where public services are almost entirely absent. Recycle Beirut, for example, was set up to find an alternative response to the rubbish crisis while the government continued to rely on makeshift landfills; it's now growing on average 10 per cent a month and employing Syrian refugees. The Chain Effect, an NGO that advocates for two-wheeled transport, has created a grassroots movement that has gained genuine momentum, with bike-hire shops and embryonic cycling lanes now a part of the cityscape. Despite municipal reluctance, activists managed to re-open the city's biggest park, Horsh Beirut, to the public after years of campaigning.

There's a lot more that could be done. For starters, park and ride schemes outside the city coupled with a better bus network would reduce traffic, pollution and road rage in the centre. A coherent urban-planning strategy would also preserve the city's considerable architectural heritage. Individual action is laudable but it can only patch up the city so much.

Anything can happen: For good and bad, Beirut is a city where rules are broken and pleasure is key – as seen at the Saint Georges Hotel swimming pool and with young divers on the Corniche (*left*)

6. Shifting down a gear
New York

The city that once never slept has learned to cycle, walk and kick back.

New York is hardly unique when it comes to impossibly tall skyscrapers huddled together in an urban core. And yet there's always something hypnotic about looking down on Manhattan from the air, no matter how many hundreds of times you've done it before (dawn and dusk are best, as the buildings twinkle in the half-light).

Perhaps it has something to do with being able to ponder just how small the island is, Lego-like down there at sea level. Or perhaps it's because up in the sky is the only time Gotham ever feels truly tethered and tame.

New York will never be everyone's cup of tea. It can take time to tune in to its frenetic tempo and can often leave visitors from more sedate metropolises yearning to get back to the quiet of suburbia. The Big Apple is blinkered pavement stomping – oversized iced coffee in hand. It's wailing police sirens and fire trucks; it's the constant honking of car horns a millisecond after a light has turned to green. It's potholes and construction. Sometimes, too, it can feel like it has time-travelled from another era with its biblical-plague medley of bed bugs, cockroaches and rats that scurry about the subway.

And yet the glory of New York is in the mix. It's somehow both a developed and developing world. It's cosmopolitan, international and about as European as any US city gets, not just because of the walking and the public transport but also because of the Italians, Greeks, Irish and Poles who have left their mark on the city. Yet New York is also about bagels and lox, US flags and trademark post-9/11 resilience. It can be tough and expensive, sure, but being from the city is a badge that even the taxi driver with the thickest of foreign accents wears with pride.

Park it: The Hunter's Point South Waterfront Park in Queens *(right and overleaf)* was built on old industrial land. It was transformed by park designers at Thomas Balsley Associates and Weiss/Manfredi alongside Arup. With a special emphasis on sustainable design, the park also provides a way of connecting bordering neighbourhoods; Pritzker Prize-winning architect Thom Mayne designed 41 Cooper Square *(below)*

"Other places are diverse, maybe even more diverse [than New York]," says Daniel Doctoroff, a deputy mayor for economic development under Michael Bloomberg's tenure. "But I don't think the notion that everyone here 'belongs' is naive."

New York has travelled a long way since the dystopian *Taxi Driver* era of the 1970s, when you couldn't use the subway at night for fear of being mugged and the city teetered on the edge of bankruptcy. As New York has cleaned up its act, there have been plenty of people who have hankered after some of the lost grit: the Studio 54 glamour with all its freewheeling; the cheap rents that encouraged artistic creativity; the time before gentrification.

That rose-tinted vision of the past does have a degree of merit. But it also fails to show the other side of the coin: the reasons why tourists want to visit its monuments and Americans from elsewhere in the country still migrate to New York to "make it". Los Angeles, Nashville and Denver may tick lots of boxes but New York is still the place where international businesses and financial organisations want to have a foothold; it's also home to arguably the best media sector in the world. And perhaps most importantly of all, it's now very safe. In 2017 the number of murders for the year dropped below

300 for the first time, with the per capita rate at its lowest in nearly 70 years. New York continues to shape-shift. If the High Line redefined urban planning and ways of regenerating neighbourhoods, the Hudson Yards mega-project on the west side of Manhattan, the eventual clean-up of the Gowanus Canal in Brooklyn and the ongoing development of the Williamsburg waterfront promise to keep redrawing the map. The danger is that the high prices and the onward march of the developers slowly erase its character, turn New York bland and that the mom-and-pop stores, niche music shops and the alternative bars continue to trickle away (as many of them already have) in favour of watermelon radish-sprinkled dishes and high-rise views.

Yet for the naysayers who protest that New York is predictable, they forget that spontaneous conversations and odd encounters do still happen. Those who claim that the Big Apple has no quality of life (apartments are tiny and kitchens even smaller, it's true) forget that you can eat and drink just about anything, anywhere, any time you want.

And they forget, too, that you can cycle to the beach in summer when the freezing winter suddenly switches to intense heat. This city may be cynical, noisy and brash, and it may be highly flawed, but we wouldn't want it any other way.

Pace changer: The transformation of an old elevated rail track on Manhattan's West Side into a linear park is a global benchmark for the reuse of existing – but unused – infrastructure. Its success is down to the quality of the project and the fact that it has captured the public's imagination with its ability to bring people together and offer a fresh perspective on the city

7. Trading places
Bangkok

In this steamy merchant hub you need to create cool places to gather.

Bangkok is like an unruly but gifted child. The more you try to control and regulate it, the more it goes its own way. Officially, the core population is eight million but most observers say it's closer to ten, and far more if you count the urban sprawl that fans out from the city limits to cover what's known as the Bangkok Metropolitan Region. But whether you live in a pricey riverside condo or a suburban prefab, Bangkok somehow manages to accommodate its ever-growing population.

In efforts to preserve or redevelop the city, successive governments have come up with a raft of ambitious development plans. The latest schemes include the extension of urban transit networks and the revitalisation of areas around the teeming Chao Phraya River and Chinatown, the nerve centre of old Bangkok. New MRT subway lines and BTS stations are opening up areas that

were once only reachable through traffic-choked streets.

There is also a programme of 250 urban-renewal projects; implemented by 2032, they'll mark the city's 250th anniversary. The latest stage in the Bangkok Metropolitan Administration's ambitious regeneration scheme ranges from smartening up inner-city parks to improving public transport.

Architecture, like urban development, is supposedly strictly regulated in Bangkok, officially limiting foreign architects to the roles of "advisers". Even so, futuristic new structures are growing like bamboo and the city is dotted with buildings designed by local and international architects such as Ole Scheeren of Germany, the mind behind the mixed-use skyscraper MahaNakhon, and the UK's Amanda Levete, lead architect of the glossy retail and hotel complex Central Embassy.

Indeed shopping malls are a fact of life in Thailand and have evolved into a particularly fine art in Bangkok. From Central Embassy, Siam Center and EmQuartier to the gleaming, riverside Iconsiam, each shopping centre has developed a distinctive personality all aimed at providing something for everyone and all delivering air-conned spaces where many young people seek their entertainment and conduct their social life away from their families.

Outside these cooled spots there are stalls selling noodles and *som tam* (green papaya salad) and motorbike taxis that still crowd street corners, ferrying passengers around for a relative pittance. Gracious colonial-era buildings co-exist with ramshackle wooden *khlong* (canal) dwellings and gleaming new condominiums. And yet there is a new sense of order in Bangkok. Food stands have, controversially, been herded into designated eating areas and those motorbike taxi riders now sport orange vests and photo IDs.

Soaring tourism accounts for some of the city's momentum. Thailand keeps its pole position with tourist hordes led by newly affluent Chinese tour groups. Chinese tourists feel particularly comfortable in Bangkok, not least because an estimated 30 to 35 per cent of the city's population is of Chinese origin, far more than the national figure of 14 per cent, reflecting the long history of Chinese migration to the kingdom.

The city has suffered some well-publicised setbacks in recent times, including coups, riots, terrorist attacks and natural disasters. From each, Bangkok has rebounded with boisterous aplomb, reinforcing the old but still relevant term "Teflon Thailand".

Escape routes: Bangkok traffic can be hellish and in this vast steamy city telling people to cycle is not a solution. But taking the elevated BTS trains or a boat on the Chao Phraya River lets you dodge the chaos (and see spots where campaigners are defending and restoring old warehouses)

8. Develop your core strength
Melbourne

The transformation of the formerly neglected laneways is a triumph.

A rhetoric that often plagues conversation about Australian cities is the comparison between Melbourne and Sydney. This need to pit one against the other feels irrelevant and acts as a disservice to both. While critics and outsiders busy themselves with who has the best flat white or biggest cultural pull, most Melbourne residents get on with their day, unperturbed by clickbait-touting headlines. It's this unique sense of self that's perhaps most seductive about the city.

This city has long built on its identity, from part of the indigenous Kulin nation to a gold rush town flushed with cash and now a migrant destination with a culturally diverse population. Modern-day Melbourne boasts a population that heralds from some 200 countries and speaks more than 260 languages, and this growth spurt is showing no signs of slowing. The city is expanding faster than it has at any other point in its history and the population that in 2018 teetered around five million is set to reach eight by 2050.

It's a prospect that has forced local government to improve transport networks and think about sustainable housing solutions. Work has begun on a AU$10.85bn (€6.86bn) underground metro tunnel (due to open in 2025), which will be a welcome addition in this car-obsessed country. Heavy investments have also been made into developing affordable homes to combat the increasingly pricey property market. Another forward-thinking approach is the introduction of regulations that help protect small-business owners and late-night licensees. It was this brand of policy-making that reinvigorated a then-stale CBD back in the 1990s.

During the 1980s, the centre of town fell victim to the "doughnut effect". Come evenings and weekends, the CBD was devoid of residents and visitors, and shops and restaurants rolled down their shutters. A central city-planning review led by city council and state government in the late 1990s sought to rectify this. Changes included more relaxed alcohol-licensing laws, protection for live-music and late-night venues and subsidising studio rent for artists.

Today the laneways and major streets in the centre are full of restaurants, shops and galleries that open in the evenings and weekends. There's also been a spike in the number of residents. It's a move that's paid off, with the city becoming more vibrant, arty and edgy. It also characterises Melbourne's commitment to its superlative cultural outposts and the ease with which it manages to layer this offering. In both the central zigzagging laneways and the patchwork of surrounding neighbourhoods, makers and indie bookshops shimmy up to buzzy bars, music venues and cutting-edge galleries.

It's little wonder then that this outward-facing state capital regularly tops international lists of most liveable cities. And while the city expands in leaps and bounds, the resident Melburnians hold fast to their laid-back lifestyle, concerning themselves more with enjoying their community rather than fuelling an indefinable debate for Australia's top city.

Back street boys (and girls):
Melbourne's laneways are a lesson in how to reinvigorate a city core

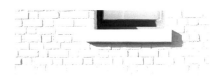

9. Leading by design
Copenhagen
The laboratory whose big ideas make it an urban powerhouse.

In the archives of the Museum of Copenhagen there are photographs of the city centre from the 1950s. In one, the main shopping street, Strøget, is choked with Opels and Wolseleys; a woman has been forced to dismount from her bike to thread her way through the traffic. Another shows Rådhuspladsen, the city hall square, looking like a scaled-up version of the traffic brain-puzzler Rush Hour. Within 10 years, though, everything had changed for the Danish capital. In 1962, Strøget was pedestrianised, one of the first capital city high streets to rid itself of vehicles. The transformation of Copenhagen to a city where, today, 41 per cent of people commute to work by bicycle, despite the dispiriting Danish weather, had begun.

Bike-mania is only one aspect of this city's human-centric urban planning. Families and younger people have been encouraged to stay in the city centre thanks to the affordable childcare, parks and sports facilities. High-rise buildings and large supermarkets have been restricted, which helps keep things to a habitable scale. There is excellent student accommodation and plenty of life on the streets. The Copenhagen calendar is filled with festivals and events, and these days there is even great food to be had. It feels like a democratic city, one in which the locals feel they have a stake and a say.

Through all of this, with Copenhagen you get the sense that most of the time there are humans working in city hall rather than accountants. Budget efficiencies and the profit motive take a back seat to questions of how to make public spaces attractive, liveable and often surprisingly joyous places to be, as with the pioneering harbour swimming pools, or the vast man-made beach and lagoon on Amager. More recently, the waterfront has been made more accessible by a couple of playful harbour bridges. And there is the radical urban park, Superkilen. None of these were farmed out to cookie-cutter,

High flyer: Stig Lennart Andersson of SLA Architects considered the success of the High Line in the planning of this elevated public thoroughfare that opened in 2017. The design delivers myriad viewpoints along its route

lowest-bidder contractors and all, in their way, contribute to Denmark's extraordinary design heritage.

The secret of Copenhagen's success lies in a very Scandinavian pragmatism. There is a balance here which means that cars are still very much a part of the city-centre mix; contemporary architecture abuts much-loved 18th-century institutions; and the demands of 21st-century living harmonise with what is still a medieval city at heart. Copenhagen juggles the demands of commerce with the needs of its inhabitants, while the privatisation of public spaces has been largely avoided. Sure, the new metro expansion is making a hell of a mess but, once it's finished, we all trust that those historic city streets and cobbled squares will be returned to their former glory.

The metro project is one way in which Copenhagen is preparing for the future. The population of the city continues to grow – a measure of its success, of course. Brownfield sites are being developed but there is still immense pressure on the nature at the city's edges. Will the city expand outwards or upwards? That is the question. (The answer is that it should expand to other cities in Denmark but try telling that to young Danes.)

Like all modern capitals these days, Copenhagen has a carbon-neutral target, in this case for 2025. There is all the usual talk of smart cities and sustainability but, unlike most other capitals, here it's not just talk. Scandinavians tend to do what they say they are going to do. And so the communal district heating systems are making more efficient use of record-high levels of wind-generated electricity; the Danes are enthusiastic recyclers; and they eat more organic produce than anyone else too.

One man more than any other has been associated with the transformation: architect Jan Gehl. He loves to show people the aforementioned 1950s traffic photos. "I have, as a Copenhagener, this funny feeling that every morning when I wake up I am quite sure that the city is a little bit better than it was yesterday," he says. "And I think it's wonderful to live in a city where you can have that feeling."

Make a splash: There's a sense of considered joyfulness in the projects being delivered in Copenhagen and a reconnection with the water that's admirable

10. Working on many levels
Hong Kong
*High-rise towers and sky-scraping
paths give an elevated city experience.*

Most of us have a specific image of Hong Kong in our minds: harbourside skyscrapers topped with advertising hoardings for banks and branded electronics. Neon-lit Hong Kong is well known but the city (or semi-autonomous region of China) is not all business. Sandy beaches and luscious green hills are both within easy reach of downtown. City and country come together in this concrete jungle and there is far more to Hong Kong than first meets the eye.

Part of the fun of living in Hong Kong, and a major source of frustration for visitors, is learning how to get from A to B through a labyrinth of subways, elevated walkways and department-store shortcuts. Hong Kong's hilly terrain, combined with an efficient use of land, has created a vertical city that exists on multiple levels and is primarily accessible by lift. Going up and down elevators in innocuous buildings rewards the inquisitive with a different menu of bars, restaurants and retail to that found at street level. Escalators operate outdoors as well as inside. The most famous example carries office workers from Central up to their apartments in the Mid-Levels, a residential neighbourhood of matchstick towers that appear to perch precariously on the side of a hill.

Hong Kong's total land mass, made up of the Kowloon Peninsula and more than 260 islands on the southern coast of China, could fit within Greater London. Technically there is sufficient space to house 7.5 million people but only 25 per cent of land is developed and some 40 per cent comprises protected country parks. Most residents want to keep it that way; hiking in the mountains is a weekend pastime that unites Hong Kongers of all ages and nationalities.

Hence the need to build upwards. Hong Kong has more skyscrapers than any other city and most of the population live in high-rises. Many residential towers are clustered together in wall-like new towns that continue to expand according to a colonial-era blueprint.

The upshot of this high-density living is a very efficient urban transport model. More than 90 per cent of trips in 2016 were made using a public transport mix of buses, minibuses, ferries, trains and trams. The "backbone" of the city is the mass-transit railway, or MTR. The government-controlled company doubles as one of the city's major property developers. Homes, offices and department stores are built above new stations, allowing residents to commute without stepping outside. This so-called rail-plus-property model sees property revenues ploughed back into the transport network, keeping fares low and increasing coverage.

Hong Kong's population has swelled by 25 per cent since the former British colony was returned to Chinese rule in 1997. Further growth is expected over the next two decades as residents enjoy one of the highest average lifespans in the world. To provide the public services to sustain this growth, from housing to hospitals, city-planners have leaned heavily on land reclamation and urban regeneration. The West Kowloon Cultural District – a collection of museums, galleries and concert venues that, when complete, will crown the city's renaissance as an Asian arts hub – sits on 40 hectares of land that used to be at the bottom of Victoria Harbour. Meanwhile, to the east, a new CBD is rising out of the old industrial neighbourhood of Kwun Tong, a former factory area that emptied out in the 1980s when production moved to China.

However, as space becomes more scarce, existing land is being made to work harder. On Wednesday evenings, thousands of people pack the stands

of the Happy Valley Racecourse to bet on the horses. But every other night of the week the land inside the racetrack is used by football, rugby and running clubs (Hong Kong's myriad public leisure facilities, from all-weather AstroTurf to outdoor swimming pools, makes it easy to get moving). All the while, beneath the horses' hooves and the hockey boots, a gigantic stormwater drain, opened in 2017, protects the residential neighbourhood from flooding during heavy downpours. Future possibilities for freeing up space above ground include developing the land underneath major parks.

The city government owns most of the undeveloped land in Hong Kong and, as a result, it's the dominant force in urban planning. Land parcels are sold off (often via the MTR) for huge premiums to powerful property developers that are controlled by a handful of tycoons. In turn, sky-high property prices keep the government flush with cash to spend on shiny new infrastructure.

At the same time, social tensions caused by unaffordable property are compounded by a projected housing shortfall. The need to free up more land is necessitating more controversial development decisions that edge closer to the city's green lungs. As such, the government has sought public input

for the first time. Additional land reclamation tends to get the broadest support, provided it's conducted outside Victoria Harbour.

One of the largest reclamation projects currently underway will house a third runway at the airport. The world's busiest air cargo hub is a commercial juggernaut in Hong Kong as well as an important lifeline, because the city cannot feed itself despite its abundant greenery. Fresh food is flown into the city from all over the world every day, another modern logistical marvel of this urban oasis that is largely invisible to the more than 70 million passengers who fly in and out each year.

Get high: High-rise Hong Kong perches across steep terrain, delivering a network of walkways that allow for swift traffic-dodging navigation

11. Moving story
Los Angeles
A place so closely linked with the car is discovering a new mobility star turn.

Los Angeles is a city of cities, interconnected but utterly distinct. Koreatown alone has a population roughly the size of Hartford, Connecticut (125,000) and that's only a tiny sliver – albeit a blooming one.

A few kilometres east, Downtown is also undergoing a renaissance (not so long ago it would have been no-go at night); New York's NoMad Hotel is here in full swing and restaurants hum with business. Across town, beachside neighbourhoods such as Santa Monica and Venice offer an entirely different style of living. Perhaps the only thing binding them is that southern Californian golden-hour light.

It can be difficult for any visitor to get a sense of Los Angeles as a whole, not just because of the geographical sprawl and fragmentation but also because it's almost impossible to extricate the city from all that is said about it. Los Angeles, as author and architect Michael Sorkin famously claimed, "is probably the most mediated town in America, nearly unviewable save through the fictive scrim of its mythologisers".

Except that today's LA is everything and nothing like the images you've been fed. Yes, there are still cafés populated by tan-limbed Hollywood species but the city is also far more urban, increasingly less car-centric and (gasp) intellectual. So how do you get an authentic glimpse?

For starters, ditch your car. Although the city's urban configuration has long existed to serve the automobile, massive investment is being poured into public transport. In May 2016, a light-rail line linking Downtown to coastal Santa Monica opened. Several months later, Angeleno voters approved a small sales tax that will fund $120bn (€103.2bn) in transport projects over the next 40 years. That aforementioned Santa Monica line may be a bit slow (roughly 50 minutes

from Downtown to the beach) but a thrilling slate of major projects loom, with many due for completion by the time the city hosts the Olympics in 2028.

The boom is also cultural: several new museums have opened in recent years, including The Broad in Downtown, with its honeycomb-like Diller Scofidio + Renfro-designed building and the cachet to pull in major attractions. A Renzo Piano-designed Academy Museum of Motion Pictures will offer cinephiles set designs, costumes and props spanning Hollywood history. And across town, film-maker George Lucas's Lucas Museum of Narrative Art has broken ground in Exposition Park.

Los Angeles is changing and it's set to change even more. But quality-of-life issues still plague the city. LA's affordable-housing crisis shows no sign of relenting without serious intervention and the city's homelessness problem has reached epidemic proportions.

And yet the city presses on with its civic transformation. By 2026, the subway under Wilshire Boulevard will finally run all the way to the Westside, allowing commuters to zip below one of the city's main, traffic-clogged arteries from Downtown to Beverly Hills or Century City in less than 30 minutes.

A watershed moment came in April 2018 when it was announced that long-time *Los Angeles Times* architecture critic Christopher Hawthorne would leave his post for a newly created position as LA's "chief design officer". Hawthorne operates from within the mayor's office to raise the quality of public architecture and urban design across the city, a role that signals the city's commitment to a new kind of visual coherence and focus on design. And the role isn't just new for LA; only a handful of cities around the world have similar positions, though more will likely follow in the future.

Fresh perspectives: The image of LA is morphing as the city successfully develops a stronger cycling and public transport culture and reshapes Downtown with projects such as The Broad museum by architects Diller Scofidio + Renfro (the firm behind The Shed, a cultural space in New York's Hudson Yards). The Broad also includes a vast public plaza

Revived: Work on Grand Park in Downtown LA (*left*) has turned it into a great public asset and a cornerstone of the area's renaissance. Host to numerous public events, its careful planting and addition of specially commissioned moveable seating have made it a much-used space by everyone from children to office workers; Venice Beach (*above*) provides space for skateboarders but sometimes these offerings need to work for a broader demographic

12. On the move
London

As the capital expands, how can it deliver quality of life for everyone?

It's not very fair. How can you compare nimble, small cities such as a Copenhagen or Zürich, both of which can navigate with speed the brisk currents of urban change like well-crewed dinghies, with a slow-to-turn supertanker such as London? Not fair but everyone does it. So, first the bad headlines: London is less safe than Helsinki, recycles less than Munich and will fleece you when you go hunting for affordable housing. It's not that city hall, the police and the citizen champions aren't there or trying. It's just that once gang crime takes off or foreign investor capital floods the market it can take years to get everyone manoeuvred into place to find a remedy.

But out of the chaos, turmoil and strained resources, good things happen. And the energy that comes from living among eight million people is of value too. Megacities may struggle with mobility but we forgive them if they deliver on opportunity, creativity and thrills. And London does that.

First, take a step back – in vantage point and time. To understand the urban wealth of London you have to realise that, despite rampant changes, so much of the city still dances to a song composed long ago. Many roads still follow paths laid down by the Romans, Regent's Park got its name in 1811 but has been a park since the Middle Ages,

and the great museums that dominate South Kensington were gifted by the Victorians. Even London's suburbs were a response to the ambitions of 19th and early 20th-century engineers, who pushed past the city's fringes with tendrils of rail and underground train lines. The gifts and decisions of long forgotten elders and kings still impact how we live today.

Yet while a walk (or run, or game of rugby) in Regent's Park on a Sunday morning may be one of those moments that make people feel lucky to be here, this city needs a new narrative, or at least a new chapter. So what will it be?

Successive mayors push for a broad vision of better public realm, more people on bicycles, more affordable housing and protecting the "green belt" around the city. But they can only fully deliver with the help of central government, powerful private players and Londoners themselves.

So, yes, the city is cycling more (even if the cycle culture is too male, fast-moving and shout-y). Yes, there is a push for more affordable homes – but the need is so huge that it will never be fully met. In the meantime, big ventures are being delivered that are reshaping the city. The vast subterranean Crossrail project will change how you traverse the city from west to east and is triggering new housing (and quite a

Route canal: Former industrial land behind King's Cross Station has been redeveloped with new offices, homes and retail projects. Despite being a largely private endeavour the area has quickly integrated into the city's life thanks to inventive urban projects such as this canalside seating

bit of hard-to-control gentrification) wherever it pokes its head out with a new station. New mixed-use projects along the southern bank of the Thames (such as Nine Elms in Battersea) are delivering walls of towers. Yet, while this is done in the name of density, there are a couple of problems: too often homes are bought by investors with no intention of moving in and some of what is being erected could have gained from better architectural teams.

But it's also good to look at the transformation of the city's East End. Over the past 20 years a trickle of projects has become a flood, shifting the whole focus of London. While some protest at the "hipsterisation" of neighbourhoods such as Hoxton, Hackney and Shoreditch, there have been many changes for the better too – from new markets and workshops to nightlife and sport. And the best of the changes has often happened in an organic way (we're not just talking vegetables). The pull to the east was also accelerated by the hosting of the London Olympics here, and there have been positive attempts at managing the legacy, with the park set to become an important cultural district with outposts for key museums and theatres, and arts education too.

Look too at the makeovers of Old Street, King's Cross, and Elephant and Castle. Now scrubbed up, connected.

So while you can carp about its failings, the city is still a place with incredible cultural institutions, a diversity to be celebrated and a history and texture that enriches lives.

Meanwhile up there on the tanker's bridge, the assorted crew from the mayor's office and big business steer this beast called London. Even at full steam they may struggle to manoeuvre it through the storms ahead but London will make it. This is a city that has been burnt down, bombed flat and attacked at every turn – it has a phoenix power that appears unwavering. And that's why, in the end, so many people are determined to call London home.

Sensing spaces (clockwise from top left):
The Hayward Gallery, which opened in 1968, was a pioneer on the south bank of the Thames; view of St Paul's Cathedral from the new Bloomberg building; cafés have taken over disused railway arches in London Fields

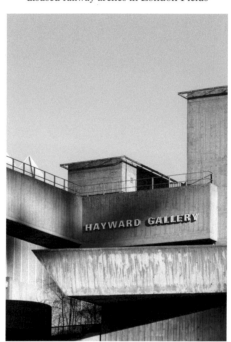

Get social (clockwise from left): The Tate Modern's Turbine Hall acts as a London square –
a place to gather, sit and maybe take in some art; the Millennium Bridge engineered by Arup;
Columbia Road Flower Market

13. Top-down urbanism
Moscow
The Russian capital has delivered a fast and furious urban makeover.

Perhaps nothing gets at both the promise and frustration born from Moscow's ambitious urban-improvement programme like the evening known in the capital as the "night of the long shovels". On one night in February 2016, without any warning or announcement, municipal agencies demolished about a hundred of the kiosks that had cropped up around metro entrances and along major thoroughfares over the years. They had become an eyesore and an impediment to city beautification efforts, a vestige of the free-for-all commercial sprawl of the 1990s.

They were torn down literally overnight, by executive decree from Moscow's mayor, Sergey Sobyanin, a figure close and relatively loyal to Vladimir Putin – but also with a vision for his city that often goes against the Kremlin's larger policy priorities. Under Sobyanin, Moscow has become a more liveable, even European, capital, with a bike-sharing programme and a thriving restaurant scene.

Sobyanin has tried, with limited success, to combat Moscow's epic traffic jams by introducing paid parking and expanding the public transport network. New metro stops – even whole lines – open with the regularity and speed that other European cities could only hope for.

The "night of the long shovels" shows both the potential and pitfalls of such city management. Sobyanin can act swiftly and decisively (narrowing the number of car lanes in the centre and widening pedestrian zones, for example) but he does so without much civic debate or public input. But independent, opposition-minded figures with seats in Moscow's district councils may be able to put some healthy pressure on that model.

Pacemaker: The city has employed both local and international talent to quickly create a Moscow that's more chilled than many would expect. There's even time to sunbathe in the chaise longues in Neskuchny Garden come summer (*above*)

14. It's all in the mix
Berlin
Being 'poor but sexy' is over and the capital now has a new global strength.

One of the oldest quips in Berlin, more tired even than jabs at the city's airport fiasco, is about the Wedding neighbourhood. *"Der Wedding kommt!"* it says, predicting the imminent rise in standing (and property prices) in one of Berlin's poorer neighbourhoods. But for many years now Wedding has stubbornly refused to do anything of the sort. Yes, small pockets have been cleaned up and embellished to attract middle-class residents. But on the whole, and despite its convenient location just north of Mitte and close to the central train station and Tegel airport, the district has resisted attempts to make it fashionable.

The question is, how long can it hold out? Rising rents and its maligned twin, gentrification, are today the issues overshadowing everything else in Berlin. A city grown accustomed to plenty of cheap space has had to grapple with changes to its way of life. Over the past 20 years, the population of the city-proper has climbed to 3.58 million. Of course, that's still a far cry from its pre-Second World War count, when the city had more than four million residents and was notorious for its cramped and unsanitary living conditions. But it's still enough to have caused something of a reckoning.

One of the characteristics that makes Berlin so attractive is its abundance of public space. It may be the city with the second-highest population density in Germany after Munich but the buildings lining its wide pavements are rarely higher than five stories, only a handful of the 2,500-odd public parks close at night and the city's playgrounds are the object of international envy. Plus, thanks to

Berlin's structure, with its many varied boroughs rather than one city centre, the city feels much smaller (and friendlier) than it actually is.

Berliners are protective of their space. A referendum blocked plans to build housing on parts of the former Tempelhof Airport, which was closed in 2008 and is now a public park. It's an awe-inspiring expanse, a luxurious space in the middle of the city. Elsewhere, too, planning offices and local politicians are locked in standoffs with residents who are resisting attempts to erect more houses on cherished green areas. Resolving the dilemma of building more housing to slow the rise in rent while also preserving breathing space is one of the biggest challenges the city is facing.

In some central areas, the planners have decided to forego the traditional model altogether. Towers have stood at Alexanderplatz and around Bahnhof Zoo for years but the ones currently being designed by architects such as Frank Gehry are intended to act as landmarks rather than the drab eyesores that currently cluster around both squares.

Berlin's recent experience with large-scale, big-investor construction is mixed – partly due to strict regulation. Berlin's chief planner post-reunification, the architect Hans Stimmann, favoured a style of "critical reconstruction" that would respect, and often imitate, the city's Prussian roots rather than allow for reinvention, and went so far as to prescribe the ratio of glass to stone on façades (40 to 60). This resulted in what the writer Georg Diez has called "a fantasy notion of an urban landscape",

Pool your resources: Opened in 2004, the Badeschiff is a playful and popular addition to Berlin. The heated pool floats in the river Spree's east harbour and is only open in summer for swimming – in the winter it gets a roof and becomes a sauna. The project was the idea of a local artist and was designed by AMP arquitectos of Spain

seen in the "bewildering" architecture of Potsdamer Platz and the renovation of the Unter den Linden boulevard.

The peak of the latter may have been reached with the reconstruction of a kitsch baroque palace on the site of the Palace of the Republic. The exception to the rule can be found, as is often the case in Berlin, in culture. Daniel Libeskind's Jewish Museum is an architectural marvel, as is the interior of the Pierre Boulez Saal concert hall. The jury is still out on the planned Herzog & de Meuron extension – which has been dubbed "the barn" – of Mies van der Rohe's New National Gallery. In Berlin, everybody has an opinion on what's happening, and not always a positive one.

Berliners like to have a say in their city's development and the results of their interventions can be surprisingly good. When the owners of the legendary club Bar 25 and its later incarnation, Kater Holzig, lost their crumbling Spree-side buildings, they decided to purchase a piece of land and build their own village-style development by the river: Holzmarkt combines housing, an open-air bar, a restaurant and even

a kindergarten. Potsdamer Strasse, a grey thoroughfare through no-man's land, has become an unlikely art and design haven with the opening of first small and independent, then large and multinational, galleries and shops. An effort to convert a side arm of the Spree canal in the city centre into a swimming pool is gaining steam. And many of the more attractive residential buildings are communal projects, planned, financed and built by their future inhabitants.

In a way, however, food culture is the most important driver of local development, mostly because it's one of the few things that Berliners will leave their borough for. Neukölln was put on the map when entrepreneurs started opening restaurants among its gambling shops and hookah bars. The young-ish inhabitants of Mitte and Kreuzberg found a reason to trek to more bourgeois Charlottenburg when new food joints started popping up on Kantstrasse.

Meanwhile, one of Berlin's best and most talked-about restaurants, Ernst, happens to be in one of its ugliest squares, Leopoldplatz in Wedding. Maybe that neighbourhood will "*kommen*" after all.

Still sexy urbanism (clockwise from right): The former Tempelhof Feld has seen the airport become a park with a 6km running-and-cycling trail and space for barbecues; street life Kreuzberg style; Haus der Kulturen der Welt

15. Taking care of its own
Singapore
The city-state is a public-housing pioneer and green-living believer.

The Pinnacle@Duxton, on the fringes of Singapore's CBD, was a game-changer when it was completed in 2009. With its zigzagging towers that stand at 50-storeys high, it was the tallest public housing complex that had ever been built in the city. More importantly, it had verdant sky gardens with running tracks and, along the green lung at the base, space for groups of elderly residents to do tai chi. It proved that Singapore's social housing could be sexy.

Two similar projects, Skyville and SkyTerrace, soon followed. They were a triumph for Singapore's public-housing policy. The programme, which started in the 1960s, now houses 80 per cent of the population and prioritises quality of life, including the beautification of public spaces through greenery.

With ecologically mindful building regulations such as landscape-replacement requirements and consideration for pedestrian-friendly streetscapes, Singapore defied the pattern of cities growing rapidly at the expense of their environments. In 1967, its then prime minister, Lee Kuan Yew, planted a mempat sapling in a roundabout as the first step towards his vision of creating a "Garden City". Little did he know that the initiative would sprout one of the world's greenest cities.

"We have almost a third of the world's 800 species of corals, more than 2,000 native plants and 392 native bird species," says Lena Chan, director of Singapore's National Biodiversity Centre. Since 2009 the centre has been planting trees and rebuilding habitats to welcome back fauna that disappeared as the city sprawled. Its efforts have been rewarded by the return of otters to the waterways and hornbills to the parks.

Singapore's leaders were prudent and pragmatic in navigating its severe physical limitations at independence from Malaysia in 1965. It lacks natural resources, including water. The nation relies on an agreement, which expires in 2061, with neighbour Malaysia to draw water from its Johor River.

And like many cities, Singapore has an ageing population that threatens to stretch these limited reserves even further. It's perhaps one reason why the leadership is anxious to keep a tight rein. The government owns 90 per cent of Singapore's territory, which means formidable veto power and red tape.

"Are we too safe for our own good?" asks Adib Jalal, co-founder of placemaking studio Shophouse & Co in Jalan Besar, a neighbourhood north of the business district. Here, cockerels crow every morning. It's known for its hardware and bric-a-brac shops, car mechanics and clan associations (places where Chinese migrants congregated in the early 20th century), not to mention brothels. But microbreweries, hotels and galleries have sprouted alongside them. In a city that has been busy scrapping old buildings and erecting new ones, Jalan Besar is an anomaly.

The loss of heritage sites has sparked some soul-searching. Regrettably, the response has been top-down, inspiring odd campaigns such as a contrived return of Singapore's "kampung spirit", the camaraderie that was once a way of life in Singapore's old villages.

High-minded (clockwise from top left): The Oasia Hotel tower by Woha architects is typical of new buildings that conform to Singapore's laws on creating additional green space when they are being developed; Concourse in the CBD, designed in 1987 by Paul Rudolph; The Interlace stacks housing and public space to create a dense, vertical village

16. Investing in the new
Toronto

Canada's dynamic city is finally out to deliver both intimacy and scale.

At the Burdock Brewery, in Toronto's west end, the first in a roster of stand-up comics at the venue's theatre has the crowd in the palm of her hands. They have been invited to riff on the theme of transport and travel. "I've only ever been violent once in my life," says the comic. "And you can guess where it took place."

The audience laughs as she reveals that her act of civic disobedience was on the TTC, Toronto's public transport system. Her tale of being pregnant among the commuter crowd and its simmering air of discontent aboard Toronto's streetcar, subway and bus networks resonates. The audience whoop and clap in solidarity, so universal is the resentment Torontonians feel about getting around their city.

Those woes, however, might be the clearest symptom of how quickly Toronto is changing; North America's fourth-largest city is also one of its fastest-growing, and its infrastructure has struggled to keep up with the pace of change. The state of Toronto's transport network – which carries nearly two million passengers every day and was lauded when it opened in the 1950s as one of the best, most integrated city public transport networks in the world – is a joke that may lose its potency soon. "Toronto is going through growing pains and it has been for some time," says Erin Kang, Toronto co-ordinator

for the Jane's Walk festival – founded in 2006 in recognition of the activist Jane Jacobs. Having started in Toronto, it's now present in more than 200 cities and allows residents to lead walks around their neighbourhoods. "In Toronto there have been a number of trends that have been hard for the city to grapple with because there aren't many examples for it to compare itself to," adds Kang.

Toronto's sense of self has been mercurial since the 1960s, when it began to emerge as Canada's economic hub. This emergence was driven in part by the exodus of people and businesses from Montréal as corruption in Canada's then-economic powerhouse reached its zenith and Québec's separatist movements began to swell.

That search for an identity has meant that extremes have flourished here, from progressive legislation that created one of the largest public library networks in the world to the election of the controversial late mayor Rob Ford, whose populist message resonated with many and alienated many more.

"Toronto has two ideas of itself, the lived experience and that more romantic notion of what the city wants to be," says Shawn Micallef, a writer on urban affairs and author of the book *Frontier City: Toronto on the Verge of Greatness*. "But there is now this positive energy here that's driving the place forward."

For your ice only: Skaters take to the ice on The Bentway, a public-space redevelopment beneath the Gardiner Expressway. **Overleaf, clockwise from top left:** Robarts Library, University of Toronto; Toronto Reference Library; OCAD University's Sharp Centre for Design

"Toronto tends to be hesitant to try things without proven success," says Christine Caruso, who co-founded the NXT City Prize in 2014, which, each year, recognises novel, design-led proposals for improving Toronto's public spaces. "But it's fantastic at smaller scale initiatives – we do wonderfully intimate, one-off projects and collaborations," she says, citing the celebrated Winter Stations programme. Launched in 2015 by the architecture firm RAW Design, along with Ferris + Associates and Curio, the programme transformed lifeguard stations along the city's beaches into cubby holes to encourage people to use the dormant beaches during the winter.

According to Micallef, unlike in many other cities of Toronto's size, change is often driven by the people rather than by city hall. "The strength of Toronto's civil society is really remarkable," he says. And that is rooted in Toronto's proudly held sense of being among the most diverse urban centres in the world. In 2001 it became one of the first cities to legally recognise gay marriage. And its long pedigree of welcoming immigrants – from refugees of the Vietnam and Syrian wars to those just seeking to study, invest or set up businesses – means that there are now some 200 languages spoken in Toronto.

The sense of what kind of city Toronto should be is still up for debate. But a sense of purpose is filtering into the decisions of city hall and developers who have set their sights on the city. Schemes such as the Bentway (which is transforming the underbelly of Toronto's unsightly Gardiner Expressway into novel public spaces such as a skating track in winter and a market in summer) are the types of imaginative approaches to public space that are found in smaller projects around the city.

On a different scale, however, is the vast project being driven by Sidewalk, a division of Alphabet (Google's parent company). The aim is to build a vast "smart" neighbourhood.

"Toronto has often been allotted as this wonderful city and it regularly makes its way onto numerous 'best of' lists," says Micallef. "And it is a wonderful place. But there are people who feel left out of that prosperity. And if that's allowed to continue as it is, that sense of greatness might not be attained."

17. Starting a new chapter
Paris

Forget the 'living museum' jibe because change here is fast and experimental.

Urban stereotypes tend to stick and Paris has long been defined by its magisterial boulevards, brusque waiters and spluttering Citroëns. It's a shrine to the blazer and ballet pumps, to little dogs in jackets and lobster bisque. Yet Paris has set about shedding the image of a coiffed, chic and predictable mademoiselle. Over the past few years, the city has pursued a quietly radical urban policy that seeks to reinvent its identity and question civic norms.

From the pedestrianisation of the Seine-side *voies sur berges* to the participatory budget that siphons off €100m of public money for citizen-led projects, the ambitious Mairie de Paris is reclaiming space and agency for its citizens. The city has launched a plan to "vegetalise" its streets, funding communal gardens and handing out permits to cultivate indigenous plants everywhere from the base of roadside trees to the tops of roofs. It has opened a nudist area in the Bois de Vincennes, rolled out many *fontaines d'eau pétillante* (sparkling water fountains) and set about boldly banning cars from its inner city.

There's a realisation that Paris cannot rest on its laurels, or fall back on its clichés, as congestion, pollution and rampant commerce spoil the *bon viveur* its citizens hold dear. It must anticipate the challenges of the modern metropolis rather than just respond to them.

Paris's urban revolution is rather subtle. It has perhaps learned from the postwar Gaullist drive to modernise, a result of which was the destruction of the magnificent Napoleonic-era Les Halles market in 1971 (it involved bulldozing a thriving neighbourhood and building a controversial, unpopular and ultimately unsuccessful mega-mall). Instead, it's seeking to revamp, renovate and re-imagine the urban landscape.

Streaming service: Two responses to Paris's wetter dimension. Les Arcades du Lac housing (*left*) by Spanish architect Ricardo Bofill and Pont Alexandre III, a bridge built with a low-slung silhouette so as not to interrupt the view

Even the Tour de Montparnasse (the butt of many jokes since it was built in 1973) is about to be overhauled. Its famous black glass will soon be replaced and a scheme by Nouvelle AOM, a group of three French architecture firms, will re-imagine its wind-swept shopping precinct and create a rooftop garden.

While Paris is determined not to ossify as a museum city, there is a consensus that the infrastructure built by Baron Haussmann between 1853 and 1870 is remarkably dense, flexible and functional, and a surprisingly pleasant model for modern inner-city life. Paris's urban schemes are geared at reclaiming space from the combustion engine, emboldening cyclists, encouraging communal collaboration and filling in the gaps with green, creative projects.

In a city that is seemingly full-to-bursting, the municipality is seeking to exploit every corner, however unappealing. A competition to "reinvent subterranean Paris" put up 34 underground spaces, from defunct metro stations to disused tunnels, for redevelopment. But another public competition, which "reinvented" 23 underused sites, was lambasted as profit-hungry development masked as social utility. Indeed, in districts such as Le Marais, where useful independent shops close down each week to be replaced by chain stores, many wondered

why a winning scheme to redevelop the historic Hotel de Coulanges includes a fashion concept store and co-working lab.

Paris has lost three Olympic bids in the past 25 years but finally scored the games for 2024 with the promise to improve its troubled banlieues. The games have also pushed the city to pursue an ecological agenda. City hall has set about ridding the Seine of pollution and litter, promising that it will be pure enough to host triathletes and locals alike in time for the Olympic Games. It has a plan called "Nager à Paris" that's revamping swimming pools and creating urban bathing spots such as the Bassin de la Villette (a Napoleonic-era artificial lake), which now hosts a free, staggeringly popular floating open-air pool in summer.

Parisians still like to do things in flocks. They holiday in August, eat *gâteau du rois* on the Epiphany and oysters for Le Réveillon. Their status quo of manicured lawns and pollarded promenades has worked well over the years. Yet they are starting to realise that they can also garden in the street, plunge into Napoleonic lakes and occupy a little slice of bucolic life in the city. They are changing an entrenched mentality and adopting an urban paradigm that puts people, not rules or cars, first. And the city is all the better for it.

Grand plans: Construction began on La Défense in the 1950s but really it's a child of the 1970s. Conceived as a way of giving the city the high-rises needed by big business, without inflicting them on central Paris, it's an area that has had its ups and downs but an extensive period of investment has given it an added role in the city's working life

In Seine: Paris has done much to reclaim its river banks for pedestrians. Around Île Saint-Louis it has created new spaces for seasonal food and drink spots, places to amble, and climbing walls and interventions for children

18. Take the middle ground
São Paulo

Downtown may be safe again but not everyone likes how it happened.

A shipwrecked sailor who washed up on the Atlantic coast in the 16th century is said to have been the first to set eyes on the site of what would become Brazil's biggest, boldest and wealthiest city. Today's visitors to São Paulo may arrive in a more leisurely fashion than the Portuguese adventurer João Ramalho but the city still provokes the same feelings of awe that he must have felt – albeit for different reasons.

This business hub of 12 million inner-city residents is quite literally a concrete jungle. Because for all its sprawl, insecurity and urban density, São Paulo is surprisingly verdant. Lush foliage drips from overpasses, colourful birds sit on pylons and the roots of fig trees rip through pavements.

But the city means business. In the 17th century it became a gateway for gold exports thanks to the persistence of the *bandeirantes*, a group of bandits who found dozens of mines. The money raised was invested in vast plantations of sugarcane and, later, coffee, transforming the metropolis and surrounding state into Brazil's commercial centre and attracting a flurry of new residents. Skip forward several centuries and little has changed: São Paulo is the place to make money in Brazil and prices reflect that.

For all the stock-exchange traders, media moguls and tech start-ups, the city hasn't forgotten the importance of culture. When coffee was first cultivated in the 19th century, out-of-work immigrants from Italy, Germany, Poland and Greece arrived. That was followed by a second migration wave in the early 20th century, with the arrival of Japanese, Arabs and Koreans. Today these third-generation communities give the megacity a global character.

São Paulo hosts the second-oldest Art Biennial in the world after Venice and is home to top museums, cultural institutes and theatres. This cultural mix is most acute downtown. Until just a few years ago the "centro" was largely derelict but a major clean-up is taking place. A regeneration project is bringing an influx of galleries and restaurants to the area, helping to rectify decades of neglect and show off some of the city's finest monuments to modernism.

It's in the newly buzzing city centre where chef Mélanito Biyouha runs Biyou'Z restaurant, serving dishes "in an African way". There's a new non-profit arts centre called Pivô, countless coffee shops and a renovated 13-storey cultural institute with a communal rooftop pool, the Sesc 24 de Maio. The grime from pollution that once covered many of São Paulo's beautiful, but neglected, buildings is being removed.

The city's plans have nevertheless sparked debate about whether urban development should aim at gentrification or help the growing number of people who are forced to live on the street and in the outskirts of the metropolis. "Since the clean-up began, hundreds [of the poor] are being forced back out onto the street," says academic Milena Durante.

Outside the centre, the city is trying to open up its urban landscape. A 15-year transport scheme to construct cycle paths, lower speed limits, expand pavements and occasionally shut off roads entirely is well underway. Paulista Avenue and the Minhocão, two major arteries, are pedestrianised on Sundays (the latter closes to traffic at night too). Since 2013, 460km of bicycle paths have been built.

São Paulo makes most other cities feel like little villages. It's huge, the social disparities are wide and the hardships can be extreme. But it's the chaos among the culture, the energy in the opulence and the greenery amid the crowds that make Paulistanos feel utterly alive.

Taming a megacity (clockwise from top left): Towers as far as you can see; Sesc 24 de Maio is in a converted downtown department store and has a pool (*see overleaf*), art gallery and free dental service; the Minhocão Park is an urban scar that's normally packed with cars but at night, and on Sundays, it's handed over to pedestrians who are short on public parks; Galeria do Rock, built in the 1960s, in Centro

19. High hopes
Bucharest
Wrecked by a dictator's follies, the Romanians are fixing their capital.

Cities that have lived through a dictatorship often need decades to overcome the anguish. In Bucharest, Nicolae Ceausescu's rule – a traumatic period that lasted from 1965 to 1989 – shaped the city's past and continues to impact its present.

Both the 1977 earthquake, which destroyed much of Bucharest's buildings, and the regime's megalomaniac plan to construct a socialist city forced Romania's capital into a series of abrupt reboots. Some of the slate-coloured, mansard-roofed art deco buildings that earned this city the nickname "Paris of the East" have managed to survive. But nowadays they rub shoulders with boxy modernist blocks on the brink of collapse and glass-and-steel towers born during the gleeful post-Communist construction boom of the 1990s.

Yet in many ways this apparent chaos is what has pushed many residents to take matters into their own hands. Urban initiatives are flourishing, including the annual Romanian Design Week, which has transformed abandoned buildings into venues for shows. Given the abundance of structures that were either built or used by the Communist regime, such as the hulking Palace of Parliament, there are plenty of spaces that can be rediscovered and reclaimed by theatres, galleries and museums with a particularly symbolic resonance.

Events such as the Street Delivery festival have begun a process of re-appropriation of the city's tangle of roads – which, with hardly a bench in sight, was never designed for pedestrians. For three days a year every June, cars are banned from stretches of central Bucharest and artists, musicians and market stalls populate them instead. All year round, there are gardens behind private houses or institutions that have turned into bars, restaurants and hangouts that provide pockets of greenery for this park-scarce city. In these hideaways, the persistent roar of traffic disappears and a calmer future for this city begins to take shape.

Another storey: There's a whole layer of most cities that often remains unloved and underused. Yet, with care, these spaces can be phenomenal – people like having a different perspective on their city from up high – and they create a connection, and a disconnection, that's unique (you can finally see your whole city just as you are slightly removed from it). This is Linea, a café-bar that has a head for heights

20. Making a splash
Zürich

*Lake and river are central to life here,
so planners go with the urban flow.*

Zürich has all the makings of a capital and yet that honour has been bestowed upon tiny nearby Bern. But the politicians don't live in Bern, they commute from Zürich by train. Who needs a chauffeured limousine when rail is so good? And who would pick Bern when you could be living in Zürich?

Switzerland's largest city boasts a population of 1.9 million but it's less dense than some Californian beach towns. The Romans settled on the northwestern point of the expansive Lake Zürich in 15BC. And they're to thank for building the paths around which the city organically grew. The top-down, car-centric model of urban planning that Robert Moses touted in postwar America never stood a chance in this bastion of direct democracy. Instead of adding to its roads, the city allocates funds to the public transport system. A long-term plan to upgrade the latter launched in the 1970s and has since transformed many streets into bike-friendly public-transit lanes and parks.

Being well-connected makes all the difference. It's why Zürich is able to retain and grow its talent pool and

why global banks and businesses such as Google flock here (the low taxes help, of course). Zürich's centrally located international airport flies to 185 destinations around the world; in less than two hours you can be in Berlin or Paris. Perhaps that's why the city is more cosmopolitan than you might expect. Of the population 32 per cent is foreign-born, only marginally less than New York or London. And while some have given Zürich a bad rep for being lacklustre, it's easy to fall in love with the city when the sun shines. In summer the streets come alive like those in a carefree southern Italian city.

The Limmat river, which snakes its way through town, lures people from all walks of life to its banks and into its cool, clear waters for a swim. On summer evenings, the lakeside is packed with people picnicking and watching the sunset beyond the Sechseläutenplatz, which stretches in front of the neo-classical Opera House. No wonder Zürich is ranked as one of the world's most liveable cities year after year.

Even so, the city doesn't rest on its laurels. Recent upgrades include

renowned architect David Chipperfield's extension for the art museum Kunsthaus Zürich and the airport's futuristic convention centre The Circle. Meanwhile, the transformation of Zürich West is creating a vibrant new neighbourhood out of an industrial wasteland. Local architects EM2N turned a historic arched railway overpass into Im Viadukt, a market hall, gallery and retail hub; while the old Löwenbräu brewery across the road has been given a new lease of life as Löwenbräukunst, an art complex that's home to the Kunsthalle Zürich and galleries such as Hauser & Wirth.

On the other side of the tracks, Zürich's old red-light district along Europaallee is barely recognisable. New shops, restaurants, cafés and an outpost of 25hours Hotels have opened up.

The beauty of Zürich – apart from its picturesque lake, sweeping mountain vistas and proximity to the Alps – is that the city still has so much potential. There's still room for growth in this comfortably sized, forward-looking Swiss town.

Doing swimmingly: The urban design of Zürich responds again and again to the lake and river setting, delivering numerous ways for residents to engage with the water – as here at Badi Oberer Letten

Flip out: Cities should impact our emotions – give us spaces where we feel secure, cosy when needed and awed on occasion too. But cities should also know how to be fun, to make us jump for joy

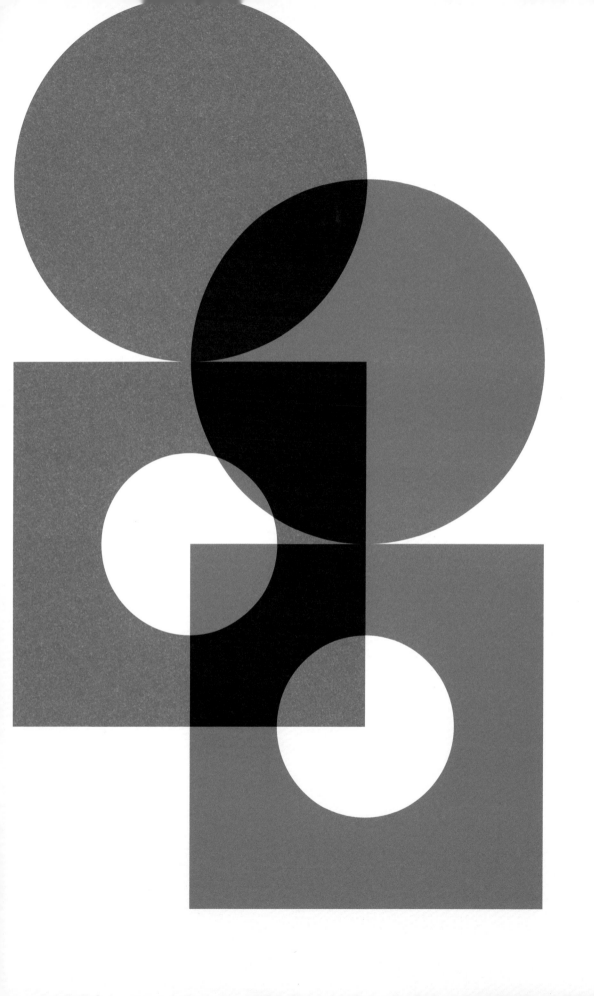

Our cities would be nothing without the people who inhabit them, build them and strive to make them better places in which to live, work and play. In this chapter we hear from 20 experts and city-dwellers around the world, who highlight the heroes of urbanism, the challenges we're facing and the improvements that need to be made.

Too often we have become enthralled with technological advancements. Instead of building cities for people, we've built cities for cars – and now the demands of tech. Instead of building cities for all, we've built cities for the privileged few. Instead of building cities that nurture nature, we've built cities that suppress it.

It took the likes of New York activist and journalist Jane Jacobs to establish that a city is meant to be our habitat, that it should be built to human scale and make everyone feel welcome. And while many cities around the world are addressing their mistakes, turning industrial wastelands into creative hubs, injecting life back into streets and riverbanks and adapting cities for young and old, there is still much to be done. Some things rest in the hands of city hall and its planners and architects but we can all make a difference.

Over the following few pages, Mike Lydon of the Street Plans Collaborative shares his tactical urbanism tips – how a comfy deckchair here and a planted plot there can transform an entire neighbourhood. Gil Penalosa, founder of 8 80 Cities, explains how we can cater to people of all ages. Helle Søholt, co-founder of Gehl Architects, shares her insight into building people-centric cities. Guy Perry, vice president of urban planning and design for McKinsey & Company, makes a case for creating cities that get their citizens moving to beat diabetes and obesity. Author Peter York contemplates the notion of living on the wrong side of the tracks, while writer David Usborne considers the missing murderers.

Kicking it all off, documentary film-maker Matt Tyrnauer looks at the legacy of Jane Jacobs and reminds us that cars, city authorities and developers don't have to define how cities look and function. The city, as Jacobs argued, is less about its physical spaces and more about how people use them. Ultimately, the city is for people, and we should embrace that.

2.

ESSAYS AND COMMENTS

Musings on cities

I.
Robert Moses vs Jane Jacobs
by Matt Tyrnauer

The modern city was born in the mid-20th century. The motorways, skyscrapers, strip malls, housing projects and suburbs that developed in these years dramatically redefined the form and function of the urban spaces of the western world, and their impact continues to ripple across the planet. When we look at the modern city, be it New York or Shenzhen, we're looking at a place based on the innovations of a time when the forces of city making were in overdrive.

Two great figures personify the way the city was viewed in the postwar years. Robert Moses, often credited as the man who built New York, was the most powerful unelected official in US history and the embodiment of the top-down approach to planning, building and rebuilding. He was the leading actor in a movement to fix the city, which at the time was seen to be in need of drastic renewal. At the other end of the spectrum was Jane Jacobs, a journalist without a college degree, who noticed that the treatments suggested by urban "doctors" such as Moses were doing harm to the cities they were supposed to be saving.

"This is an unfortunate period for the city," said Moses in a radio interview when he was leading urban-renewal efforts in New York in the wake of depression and war. Such efforts generally took the form of planning motorways and building public-housing projects in place of dilapidated (but often thriving) low-income areas that he saw as a cancer on the city. "We've done an immense amount to cure these diseases and we have much more to do."

Jacobs pushed back against this perception of the city as a problem to be solved. "It is so easy to blame the decay of cities on traffic, or immigrants, or the whimsies of the middle class. It goes right down to what we think we want, and to our ignorance about how cities work," she wrote in her landmark 1961 book on urban planning and city making, *The Death and Life of Great American Cities*. Arguing for the organic nature of cities, built by and for the people, her book landed with the power of an A-bomb in the cosseted worlds of top-down city-planning.

These opposing views would become the two sides in a series of battles over development in New York in the 1950s and 1960s – and over the future of the modern city itself. It began in 1955, when Moses targeted Jacobs' neighbourhood; he wanted to build a road through Washington Square Park, Greenwich Village's main public space. Jacobs joined The Joint Emergency Committee to Close Washington Square Park to Traffic to stop the project and quickly became one of its leaders. Ridiculed by city authorities as a "mere housewife", she revealed herself to be a brilliant strategist, staging protests, gathering petitions and painting Moses as a bully. Thousands of New Yorkers joined the opposition, including famed neighbourhood residents such as former first lady Eleanor Roosevelt. Ramming a road through a public park, they argued, would damage Greenwich Village and the city as a whole. It was an argument many agreed with, gathering enough clout to make the road politically unviable. By October 1958, the plan was dead.

The city Jacobs fought for is one of variety, potential and opportunity, built and rebuilt to meet the needs of its people. But while many modern cities are pursuing this people-focused approach, even more are not and the ramifications could be devastating. We are currently seeing the greatest building boom in human history. Urbanisation is occurring rapidly across the planet, turning formerly small enclaves into high-rise megacities and transforming hordes of people into urbanites. Roughly four billion people – about 55 per cent of the global population – now live in urban areas. By 2050 the urban population is set to grow to more than six billion.

Many of the cities being built today are repeating the mistakes of the past. Public officials in collusion with private developers in countries such as China and India are looking to the example of Moses as they scramble to handle mass migration to their cities. In the process, history repeats itself with miles of new but poorly planned urban fabric. Forests of banal towers are rising rapidly in cities across the developing world, creating single-use districts where life on the street is all but non-existent.

That's why it's so important to remember that Moses and his approach to city building ultimately failed. His approach was shown to be harmful, anti-democratic and anti-human. Jacobs, through her writing and activism, helped people to realise that this form of city making doesn't have to be the only way. The movement of cars, the profits of developers, the orderliness of spaces: these don't have to be the elements that guide how cities look and function. The city, she argued, is less about its physical spaces and more about how people use them.

It's a lesson that the emerging cities of the developing world need to learn before it's too late. If left to develop in the Moses style, these cities will be doomed to a fate of prescribed neighbourhoods planned without people in mind and without the potential to experience the serendipitous interactions of vibrant spaces. Jacobs' vision is the one we need and deserve in the 21st century – and through collective efforts it is the one that we can achieve.

Matt Tyrnauer is a writer and director. His documentary 'Citizen Jane: Battle for the City' looks at cities through the lens of the titular journalist and activist.

2.
Take small steps
by Mike Lydon

Jaime Lerner, architect and former mayor of Curitiba, Brazil once declared: "To innovate is to start." It's a simple but powerful assertion that casts light on an overlooked reality: the improvement of urban life can't rely on formal studies and long-term plans. Such efforts have value but are too often out of date by the time political or economic resources allow them to be implemented.

The conventional planning process is slow and expensive, constrained by political leaders who struggle to balance future vision with tangible results. It often excludes swathes of the population, resulting in a lack of trust in government institutions and untold sums of unrealised value creation. In short, it lacks tactics for addressing the challenges city-dwellers face today. Our cities are suffering because there is too much planning and not enough doing.

Tactical urbanism is a collaborative approach to building cities using short-term, low-cost and scalable projects intended to catalyse long-term changes in infrastructure, policy or ideally both. Typically, tactical urbanism projects serve as proofs of concept that legitimise the viability of more permanent projects desired by neighbourhoods. In doing so, they often speed up the implementation process. Sometimes sanctioned by cities, sometimes not, they can be instigated by anyone: artists, community groups, NGOs, small-business owners and, yes, even architects and urban-planners.

In less than a decade this approach to improving city life has moved from the fringes and is often heralded as a legitimate methodology for building a more inclusive, citizen-driven city. Here are three examples of cities that are experimenting with tactical urbanism projects:

Unsanctioned to sanctioned
A small group of frustrated citizens in Hamilton, Ontario used traffic cones topped with daffodils to extend the pavement width at a dangerous intersection. The city removed the cones, only to return a few weeks later with a "pilot project" formalising the initial act. The pilot was a huge success and two years on, the city had replicated the effort at more than 100 intersections.

Tactical resilience
The earthquakes of 2010 and 2011 nearly decimated Christchurch, New Zealand. While the government responded with long-term plans to reconstruct the city, more than 100 citizen-led projects filled the voids left behind. These small-scale efforts – community gardens, bike-repair kiosks, container markets, temporary co-working pods and more – brought activity back to the core of the city, speeding up its recovery and informing government investments. Whether lasting for days or years, each project proved that a community's physical resilience is only as strong as its social resilience.

Short-term action for long-term change
Finally, the evolution of New York's Times Square from a car-choked nexus of streets into a pedestrian haven began with $15 lawn chairs. The three-day project invited people to sit in the middle of the temporarily car-free street, effectively putting "the square" back into Times Square. An instant success, the city and its partners invested in an interim version of the project – colourful painted asphalt, tables, chairs, umbrellas and planters – while long-term plans could be drawn up and implemented in the near future, permanently transforming Times Square as a place for people.

Cities will always have unmet needs and unexploited opportunities to enhance public life. That said, tactical urbanism won't solve every urban problem. What it can do is get planners and architects out of city hall and design studios, and back into the streets where the foundation for social, political and economic capital is built. It can also cut through outdated bureaucracy and break big plans down into many manageable projects. If we – city leaders, citizens, private sector leaders and community advocates – can't work together on a small scale to improve urban life, we'll certainly have a hard time responding to the larger financial, civic and environmental challenges our cities must solve.

Mike Lydon is a planner, writer, speaker and advocate for liveable cities. He runs the New York office of urban planning firm Street Plans and is the co-author of 'Tactical Urbanism: Short-Term Action for Long-Term Change'.

3.

Ageing in place
by Sophie Grove

I have a running joke with my nonagenarian neighbour across the hall. "How's le Brexit?" he asks when I meet him on the landing of our Parisian apartment block. "And how are Winston and Elizabeth?" (His pet names for my children.)

A resident for 40 years, he is bright, brisk and courteous. He walks stick in hand to the boulangerie each day and buys *Le Monde* to read after lunch. Urban life suits him. And why shouldn't it? There is a lift, public transport and cafés. Much has changed in the 6th arrondissement but there are

Traditionally, many urban elders would have retired to the coast or the country. But this is changing. Older residents are staying put and there is anecdotal evidence that affluent retirees are migrating back to the city in search of a dynamic social scene, a rich cultural life and proximity to grandchildren.

"We're seeing a blurring of life phases," says Deane Simpson, an architect who teaches at the Royal Danish Academy of Fine Arts in Copenhagen and has studied the urban retirement towns of Florida (and even a Dutch-themed residential community at Huis Ten Bosch in Japan). "Many people want to continue to work well after retirement. People are generally not as likely to move to Florida or Spain. They are more interested in staying in their social and spatial networks."

other NORCs in the city (including Knickerbocker Village and the Big Six Towers in Queens) to assess how and why these urban high-rises are so inadvertently successful for the old.

Developers, architects and city-planners are facing up to the need for an age-friendly urban landscape. Yet the private sector seems slow to realise the potential for an urban retirement concept that leans on the amenities of the city and its adaptable housing stock. "Developers are often really conservative in what they think works," says Simpson. "In Denmark there is a lot of research into what's stopping the market from realising adaptable, collective housing."

In the Copenhagen district of Nørrebro, Danish architect firm CF Møller is creating a project known as Sølund, a multi-generational development that

still quiet bookshops and a puzzling density of pharmacies.

It's strange that the inner city has become so synonymous with youth. Undoubtedly, frenetic urban landscapes appeal to a fit, fun-loving, working-age demographic. Yet city life, with its tight social structures and proximity to healthcare, parks and shops, is really just as suited to the old.

In any case, data shows that our cities are ageing fast. A recent report shows that the number of urban-dwelling over-65s in OECD countries rose by 23.8 per cent between 2001 and 2011 versus 18 per cent in non-urban areas (cities themselves grew by 9 per cent). In places such as New York there are now more people over the age of 65 than there are children under five, whilst London's 60-plus demographic is expected to expand by 48 per cent by 2035.

This idea of "ageing in place" is fast replacing the concept of housing older people in faraway communities. There's even an acronym, NORC (naturally occurring retirement community), to describe the urban settlements that have become magnets for an older crowd.

In 2010, Brooklyn-based architects Interboro Partners published an essay called *NORCs in New York* looking at New York's Co-op Village, a development designed by Herman Jessor in the 1970s, where 4,060 of its residents were over 60. They insisted that red-brick blocks had added years to their lives. Some had even moved into assisted living and then returned to the autonomous city. Others had friends who joined them after hearing great things about the quality of life. Interboro is looking to identify

will house the city's largest care centre, a nursery, youth housing and a senior community by 2022. Here, every detail has been configured to make sure generations collide and interact. "It's about creating halls and corridors that act as social hubs where people can stop and form relationships," says Sølund's project leader, Mads Mandrup Hansen.

Architecture is key but making cities more age-friendly requires a political and cultural shift. After all, what's the point of beautiful parks if young people jog aggressively through them within a whisker of someone recovering from hip surgery? It's about reimagining the public sphere.

"You have to get the highest political support," says Paul McGarry, who is in charge of the

Greater Manchester Ageing Hub and has been working in the field for decades. "You have to create a platform for older people to be involved in decisions at a civic level. You've got to find space, make an effort and give people agency."

Manchester is one of the World Health Organisation's Age-Friendly cities and is working with Barcelona, Gothenburg and Amsterdam to raise the bar. McGarry describes a push at every level, from infrastructure to health and city planning, all with older residents in mind. Getting businesses to understand the potential that older people represent, as customers and entrepreneurs, has been key.

We don't want our cities to be giant temples to youth. It's clear that a dynamic, intergenerational mix is vital to a healthy, happy,

balanced society. The very old and the very young change the pace and timbre of life for the better. Instead of being siphoned off from each other they should be brought together to exchange thoughts, jokes, reassurance and historic perspectives.

"I've been a Gaullist since 1941," my neighbour exclaimed the other morning as he insisted I take the lift up before him. "Churchill was an exceptional man. You see, I'm an Anglophile, despite le Brexit. You will always be our allies."

Sophie Grove is Monocle's senior (not that kind of senior) correspondent, based in Paris. She has been with the magazine since 2009 and reports on everything from diplomacy to design.

4.
Q&A with Gil Peñalosa

Gil Peñalosa, founder of non-profit 8 80 Cities and chair of World Urban Parks, started his career in urban planning as parks commissioner of Bogotá. Since then he has inspired and advised leaders in more than 200 municipalities across all continents on how to create healthy, happy and sustainable communities. Here he tells us his secret to building cities fit for everyone from eight to eighty years old.

When did you first become interested in urban planning and how did that lead to the foundation of 8 80 Cities?
I was exposed to it in my early years. My mother was a landscape gardener so I came to love nature through her, and my father was head of UN-Habitat. Before moving to Canada I was commissioner of parks in Bogotá and that sparked my interest in issues related to cities. That's why I founded 8 80 Cities. It has a simple but powerful concept: what if everything in our cities – pavements, parks, schools and libraries – had to be built for an eight and an 80-year-old? If it's good for both an eight and an 80-year-old, it's going to be good for everyone. We need to stop building cities as if everyone's 30 and athletic.

What are some of the key areas for improvement?
People are suffering from poverty, depression, loneliness and obesity

– and a lot of this has to do with the built environment. The most vulnerable people in cities are pedestrians. Walking is the only individual mode of mobility; it should be a human right, unless you think that only those with the money for a car have the right to individual mobility. Walking should be safe and enjoyable. Unfortunately, it's not. A pedestrian is killed by a car every two hours. We have not been doing cities right if that is happening.

How can we improve our cities for everyone?
Streets are a city's biggest public space: they make up between 30 and 40 per cent of its area. When I was commissioner in Bogotá, I started a programme called Ciclovía, which turned the city's streets into the world's largest pop-up park on Sundays. From 07.00 to 14.00 cars were banned and people could walk, cycle, skate and run down some 120km of car-free roads. People met each other as equals on the streets. This concept has taken off like a positive virus; you now see it in France, in Mexico, in the US. But often it's only implemented a few days a year. In order to really get the benefit, you have to do it every week.

What further advice do you have?
I tell leaders that they should be like guardian angels for the young, the elderly and the poor. We need to elect the best people possible in government. And citizens can no longer be spectators; they need to participate. I also think we need to create broad alliances between people across different sectors and communities, from city officials and environmentalists to the public. When you do that, you can develop a shared vision and take action. It's important to realise that when you say no to a park or cycle paths, you're saying yes to sprawl, pollution, mental health issues and obesity. There are no easy decisions but we need to create cities for people – not just for the people here today but also for the billions who will be living in our cities tomorrow.

5.

In praise of the lift
by Matt Alagiah

Elisha Graves Otis may not be a household name but he has arguably done more to shape cities around the world over the past 160 years than any mayor, president or planner. While he wasn't actually the inventor of the lift as many erroneously believe, he did devise the safety brake in 1852, which meant elevators could be trusted for the first time.

Before then, constructing buildings of more than six or seven storeys was pointless, because few people were willing to trudge up that many flights of stairs. With the emergence of the safe lift all that changed. Ever since, our cities have bloomed, growing upwards as fast as outwards and scaling new heights worldwide. Thanks to the humble lift, the tallest buildings in the world are today hundreds of metres high and plans for the first 1,000-metre-tall tower are underway in Saudi Arabia.

While it's important to remember that the most pleasant cities around the world retain a degree of human scale, it's impossible to deny that our cities have needed – and will continue to need – to become denser to accommodate growing populations. The lift has helped us achieve that and will do so even more in the future.

If it's astounding how much the lift has shaped our cities over the past century, it's equally astonishing that the basic technology that transports human beings up and down buildings has barely changed since Otis's day. The same four fundamental ingredients (ropes, brakes, a counterweight and a cab) are still used in almost every lift in the world.

But that, too, is now changing. The engineers at ThyssenKrupp Elevator (one of the four big global lift manufacturers) have come up with a design called the Multi, which disposes of ropes and instead drives through a system similar to magnetic levitation (used by some modern trains). And whereas most lift shafts can only accommodate one cab, the Multi's shafts will be able to carry multiple cabs, which will be able to move both vertically and horizontally. If none of this sounds particularly groundbreaking, allow me to wheel out an industry heavyweight. The editors of leading industry publication *Elevator World* have described the removal of ropes from lifts as the industry's "Holy Grail".

ThyssenKrupp's invention will once again shift the economics and possibilities of the construction industry, enabling developers to build towers that reach more than a kilometre in height. And whether we like it or not, we may well need such soaring skyscrapers in the future, as our cities become megacities and our megacities become something that we can scarcely imagine today.

But don't take my word for it. Executives at major lift manufacturers are confident about the future – they know their market is only set to grow in the years and decades to come. Let their confidence be a sign. We'd better get used to living at greater and greater heights.

Matt Alagiah is Monocle's executive editor and has covered new trends in the property sector for several years. He didn't find lifts particularly interesting until visiting ThyssenKrupp's headquarters. Since then, his appreciation for the unassuming lift has soared.

6.

My troubled love affair with Rome
by David Plaisant

To call the current state of Rome disastrous would be an understatement in a city accustomed to magnificent superlatives. Every day seems to bring news of yet another urban calamity. Large chunks of streets – and their haphazardly parked cars – disappear into sinkholes, then the effects of snow and ice bring the city to its knees; and, most dramatically, a total lack of maintenance causes buses to explode on central streets and avenues. These are but a few of the incidents that Romans are expected to take in their stride.

Rome is often described as ungovernable, and as a new resident to the city this was hard to come to terms with. Yet its hint of lawlessness and adamant informality also means that Romans you've just met will happily invite you to dinner that night – and insist you bring a friend too. In the streets and piazzas a choreographed chaos pervades; here you can have a cappuccino (no flat whites, *grazie*) in a tatty café or opulent bar and it will taste the same – resoundingly delicious.

Of course the daily grind in Rome throws up plenty of challenges. If you're reliant on public transport the general advice is "don't be" but the thousands of potholes dotting the city's ancient streets also make getting around by scooter or bike an increasingly precarious activity.

Then again, everyday life is infused with flavours that go a long way to making up for those transport trials and rush-hour mayhem. Indeed, that a good plate of seasonal and locally grown delicacies nourishes the soul in a way that no chain restaurant ever could is emblematic of the lack of showiness that dominates the Roman way of life. Just because a Negroni costs €3 and might be served in a plastic cup doesn't make it any less delectable. As spring brings blue skies and perfectly agreeable evenings, residents revert to the outdoors and those who are fortunate enough to have a *terraza* often assume the role of host by default.

For those who like rules and a sense of civic order, the Italian capital may be too much to stomach. Certainly, the parlous state of the city's finances and public services is not something to shrug off; that would seem glib given the inconvenience and waste that this city's *degrado* (deterioration) is causing its inhabitants.

Yet just as Roman infrastructure and urban complexities throw a spanner in the works of efficiency, the Roman cuisine helps to slow the metabolism to a pleasantly unrushed pace. In Rome, residents can only hope to be happy if they let the rhythms and routine of the city hold sway. In the Eternal City that's the difference between eternal frustration and eternal fulfilment.

David Plaisant spent more than five years at Monocle, writing for the magazine and producing 'Section D' and 'The Stack' for M24. As Monocle's Rome correspondent, he can regularly be found boarding Frecciarossa high-speed trains to report on stories from Trieste, Taranto and beyond.

7.
Why I built a park
by Bénédict GF Hentsch

The story of Le Parc Gustave & Léonard Hentsch dates back to 1925 when my grandfather, captain and goalie of the Servette Football Club, decided to build a stadium for his beloved club. The chosen site for the Stade des Charmilles was in the middle of Geneva's thriving industrial zone.

From its inauguration in 1930 to its complete closure in 2002, the stadium hosted 2,500 matches and some of the world's leading football teams. Its sudden demise, mainly due to safety reasons, raised the question of what to do with the area. Should the stadium be replaced with yet another property development?

By then the neighbourhood, which had been dotted with factories, had transformed into a dense residential district. And I realised what it needed: a park. A place where people could meet, play and relax.

Before work could begin on the four-hectare property, a new football arena had to be built. The new Stade de Genève, which cost CHF120m (€103.2m), was inaugurated in 2003 and attention then turned to the park.

I decided to name it Parc Gustave & Léonard Hentsch after my grandfather and father, who had witnessed the ups and down of their beloved Servette Football Club on its pitch. And I would gift it to the city. Now came the hard part: turning a former football stadium in a post-industrial part of town into a bustling green space.

A park should be a reflection of the neighbourhood, a place where all generations can interact. In a "good" neighbourhood people from different social backgrounds congregate and mingle. And a "good" park should be used by everyone as if it were their own garden. Parc Gustave & Léonard Hentsch opened in 2015 and the neighbourhood has claimed ownership of the space as if it had always been there. Now it's time for the trees to grow and the birds to start singing.

Bénédict GF Hentsch is the retired co-founder and chairman of the former Banque Bénédict Hentsch in Geneva. He was previously managing partner at the family-owned private bank Darier Hentsch & Cie, which merged with Lombard Odier in 2002.

8.

Night mayors
by Shain Shapiro

Walking through Melbourne's CBD on a weeknight gives you a glimpse of its well-oiled night-time economy. Punters fill the streets en route to gigs, comedy and theatre shows; restaurants are packed; street performers entertain audiences; and the streets are well-lit. As vibrant as nights in Melbourne are, just imagine what they could be like if a night mayor ran things after sunset?

Melbourne, which is regularly ranked as one of the world's most liveable cities, is late to the party. Cities such as London, New York, Amsterdam and Vilnius have created the post of night mayor to protect, promote and support everything from nightlife and health and safety to workers' rights after 18.00.

A decade ago, a night mayors' summit would have been a lonely affair, attended solely by the Dutch. These days being appointed a city's "night czar" is a coveted prize. The question is, do cities really need one?

It's the same question that was asked when villages evolved into towns and towns into cities, necessitating the appointment of mayors. Someone had to keep an eye on public spending and services. But the planning laws that govern our cities often neglect the night-time economy. We traditionally manage and evaluate our cities based on what happens during the day. Our laws have not been set up to support what happens after dark.

Across the UK, sound is first and foremost an environmental health issue. And in Melbourne, live-music venues were deemed risky no more than 10 years ago because of the alcohol-related incidents that occur there. When it comes to planning and city management structures, alcohol is regulated independently, without taking the wider ecosystem into consideration. As a result, we've built cities where bars remain open until 04.00 but where there's no way of getting home without a car. We accept locking disorderly punters out of venues, even though such spillage onto the streets only escalates the issue. This is down to our urban governance systems, which rely on daytime solutions to solve night-time issues. Our night requires its own management policies, and yet these are few and far between, even in the cities that are recognised as the world's most liveable.

So the creation of a role or a department designed to manage issues after sunset is a necessary requirement for a growing, global city. As of yet there's no blueprint. In New York, an Office of Nightlife was created within the city's Media and Entertainment division, and its executive director acts as the de-facto nightlife ambassador. In Geneva, Toulouse and Zürich, advisory boards assume the role. In Pittsburgh, the role sits within the police department. Not only is the process variable, so are the objectives of the role. In Amsterdam, Berlin and New York, for example, the night mayor's role is to safeguard, legitimise, improve and support healthy, safe and fair nightlife. In London, Pittsburgh and Tbilisi, the night mayor is responsible for the entire night-time economy, which includes transport, logistics and workers' rights alongside nightlife.

Despite many cities moving in the right direction, no recognised night-time economy policy exists within the UN or any other global administration. For every city that elects a night mayor, there are hundreds that have yet to realise its importance and accept its legitimacy.

Our night-time makes up at least half of our day. I say, bring on the night mayors.

Shain Shapiro is the founder and CEO of Sound Diplomacy, which advises cities on music and night-time strategies. He's also the co-founder of the Night Time Economy convention.

9.

Asia's outdoor living rooms
by James Chambers

Shanghai is China's ultra-modern city of neon lights, commerce – and sprightly seniors going for evening strolls in their pyjamas. For me, witnessing this nocturnal activity was an early introduction to how the streets in Asian cities are an extension of individual living space.

Growing up in the West, hanging out on the street was considered anti-social, bordering on criminal, behaviour. By contrast, in Asian cities everything is allowed to hang out, from washing in Hangzhou to badminton nets in Hanoi. Kids play, businessmen hawk and car horns honk. Street life in Asian cities is more lively than in the West and it's not just amid the dust and detritus of developing cities in Southeast Asia.

The thing that struck me most when I moved to Hong Kong from London is just how much time I spend outside. Weather certainly plays a part, although "outside" does not always mean outdoors. Teenage couples, for example, are a common sight in shopping malls, late at night, once all the shop shutters are down.

Cities such as Jakarta, Manila and even Singapore are routinely ranked the world's most densely populated urban areas. With living space at a premium, private life naturally spills into the public realm. This is nothing new – but the traffic is. Chu Kim Duc co-founded Think Playgrounds in Hanoi in 2014 to provide a safe place for children to play in the Vietnamese capital. "When I was a child we didn't have playgrounds," she says. "We played on the empty streets."

As cities grow, mayors and urban-planners will have to get creative. Indonesia's third-largest city of Bandung has set a useful precedent. An initiative from city hall called the Taman Film Bandung installed a cinema screen underneath an overpass and covered the ground with artificial grass. "People took off their shoes and stopped littering and it became an urban living room," says its co-designer Daliana Suryawinata, a director of architecture firm SHAU.

More Asian cities should focus on providing a pleasant, safe outdoor environment for its residents rather than pushing everyone inside an air-conditioned box and labelling it progress. Spotting a pyjama-clad senior in Shanghai is less common nowadays – and that's a shame.

James Chambers joined Monocle as Hong Kong bureau chief in 2015. When he's not at the office, he can be found exploring the streets of Hong Kong.

10.
Time to cool it
by Tyler Brûlé

How to have a more relaxed approach to city living.

1. Take your clothes off
There's a reason why the likes of Munich, Zürich and Vienna do well in MONOCLE's liveability ranking: they create places for people to strip off and cool down. As a result, they're cities where everyone feels they can show off as much or as little as they like. Plus, having great public settings where people can take a few minutes to literally chill out makes for a more harmonious urban environment.

2. Return to civil pleasures
We're not suggesting you take up the smoking habit but a trip to Beirut reminded us that there are too many rules applied to moments of the day when we should be able to lean back and relax. We need to engage with those around us and be civil about basic pleasures. "Do you mind if I light up? Would you like one?" At the same time we should be mindful of other things that can spoil the mood, such as people watching video clips on their phone with the volume on full. We don't need rules to guide every aspect of a good night out, we just need to read the room and gauge the mood of those around us.

3. Drink when you want
Sydney gets a drubbing for not letting people sit outside late at night and order a final cocktail. Too many cities take the same view: you are

not to be trusted to decide when and what to drink. A few violent drunks should not change the rules for all.

4. Add to the street
Some of the best public squares and neighbourhood stretches are those that have been adopted by residents or local business owners. The trees planted by the council might look healthy but they're enhanced because someone has set out their collection of cacti for some morning sunlight or a few Embru loungers have been added so that visitors can take in the sun. Cities can still have rules about where and what to plant but they should also accept when something looks good and allow it to flourish.

5. Properly enjoy the park
Our favourite parks are those that have a metabolism from sunrise until last light. In the morning it's joggers and nude sunbathers, at midday it's business folk enjoying lunch on a bench or kids kicking a ball around, and on sunny evenings there are picnics and plenty of rosé. We prefer park rangers to gently nudge rather than enforce. Give citizens the tools to work with and they'll follow suit.

6. Trade when you like
We're all for a day off but we also believe that a modern city should allow its entrepreneurs to open when they want. No one is telling Amazon that they need to close after 19.00 and that orders can't be taken on Sunday. If local shops are to flourish then they need a more even playing field – and that means the city not getting involved in trading hours.

Tyler Brûlé is Monocle's editor in chief and chairman.

11.
Communist to capitalist
by Annabelle Chapman

Warsaw is a city of layers. For a snapshot of its eclecticism, stop by Grzybowski Square near the main train station. Around the perimeter, glassy blue skyscrapers jostle with nondescript blocks of flats built during the communist era, the red brick of pre-war tenement houses, a renaissance-style church and the site of the Jewish Theatre (with the city's last functioning regular Orthodox Jewish synagogue behind it). Peeking through a gap in the buildings is the Stalinist Palace of Culture and Science, completed in 1955.

The city bears the scars of Poland's history: foreign occupation, wartime devastation and communist rule. Most of its buildings were destroyed by the Nazis during the Second World War, with swathes of the city razed to the ground. Hundreds of thousands of civilians died, including most of the city's Jewish inhabitants. On the rubble of the Warsaw Ghetto, Poland's new communist authorities built a ponderous housing estate. A socialist realist housing complex was constructed along the city's main thoroughfare, its façades decorated with relief carvings of the proletariat. And the Old Town was gradually rebuilt, with planners consulting the Warsaw cityscapes by 18th-century Venetian painter Bernardo Bellotto.

After the fall of communism in eastern Europe in 1989, capitalism swept in, bringing fast-food chains and sprawling shopping malls. A metro – planned during the 1920s – was finally realised. Skyscrapers sprouted around the Palace of Culture and Science, which continues to spark mixed emotions. Some people see it as an ugly reminder of the communist past when Poland was subordinate to the Soviet Union. There have been recurring calls to tear it down but no consensus on what could replace it.

The city's new openness is felt most strongly in summer. People get out more, unlike under communism, when wining and dining options were limited. Cafés move out onto the streets, as part of what is known as the "Mediterranisation" of city centres. On Zbawiciela Square, bike-toting millennials mingle over drinks while old market halls and factories have been transformed into mixed-use spaces serving Asian-style street food. The Vistula embankment has had a facelift, complete with a new promenade and riverside dance spots. On the river's wild eastern bank, sandy beaches offer a view of the city; and neon lights attached to one of the bridges spell out *milo cie wiedziec*, Polish for "nice to see you".

Challenges remain, including the smog in winter – the result of traffic pollution and Poland's dependence on coal. Hardy cyclists don masks and peddle on. The city centre can feel intense; a hot plateau in summer and a frosty expanse in winter but refuge can be found in the leafy districts of Mokotów, Zoliborz, Ochota and Saska Kepa, which retain Warsaw's pre-war charm. These days, their modernist flats built in the 1920s and 1930s house creatives, young families and old-timers, some of whom remember the city before the war. Praga, on the opposite bank, has a more unpolished feel, with century-old tenement houses built around shady courtyards. Some have gaudy shrines to the Virgin Mary, decked with flowers.

Warsaw may lack the historical charm of Poland's second-largest city Kraków, with its preserved medieval centre. But one thing the capital isn't short on is resilience – through war, the communist years and beyond. From the ashes, it has become a thriving city geared towards the future.

Annabelle Chapman is the Poland correspondent for Monocle and 'The Economist'.

12.
Cities as places of refuge
by Carlota Rebelo

When the refugee crisis knocked on Europe's door in the months leading up to the summer of 2015, it didn't prompt an immediate response from officials. It took the capsizing of a makeshift raft off the coast of Libya, which claimed the lives of nearly 800 people, along with the tragic photograph of Alan Kurdi, the three-year-old Syrian baby who drowned on a Turkish beach, for any real action to kick in.

Prompted by the prime ministers of Italy, France and Malta, an emergency meeting between EU interior ministers was called and one of the key decisions made was that each European member state would take in a set number of refugees – the infamous "migrant quotas". In the months that followed, many cities opened their doors (of schools, community centres and public housing) and became veritable havens of safety.

In 2018 the UN high commissioner for refugees estimated that more than half of the world's 22.5 million refugees live in urban areas. Yet often a city's officials, planners and architects are brought into the conversation too late and end up working towards minimising bad decisions rather than initiating positive solutions.

This is one of the main reasons behind the failure of refugee camps, according to expert Kilian Kleinschmidt. He used to run the Zaatari refugee camp in Jordan and believes that they should be planned like a city from the very beginning. "The reason refugee camps are not working is because they are set up as temporary solutions but almost all end up becoming permanent."

In the absence of urban-planners, it's often up to savvy entrepreneurs and local activists to step up to the challenges. Robert Barr is the CEO and founder of jobs4refugees in Germany. Originally from Munich, he decided to create his company after witnessing hundreds of refugees arriving at the city's main train station in 2015. "Our goal is to even the playing field," says Barr. "We want to help refugees find work, overcome the cultural and language barrier, and navigate any bureaucratic hurdles."

At one point during that summer, a reported 10,000 migrants were arriving in Germany every day. So it's no surprise that many of these quick-thinking grassroots organisations came into being at that time. It was then that Mareike Geiling and Jonas Kakoschke created Refugees Welcome, a sort of immigrant Airbnb for new arrivals that matched people who had spare rooms with those in need of shelter. A number of cafés, clubs and restaurants across Berlin displayed a "Refugees Welcome" banner, inviting newcomers into the city.

Long before the photographs of refugees crossing Europe on foot were splashed across front pages around the world, the crisis had been quietly unfolding on the shores of the Mediterranean. Greece, along with Italy, was one of the first entry points for many migrants. And it's in cities such as Rome, Naples, Athens and Thessaloniki – all of which were, at the time, grappling with their own challenges through budget cuts and years of austerity – that integration becomes even more essential.

Giorgos Kaminis was at the start of his second term as mayor of Athens while the crisis was unfolding. For him the biggest issue was that it was impossible to measure what the magnitude of the situation would be. But while those first months were rough, with his city seeing a record number of migrants sleeping on its streets and in its squares, city hall stepped up to the challenge. Kaminis's office created temporary accomodation to house 3,000 refugees and the municipal radio station, Athens 984, started broadcasting news bulletins in Arabic as well as Greek.

The infrastructure for coping with refugees in European cities has come a long way since the summer of 2015, in part thanks to local urban heroes. New enterprises have ranged from an Arabic-language bookshop in Amsterdam to a Syrian restaurant in the heart of Lisbon and a theatre company thriving at the heart of the now-defunct Calais camp in France.

Refugee or not, we all move to cities looking for something – be it a better job, a journey of self-discovery or an improvement to our quality of life. And the reason the move works is because cities quickly make us feel at home.

It's paramount that those who are responsible for making cities, from planners and architects to activists and academics, are engaged from the start. History is cyclical and as our urban areas continue to grow it's likely that another refugee crisis will emerge not long after this one. When that day comes, cities have to be fully prepared to be what they have always been: places of refuge.

Carlota Rebelo is a producer for Monocle 24. She's been producing our flagship cities programme, 'The Urbanist', for the past four years and has interviewed many mayors, planners, activists and urban leaders on what makes a city tick.

13.
The wrong side of the tracks
by Peter York

I live on the wrong side of the tracks in London. I used not to. I've moved here recently. I've lived on the right side. Both right sides in fact, because the tracks in question describe a 90-degree turn, to form two sides of a square of cruel isolation.

Living on the wrong side of the tracks is a staple of class imagery and rebel romance. According to online sources, there are just under 9,400 "wrong side of the tracks" lyrics and 100 albums that address the subject. It used to be the absolute concrete and clay symbolism of social distance and social mobility. What social mobility meant then was undeniably, emphatically geographical. In the old London, the pre-1980s London, there was the idea of making it from the hopeless corners of "south of the river" to the rich and verdant bits of north London. Or "rising in the east and sinking in the west" by moving from London's old East End, centred on the Docklands, to somewhere plutocratic in the West End. I had rich friends at school whose widowed grannies had taken that journey in their lifetimes.

Social determinism meant, until fairly recently, that you are where you live. It was the basic assumption of postwar planning. If geography was destiny then a generation of high-minded postwar planners and architects was determined to change it. In the 1950s and 1960s that meant slum clearance, tower blocks and new towns. Swathes of 19th-century housing stock, poor and not-so-poor, were bulldozed.

Postwar planning utterly destabilised life on the wrong side of London's tracks. Some of the "slum" people were decanted into tower blocks (some of them became "slums in the sky") and others went to more modest outer suburbs. In the 1980s, British prime minister Margaret Thatcher's "right-to-buy" legislation meant that council tenants often bought and resold their council flats and moved to the suburbs as proud first-time owners, leaving their previous homes empty.

On the whole, they remained empty until a combination of unstoppable social forces developed in the 1980s. There was retro romanticism, which turned the tropes of 19th-century developments into "period features". There was the owner-occupier housing boom of the 1980s and what author Richard Florida coined "the rise of the creative class". Young, aspiring middle-class buyers, who couldn't afford, or rejected, their parents' comfortable suburbs or smart right-side central places, wanted somewhere affordable, chic and edgy.

In this spirit of pioneering romance and torrential mortgage money, practically everywhere became redeemable. We came to see the design-literate beauty in 1960s brutalist tower-block flats – whose occupants had fled to the outskirts – or in 19th-century artisan houses with their cast-iron chimneypieces.

I live on the wrong side of the tracks from Belgravia and almost anything adjoining. My area of Pimlico was developed for the Grosvenor family by Thomas Cubitt, the biggest builder in the world in the first half of the 19th century. Its stucco cliffs and oversized porches were designed to appeal to the aspirant upper-middles; like South Kensington 20 years later, Belgravia itself was built for full-on toffs. Then the railway came in the 1860s and cut us, the people of Pimlico, off from the world. (We still live in approximately 1979.) I've resented it ever since.

Peter York is a cultural commentator, management consultant, author, broadcaster and contributor to Monocle and M24. He co-authored Harpers & Queen's 'The Official Sloane Ranger Handbook' in 1982 and has since published books such as 'Peter York's Eighties' and 'Authenticity is a Con'.

14.
Where have all the killers gone?
by David Usborne

Cities across the US are racked by crime; international gangs such as MS-13 are on a rampage while drug trafficking and porous borders mean more killers are flooding in. That's what you'd think listening to Donald Trump, who campaigned on a tough law and order platform; at his inauguration he vowed to stop the "American carnage".

Compelling, to be sure, but many voters knew better. Or should have.

Mass shootings in public places have united the country in grief with disturbing frequency. Instances of police violence against minority citizens have been grabbing the headlines. But it's not the bad old days, not by any means.

When were they exactly? The late 1980s and early 1990s, when big metropolises were virtually synonymous with murder and mayhem. If you weren't directly living it, you saw it on TV police shows such as the *Hill Street Blues*.

But Gotham doesn't need Bruce Wayne anymore. Just as Trump took office, New York saw its murder rate fall to levels not seen since the 1940s. The NYPD spoke of a "New York miracle". Chicago and Houston also saw a calming of the criminal waters. Some cities lagged but the direction was clear.

What's the US doing differently? The economy and available wealth matter. And confidence. In the prosperous 1990s, investors pushed past recognised urban frontiers of Washington, putting their money into areas they once saw as no-go zones and transforming the nature of downtown in the process. The same dynamic occurred in Harlem.

Police tactics count too. Soon after Rudy Giuliani became mayor in 1994, New York attracted attention not for its violence but because of what it was doing to stop it. It turned successive NYPD police commissioners into international stars of urban crime fighting. First among them was Bill Bratton, who embraced the "broken window" approach, which held that no crime was too small to ignore.

There's also been a new focus on using technology such as CompStat, a system that collects and drills down into data that allows commanders to identify areas of high crime and respond with resources. As the years passed and the statistics improved, the NYPD also began to prioritise the human side of its mission. Instead of being deployed depending on what day it was, officers were assigned neighbourhoods and kept there over long periods. They would get to know them like the residents did and the residents would get to know the officers and, with luck, trust them.

Cities in the US will never beat all crime. Gangs still fight for turf and lives are lost in the crossfire. The cocaine epidemic of the late 1980s is a distant memory but drugs persist. Nevertheless, the fear that so many urban-dwellers in the US once harboured has receded.

David Usborne was a correspondent for 'The Independent' for 30 years and now writes for Monocle and other titles. He lives in New York with his partner.

offshoot of Google's parent company Alphabet), which is building the first data-driven urban development in Toronto. Here energy will be recycled to heat and cool buildings, and driverless cars will be used to save space and combat pollution. This technology bears the promise for a safer, cleaner and happier urban future. It has something of the utopia that Walt Disney presented in his plans for the Experimental Prototype Community of Tomorrow in 1966 and what Mark Zuckerberg is trying to create with Facebook City, a mixed-use hub inspired by idealistic architectural theories.

15.
How to fix yesterday's mistakes
by Alice Cabaret

With centuries of city building under our belt, we're still no closer to that holy grail of urbanism: the "ideal city". And no wonder. Cities are inherently flawed, chaotic reflections of their creators. But would we want it any other way? Past attempts at achieving urban perfection have resulted in sterile and oppressive environments, from dysfunctional grand ensembles to lifeless new towns. Jane Jacobs said that cities are "immense laboratories of trial and error, failure and success" – and maybe that's the way they should be.

Some may argue that technology brings us closer to an urban ideal. One example is Sidewalk Labs (an

These living laboratories are all after the same thing – perfection – but perhaps that isn't what we should be striving for. After all, the very spaces inherited from our past mistakes provide platforms for some of the most innovative initiatives. New spaces are rising from the post-industrial rubble, transforming warehouses into fertile breeding grounds for entrepreneurs and motorways into blossoming urban parks. Urban innovation is not merely a result but a process that calls for forward-thinking start-ups, artists and local communities.

Celebrating our freedom to fail may be the best way in which to address yesterday's mistakes. It's only through experimentation that we'll be able to tackle the unprecedented complexity and growing challenges faced by our cities today.

Alice Cabaret is the founder and director of The Street Society, an agency that specialises in property development and urban transformation.

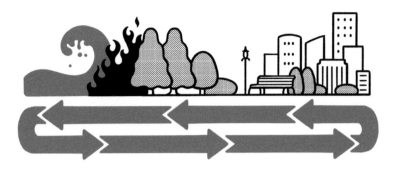

16.
Going green
by Shelley Poticha

Just as with any true love, to adore a city is to adore all of its parts. That means the iconic buildings, streetscapes and cafés, of course, but also the grittier side, the curbside yelling matches and honking horns. Whether a commitment or a fling, getting to know a city contributes to how we get along in the world. Cities, in fact, are touchstones in our human interactions: "Oh, do you know Detroit? How is it these days?"

But just as we would ask about a significant other who has become ill, so should we be worried about cities as their urban immune systems are pushed to the limits. We've all noticed it. As more of us crowd into cities, cars are straining roads and resources, temperatures are ever more extreme, air quality is suffering, green space is shrinking, walking and biking is riskier, housing is more expensive and transit is overcrowded. In some cases, lives and neighbourhoods are being wiped out by monster storms, flash floods and fires. Our cities and the people in and around them face challenges at the hands of many forces – but a chief concern underlying all of these issues is climate change.

There is a seemingly growing voice in the US that climate change isn't real or that its effects aren't knowable or seen. But, be it a blessing or a curse, when one is an environmental urbanist with a background in city planning and development, one "sees" climate change everywhere. Also, one notices what cities are doing about it.

While it's true that cities are at the nexus of all that climate change has wrought, they are also the best and most likely leaders in sustainability and resiliency. What most of their leaders and stakeholders understand is that if cities go down, we all go down, and what some metropolises are trying to do to prevent that is astounding.

Sometimes it's a result of lessons learned. Hurricane Sandy humbled current New York mayor Bill de Blasio, who is working to cut the vast amounts of energy waste in Manhattan's beloved skyscrapers to reduce the global temperature warming that's contributing to such storms. And even Houston, after watching Hurricane Harvey turn parts of the city into a "Waterworld", is rethinking its freewheeling approach to development, or at least giving green infrastructure a chance.

It's also the realisation that climate change prevention and adaptation are key to future prosperity. Some statistics: from 2014 to 2016, sustainable investments grew by more than $2trn; by the Federal Emergency Management Agency's estimates, for every dollar invested in climate resiliency, we save at least $4, and energy efficiency could save the US economy $327bn (€280.6bn) a year by 2030.

Cities such as Austin and Portland, Oregon are aware that going green and taking action on sustainability adds to their appeal. Austin's focus on renewable energy, green jobs and the environment is partly why business is flocking there.

Some have gone so far as to call this the age of New Localism – a kind of cultural antidote to the rise of populism. But our cities' efforts to become more sustainable aren't about politics or cultural theory. Climate change effects are a clear and present danger. Fighting back, and adapting in ways that only cities can, will mean that we can stick around to fall in love with cities and their way of life again and again.

Shelley Poticha leads the Natural Resources Defense Council's Healthy People & Thriving Communities programme. She works with local, national and global leaders to build resilient communities and make cities part of the answer to climate change.

17.
Why diversity matters
by Alexandra Hagen

You know it, big brands know it and politicians know it: the ability to innovate is paramount for any and every business. Innovation is a key driver of prosperity. The question is, how can our cities contribute to the growth of innovation?

Let's begin by examining what prosperous cities have had in common for centuries: trade. Trade with strangers, who over time ceased to be strangers; trade of pearls, seeds and silk but also of values, traditions and languages.

For thriving cities, this openness and diversity is a necessity. Bringing together a mix of people with their unique experiences, know-how and culture is a source of innovation. And there's no lack of evidence to suggest that businesses with a more diverse workforce outperform others. Without this diversity, a city's financial growth and quality of life declines.

According to the Knight Foundation's "Knight Soul of the Community" study, the most important factors for attracting talent are social offerings, aesthetics and openness. The latter, in particular, is often sacrificed for security, despite research showing that political and social polarisation divide a city and increase the risk of conflict.

My solution for building an open city is to invest in these four elements:

1. Connectivity

Prioritise people over cars. Bike lanes and pedestrian routes are an asset to all inhabitants and contribute to better health. The transformation of Bogotá proves that the increased presence of bike lanes and pedestrian zones improves safety and lowers crime rates.

2. Culture

A rich cultural offering encourages social interaction and promotes a city's brand beyond its borders. After the 2008 recession, the number of "staycations" in the US increased and the most popular destinations were those that invested in culture.

3. Public spaces

Investing in timeless design improves less popular areas and connects people with their communities. With Bryant Park in New York, for example, some landscaping, design and maintenance have changed the reputation of the neighbourhood.

4. Affordable housing

A city cannot function without a variety of people doing a variety of jobs. Berlin has grown as a hub for start-ups and innovation in large part because it has been able to provide and sustain affordable housing. Cities benefit from erasing segregated living conditions, where people with high and low incomes are separated.

Ghettoisation contributes to polarisation, which in turn fuels distrust. Trust is the currency of democracy and the foundation for a peaceful and safe society. In order to build a prosperous city, diversity and trust are vital.

Alexandra Hagen is an architect and the CEO of White Arkitekter, specialising in designing sustainable architecture.

18.
City as gym
by Guy Perry

I did it again this morning. I pedalled nearly 20km on a bicycle but went nowhere: 450 calories burned in air-conditioned comfort while staring at a TV screen. I do this stationary cycling often these days to offset the sedentary lifestyles that the city imposes on us.

Urban environments engineered over the past few decades are primarily the habitats of cars, and the heart of the most cherished historic cities can often fit within the area of a motorway interchange. Even in those places where cycling was once a staple of mobility it has become a life-threatening exercise. Driving isn't much better: not only are road death tolls high but each hour spent in a car per day on a regular basis increases the risk of obesity by 6 per cent.

Both of my grandfathers walked or cycled to work, because they could. One in a US university town, the other in a leafy suburb west of Paris. Walking and biking were the fastest, safest and most pleasant ways in which to start and end the day. They both stayed trim without a gym, ate whatever they enjoyed and lived well into their eighties. Passing away in the late 20th century, they predated another physical challenge of the modern city: virtual connectivity. They did not have the health burden of spending seven hours a day online.

Human anatomy evolves slowly compared with the technologies we create and the environments they shape. We're still conditioned for the 15km that hunter-gatherers walked and sometimes ran each day to survive. Until a century ago we would often get around on horseback. The farther we get from a balanced range of daily physical activity, the more our bodies – and eventually our minds – suffer.

Lives lived in the world's fastest-growing cities are increasingly spent in vehicles, lifts and the virtual sphere of screens and smartphones. Too many well-educated, well-paid professionals in emerging markets are afflicted by avoidable diseases before their time. In India, for example, moving from the countryside to the city brings with it a four to six-fold increase in the likelihood of being diabetic. Ironically, the comfort of the "good life" often shortens it.

Today, a growing engagement with the virtual world has made us more sedentary than ever before, so it's crucial that we build cities that coax us back onto our feet and into a human-scaled urban habitat. When I lived in Paris, Tokyo, Barcelona and Cambridge, Massachusetts, I used to gingerly crisscross town on a daily basis. I cannot say the same for my new home.

Guy Perry is the vice president of urban planning and design for management consulting company McKinsey & Company. As architect, designer and developer, he focuses on creating sustainable urban environments.

19.
An ode to suburbia
by Jamie Waters

warm evening in December, the air still and lights from waterfront homes sparkling, Perth is a hard place to top.

People from other Australian cities refer to the Western Australian capital as a "big country town" and there is some merit to that: it has always felt sleepier than its sizeable population (about two million) suggests. This is attributable to its isolation and, historically, the lack of

Belmont Park racecourse that, once completed, will provide 4,500 apartments.

The boom may be over but it has left Perth with this impressive hardware and brought life to the city centre. There are more attractions for tourists and locals alike. Inner-city living is now the norm for young people, who have moved into red-brick townhouses in CBD-abutting

Growing up in Perth in the 1990s meant growing up in sun-kissed suburbia. We played on streets lined with weeping peppermint trees and rode our scooters to the tennis club after school. We stuck to the leafy suburbs, which are flanked on either side by stretches of water: the Indian Ocean and the Swan River. Visits to the "city" (or CBD) were rare; trips to the beach were frequent. Imagine if *American Beauty* was transported to the seaside and you get the gist.

Our scooters were soon replaced with secondhand cars. Obtaining a driver's licence is a big deal here. This is a car city: the suburbs are strung out along the coast, connected by parkland and motorways, so there's a sizeable distance between hubs. Each outer neighbourhood (or clutch of outer neighbourhoods) has a village-like nucleus, whether Claremont in the affluent "western" suburbs or Fremantle, the historic port, to the south.

Perth is best enjoyed in a car with the windows down and the radio up. During high school and university, summer nights were spent driving around with friends. Inevitably these trips ended with us sitting on the bonnet in one of the parks overlooking the Swan River, the blue lifeblood of the city. At its best, on a

a bustling CBD. There is a high quality of life here – it's one of the wealthiest and sunniest cities in Australia – and the pace is slower. Businessmen surf before work and families have riverside picnics for dinner.

In the past decade, however, the world's most isolated (state) capital city has experienced a shift. It has grown up, shedding some of its languid vibe, and become more "big city". The mining boom that started in 2009 and soared until 2014 brought huge injections of cash and people to the city. While the rest of the world plummeted with the financial crisis, Western Australians were rolling in iron-ore money. There was much chatter about "cashed-up bogans" – men who did shift work in mining towns and splashed cash on waterskis and holiday homes. At its peak, in 2012, the mining industry was worth AU$120bn (€75.8bn).

With the mining money came big infrastructure projects: two state-of-the-art hospitals; a new stadium; the Elizabeth Quay waterfront development; a public library (the first civic building to be erected since the 1970s); and a gilded hotel and casino called Crown Perth. What will be the biggest building in the city is currently under construction: a multipurpose development at

neighbourhoods. Projects such as the five-starred Como the Treasury hotel have brought razzmatazz. And the scene has been bolstered by the relaxation of drinking laws, which has seen small bars spring up.

Perth possesses extreme versions of all the characteristics that are particular to Australia. Australia's weather is good; Perth's is exceptionally so. Australia is isolated – yet no city of comparable size is more isolated than Perth. This isolation is both its greatest asset and Achilles heel. On the one hand it gives the city a sense of escapism and means there are plenty of jobs: many international companies have Perth branches because the city is so far from anywhere else. Yet with isolation also comes parochialism, claustrophobia and a brain drain of talent to Sydney, Melbourne and London.

This oil painting of a city is bigger than ever with its new CBD. Yet the real heart of Perth is not found in these multibillion-dollar developments but in the small suburban hubs dotted along the water – in the beach cafés, riverside bars and sun-drenched tennis clubs.

Jamie Waters is Monocle's fashion editor and grew up on the sandy beaches and grass tennis courts of Perth.

20.
Q&A with Helle Søholt

As co-founder of Gehl architecture practice, Helle Søholt has gained a unique insight into how to build cities. Together with the celebrated Danish architect and urban-planner, Jan Gehl, Søholt has helped cities from Buenos Aires to Shanghai create a more people-centric design. Here she tells us how we can build better cities and why it's such an urgent issue.

What inspired you to become an architect?
I think for me it was the opportunity to have an impact on society and find creative ways of solving problems. When I studied in Copenhagen I was fortunate to meet Jan Gehl, who was a professor at the time. In Jan's department for urban design I was introduced to a range of international thinkers and in 1998 Jan invited me to join his one-man studio. We started working on projects together and in 2000 he invited me to co-found Gehl Architects.

Should we model all cities on Copenhagen?
I don't think so, even though there are a number of things that we can learn from a city such as Copenhagen. It's relatively small compared to many other cities around the world and it has been experimenting with a more integrated and people-oriented approach to urban design for years.

Jan started impacting that journey way back in the 1960s. For that very reason, Copenhagen has come far and can be an inspiration – but we don't go around "Copenhagenising" other cities. In fact, we have a strong methodology that's rooted in an anthropological approach to surveying and understanding what's important, what's at risk and what cultural opportunities a city has. We use Public Life Public Space surveys to map what's going on in cities. We also investigate the quality and nature of life itself. It's only by understanding the unique qualities of life in every place that we can make a positive difference.

Why has it taken planners so long to understand that cities should be built for people?
History and society go through different cycles and I think for a long time there's been a focus on a more isolating, systematic approach. Cities all around the world are experiencing extreme densification these days and many are struggling with the same problems, including climate change, traffic congestion, lack of financing, ageing populations, an increase in obesity and so on. These issues share one common denominator: we're the cause, so we have to adopt a more multidisciplinary, holistic and people-centric approach to urban planning and design.

Are you finding that more cities are adopting this approach?
A shift has happened over the past 10 years and we're seeing a push towards this approach across the world. When we started out in 2000 there wasn't much talk about the social values and issues that cities

struggle with. The main problem that cities – and companies – face today is social inequality. It's a huge risk to our societies if we don't find ways of engaging people and ensuring more transparent decision-making.

How many cities has Gehl worked with to implement this strategy?
We've worked with 250 cities and are trying to focus on what we call "reference cities" – those that others look to for a solution. Lately we've been working in China. The country is building a huge number of new towns and, in these new towns, the streets have disappeared; in their place, enormous roads and tower developments have been built. If you study how Chinese cities historically worked, you'll find that the streets brought everyone together; it's where trade and community were at home. Their new cookie-cutter model could potentially have a culturally damaging effect on society. We've been working with city governments to ensure that there is, in fact, life between buildings. In Shanghai, for example, we're looking at how to allow public access to the Huangpu River and make sure public spaces and cycling routes are developed along the entire river.

How can we build better cities?
Urban projects take a long time to implement. Even in a city such as Copenhagen the metro system we're building was planned in the 1990s. You might make a decision and only see the results 10 to 20 years later. We're advocating for a framework-type approach to planning, instead of traditional master plans, to allow for the revision of plans after every implementation phase so that you can see and learn what works. If we want to achieve climate-neutral and sustainable communities, we need to effect a change in behaviour at the individual level and we need to learn from what we're doing. I think cities, governments and companies must find new ways of collaborating because we don't have time for everybody to reinvent the wheel by themselves.

Cities too often get slated for being lonely, anonymous places but they are, contrary to what the nay-sayers think, inherently social: they were born out of their residents' willingness to join a huge group of people and engage with the endless possibility of encounters that this concentration of humans affords. Some cities may have always been laid out following this convivial principle (take Rome and its piazzas, for example) but others have had to adapt and set aside some room where citizens can get together. Sometimes it's a matter of reclaiming a space that was colonised by traffic for too long. Often, though, the urban equivalent of a living room where people can linger, sit down and chat comes in the shape of a park.

No matter whether they're big and centrally located or tiny and tucked away between towers, parks are fundamental to a city's metabolism – and not just because of their obvious anti-pollution credentials. Greenery's power to boost an urban-dweller's mood is well-documented by now. In many ways, parks act as pockets of nature amid the cement but still adhere to a city's rules and rhythms. Like the streets that surround them, they're often busy all day long, with everything from morning dog walks to sunset picnics. And, like the cities that they belong to, they play host to all sorts of people and activities. Parks are, above all, democratic spaces where enjoyment comes for free – just as it does at urban beaches, lakes and swimming pools. Forever enticing, especially when the summer mercury starts rising, a city's aquatic areas offer refuge and relaxation to those who don't have the time or money to leave the metropolitan boundaries. Long left to run their course, rivers are also being rediscovered as refreshing retreats and are increasingly being redeveloped and purified for residents to take a dip.

Away from the cars and surrounded by trees, spaces for sport are at their best when they double up as meeting points and make exercise an excuse rather than a chore. In this chapter, we explore why a sense of community is a cardinal factor in relishing our city's public hangouts. Follow us at your leisure as we guide you through the spots that help to ensure that living in a city is always a pleasure.

3.

LEISURE AND PLEASURE

Parks, squares and pop-ups
Let's get together

That being around greenery has a positive impact on our mood is obvious from any memory of a lunchtime spent lounging on the grass. Parks are often one of the main criteria we use to judge a city's liveability and since the Victorian era London's urbanists have been aware of their potential to transform entire neighbourhoods.

It wasn't until 1984, though, that the biologist Edward O Wilson formalised this idea and called it "Biophilia", a theory that views the natural world as a calming influence on humans. It may be unrealistic and unnecessary for cities to strive for a complete communion with nature but the concept of "seeing out" still has a bearing on our state of mind. That's why investment in greenery is essential for our cities, no matter how expansive or diminutive the plot, and it's also why skilful and far-sighted landscape architects such as Kathryn Gustafson and Thomas Woltz are fostering an ever-growing portfolio of municipal commissions.

Beyond their physiological benefits, parks are a natural haven where people can come together. And spaces that lend themselves to community gatherings are always worth fighting for, whether or not they're filled with foliage.

1.
Olympiapark, Munich
Time to reflect

More than just a way of bringing nature into the concrete jungle, parks are an integral part of the urban environment. So much so, they become one of a city's symbols: imagine New York without Central Park, Tokyo without Yoyogi or Madrid without Buen Retiro.

That's also true of Munich and its Olympiapark, built to host the city's 1972 Summer Games. German firm Behnisch & Partner created an undulating landscape that mimicked the topography of the nearby Alps. And when the Games wrapped up, Olympiapark managed what many other huge infrastructural projects have struggled with: it transitioned into a popular public park.

Decades later there's an aquarium, another sports hall, a restaurant and a sausage stand in its grounds. In 2017 the number of visitors was estimated at almost four million, making this one of the most visited Olympic park in the world and proving that evolving, upgrading and taking care of your assets is the best route to a lasting legacy.

Trees that brand a city
Urban roots

1. **Jacaranda, Mexico City:** After Washington DC received cherry blossom trees as a gift from Tokyo in 1912, Mexican president Pascual Ortiz Rubio asked the Japanese government for plants too. The cherries failed to blossom in Central America, so master gardener Tatsugoro Matsumoto chose the more suitable jacaranda; they still turn the city a brighter shade of purple every spring.

2. **Palm, Los Angeles:** Flick through old black-and-white photos of LA and you'll notice that one key feature is missing: the palm trees crowned with comical tufts of hair-like fronds. Now iconic residents, they took up their famed posts when city hall methodically planted them to beautify the broad boulevards ahead of the 1932 Olympics; an estimated 40,000 were planted at intervals of 12 to 16 metres. The swaying trees soon became synonymous with the sunny city and still play a leading role in LA's visual identity.

3. **Plane, London:** Despite not being native, this mottled trunk appears so frequently in the UK capital that it's now dubbed the London plane. Though this kind of tree is thought to have been introduced during the 1500s, most of the planes in London's parks and footpaths were planted in the 19th century to add a dash of green to its growing network of streets. The bark's tendency to peel and shed is said to be the reason behind the species' ability to weather city pollution.

4. **Ginkgo, Tokyo:** The fleeting sea of powder-pink cherry blossom that colours Japanese cities in spring is matched in beauty only by the amber glow of ginkgo leaves come autumn. Before the grey of winter descends, Tokyo is broken up by golden bursts of this tree's spoils; in their final act, the fan-shaped leaves litter pavements, parks and temple grounds. The ginkgo is thought to have relatives dating back 270 million years and is a symbol of endurance and longevity; some trees live to be 1,000 years old.

5. **Gum tree, Brisbane:** There's hardly a city in Australia that's not shaded by gum trees. The narrow trunks stretch skyward and are topped by spindly arms sprouting perfumed grey leaves. In Brisbane many varieties appear on the banks of the river, on empty land next to motorways and at the centre of roundabouts. They are so ingrained in the urban landscape that children's author May Gibbs created an anthology of tales about them, *Snugglepot and Cuddlepie*, essential reading for any Aussie child.

2.
Pocket parks, Global
Planting the seed

Parks are a precious resource but, as our cities get busier, catering for an expanding population often means high-rises are built where trees used to stand. Densely built neighbourhoods that no longer have space for expansive fields need not give up on carving out room for green spaces, though. No matter how pint-sized the patch, frequent dots of foliage can make vegetation accessible to residents. Nooks, crannies and corners can only improve by turning from cement to grass: pocket parks can fill gaps between buildings with picnic benches, pathways and plants.

Some emerge in disused stretches: in London's red-brick Bethnal Green, one now thrives in a former dead end that's been transformed from a fly-tipping spot into an expanse filled with flowerbeds. Devised in partnership with the local authority by landscape architect Luke Greysmith and John Ryan, the CEO of the area's community centre, the narrow alleyway of Derbyshire Street hosts residents' street parties as well as their daily chit-chats.

The UK capital is commendable for its investment in this kind of space. Between 2012 and 2015, city hall's pocket parks programme allocated a healthy £2m (€2.2m) to create more than 100 such projects in its boroughs.

In New York, meanwhile, pocket parks often crop up in the shape of privately owned public spaces, where a building's courtyard or rooftop is redesigned to welcome both people and greenery. Voluntary community groups such as the East Village Parks Conservancy have also been working to upgrade and expand the tiny plots in lower Manhattan. Similarly, on the West Coast, architecture firms such as Perkins+Will have included green space in new landscaping projects. When designing a station for Los Angeles Police Department, the studio added a pocket park to help the community feel more connected with the officers.

Thanks to their size and proximity, these small patches of foliage give residents a sense of responsibility and ownership of their verdant refuge wherever they sprout.

High point: Parisian mayor Anne Hidalgo's "licence to green" initiative not only improves the look of the French capital's streets but is also helping to increase the biodiversity of flora and fauna

3.
Neighbourhood gardening, Tokyo and Paris
Grow your own

Not all local governments make greening the streets an investment priority so residents are grabbing their shears and fighting for their own right to vegetation.

Tokyo's citizen gardeners have made their DIY plantings a feature of their cityscape for more than a century. Typically their patches feature no more than a collection of potted plants, spilling from doorsteps onto the pavement. Officials tend to oppose them, griping that these micro-gardens blur the line between public and private property (and are sometimes scruffy). Admittedly, such random acts of greening can produce mixed results. But cities can only benefit by getting residents involved in the upkeep of neighbourhood plots.

In Paris, as part of a government scheme to add 100 hectares of vegetation to the city's streets, citizens can apply for a "permit to vegetalise" plots across the arrondissements. As well as turning the bases of trees into gardens, they can also install tubs and planters in public spaces – outside shops, cafés and schools – with soil and seeds provided by city hall. The project's social effect is blossoming, bringing together colleagues and neighbours who rarely spoke before.

Chapter 3
Leisure and pleasure
Parks, squares and pop-ups

4.
Balconies and terraces, Beirut and Milan
Cherry on top

A city's green credentials are often measured by how much verdant space it offers at street level. What's often forgotten is what lies hidden above eyeline: plants, flowers and trees on people's balconies, rooftops and terraces.

Look skyward in Beirut and you will see greenery spilling from balconies of both villas and apartment blocks. In a city suffering from a public-space crisis (there are next to no communal parks, let alone planted ones) these spaces have become surrogate gardens. Individuals rather than the authorities are doing the city a service: the plants growing on their terraces improve air quality, perfume the streets, provide shade and soften some of the city's less appealing landmarks. Other than creating a diffused refuge from what Beirutis call *a'jja* (the crowded, polluted side of the city), these planting efforts afford residents some privacy, and in their befuddling variety they also reflect the Lebanese capital's manifold personalities.

On terraces across Milan, citizens have also created their own patches of personal botanical gardens to make their city that much more liveable. Vegetation runs from wild fennel and roses to bougainvillea and cacti, and herbs, vegetables and fruit are grown to be used in kitchens. All this flora attracts and feeds the butterflies, bees and birds who manage to make the city their home.

With these efforts, residents have helped combat Milan's image as a dour, grey city that lacks the beauty of Rome and Florence. Milan is also where architect Stefano Boeri decided to create his Bosco Verticale, a pair of green-studded apartment towers that have become an oft-replicated model of vegetation-clad housing. The buildings' balconies are home to 20,000 plants and up to 900 trees (some as high as nine metres), which also do their bit to fight against smog and CO_2 emissions.

On a high: These private spots – all in Milan – also add to the common good by shading roofs, limiting the need for air-con

5.
Office greenery, Global
Cultivating productivity

Ferns and cacti may have recently become a fashionable addition to offices but the idea of bringing greenery into a workplace dates back to the 19th century. Back then, the UK's business owners often built "factory gardens" for their workers; they were guided by a belief that happy workers are also productive ones. Recent studies have proven them right. Filling an office with plants is a cost-efficient method of boosting memory and concentration, if only by improving air quality. Some research claims that greenery can be responsible for a 15 per cent uptick in productivity.

So it's not surprising that many companies have rediscovered the value of keeping plants in their offices. Apple's Californian base is built in a circle around trees and lawns. Plans for Google's new offices in London's King's Cross reveal a linear rooftop park with a running track, while Amazon's Spheres in Seattle have their own in-house horticulturist. Smaller businesses are following suit: despite a tight budget, Dutch pram-maker Joolz (*pictured*) has added three greenhouses to the office floor at its Amsterdam HQ. These spaces contain meeting rooms and work spaces brimming with tropical foliage.

6.
Tactical urbanism, Budapest
Reclaiming the streets

Parks and green spaces may offer a naturally conducive environment for get-togethers but shared space in a city doesn't always need to come accompanied by foliage. Nor does it need to be neatly set aside for that purpose by town hall. With or without the approval of government, groups of residents in many cities have been reclaiming their streets from traffic, even if the results are not permanent.

Citizens-turned-urban architects have proved time and again that bursts of action can have powerful and positive effects. Tactical urbanism, as it's often referred to, can have the most impact when its scope is limited: the temporary, pop-up appeal applies to urban interventions and not just restaurant openings.

In Budapest a successful act of citizen-led urbanism first took place in 2016, when traffic on the city's famous Liberty Bridge was halted due to nearby construction. People claimed the road for themselves and began gathering on the bridge to drink wine, practise yoga and play cards. Word spread, more came and as the summer drew to an end the people weren't quite ready to hand the bridge back. This place had turned into the best-loved plaza in the city.

Eventually the bridge had to reopen to traffic but a year later a deal was struck between officials and a collective of architects, engineers and musicians. For four weekends over the summer, cars would be banished again and hundreds of citizens would be allowed once more to walk, sit and chat on top of the steel supports of this art nouveau treasure.

Initiatives like this skirt a boundary between protest and celebration. They're joyous and festival-like but they're also intended to make city hall take notice – and further action. Bogotà's Ciclovía (*see page 113*), where roads are closed to car traffic on Sundays, and Singapore's walking road takeovers function in the same vein. Cities may often consider costly proposals to create public space but, as Budapest demonstrated, sometimes all you need is a mundane road closure and a bunch of determined citizens.

Winning looks: This project's success lies in the structure and location of Liberty Bridge. Its steel supports, which swoop down almost to the pavement, provide seating and shade. Wide pavements become bike lanes while the main road beckons foot traffic. And noise pollution from the crowd is not a problem due to the bridge's position far away from homes

Piazza the action: Rome's piazzas are popular with locals who come for fresh produce, a morning cappuccino, conversation and a glass of wine at the end of the day. It's worth noting, however, that some have been used for public executions and today have to contend with the odd rowdy tourist drunk. Sometimes a bit too much life can take place in these squares

7.
The piazza, Rome
Fair and square

Because they're born out of residents' needs, urban spaces where people spend time together often have a joyously spontaneous feel and an in-built sense of vibrant liveliness. When it comes to planning a communal space from scratch, though, the danger is ending up with something sterile and artificial.

To find the perfect example of a space that promotes social life, developers should look no further than the Italian piazza. On the face of it, a piazza is nothing more than a paved opening surrounded by buildings. But this urban form has rules and characteristics that distinguish it from any old square. It's no coincidence that many master urbanists (including Jan Gehl) look at this archetype when researching ways to create a human-focused city. With its origins in the Greek *agora* (a designated space for citizen gatherings), the piazza has always had community building as its founding principle. Since renaissance times, piazzas have held steady as the focal point of an Italian town's goings-on by becoming the combined seat of all its commercial, political and religious activities. Built to surround a municipal hall or a church and often to host a market, the piazza's key asset has always been its many uses.

Fundamentally, piazzas were always conceived as pedestrian-first spots where interaction between people is not predetermined by set-out paths but encouraged via a series of focal points such as a fountain, some benches or a monument's steps. At their best, squares are spacious but not too large; people feel comfortable in areas that feel contained and that can be easily surveyed with one single look. In their architecture, piazzas need to feel consistent and seamless. This way, they can become the flexible, buzzing living room of the city. With enough small shops and a few cafés (with outdoor seating, of course), this exemplary slice of urban planning still shows that the best kind of interaction is always born out of variety.

8.
Pavement parks, San Francisco
Crossing the line

While streets make up the majority of public space in a city, they're generally only used by pedestrians rushing from A to B. But savvy citizens have begun laying their hands on parking spaces to create places where you can finally slow down and take a break.

Most have San Francisco's Pavements to Parks initiative to thank for coming up with the idea. The project – known as "Park(ing) Day" – began in 2005, when landscape architect Blaine Merker and fellow artists Matthew Passmore and John Bela decided to pay a couple of hours' worth of metered parking space on Mission Street and turn it into a tiny public park, effectively renting 18.6 sq m of prime urban real estate for $2 an hour. They unrolled turf on the asphalt, placed a large tree and bench within the white tick marks and waited. Soon enough, people came, kicked off their shoes and sat down. This original "Park(ing)" installation then turned into an annual event and, later, into semi-permanent fixtures called "parklets". They don't always feature grass and plants: many of the 50-plus installations across San Francisco consist of cheerfully designed seating areas. Now, in cities from Montréal to Melbourne, "parklets" function as anything from croquet pitches to libraries.

9.
Dog runs, New York
Paws for thought

Having a dog trot by your side does wonders to combat a city-induced sense of loneliness – and not just because pooches are faithful companions. Dog-owners are a peculiar tribe who inhabit almost-empty parks before sunrise. They congregate daily in dog runs and often end up making friends too.

Many of the 140 public off-lead areas in New York have become busier morning meet-up places than some neighbourhood cafés. In the heart of Manhattan's East Village, the Tompkins Square Dog Run is the oldest in New York. Opened in 1990 in place of a run-down square, the park has always been funded and managed by volunteers. Tompkins's granite sand, ample runs, bone-shaped paddle pools, fresh-water hoses and picnic areas still make this the city's best canine oasis.

While most other New Yorkers are getting ready for their daily commute in a jam-packed subway, here residents of all stripes can get together and enjoy an early-morning natter. Some (having just rolled out of bed) keep to themselves. Yet no matter the hour, dogs are consistently enthusiastic; this is their chance to roam free in their own little piece of Manhattan.

Runners-up:
Other New York doggy favourites include Washington Square Dog Run in Greenwich Village – with its circular benches for both humans and their four-legged friends – and Battery Park City's Sirius Dog Run, known for its refreshing pool

Urban canine companions
Five furry urban friends

1. **Wire fox terrier:** The wire fox terrier is gentle and sociable with both people and pooches so trips to the park may well end in making new friends. Its small stature and laid-back attitude mean it's also content to relax with you indoors. But this is not a dog to be neglected; it needs a good brush every now and then and regular trips to the salon, please.

2. **Whippet:** A little smaller than a greyhound but equally slim and fast (and we mean *really* fast), the whippet is a graceful, well-tempered companion. Highly strung and muscular, it's not the breed for couch potatoes: while it may have a placid disposition when inside, the whippet loves a good sprint around a park and won't be happy unless it has regular outings. Its silky, short coat means little maintenance is required (so no expensive grooming bills).

3. **Cavalier King Charles spaniel:** If you're not sold on the regal name alone, this breed's loving and loyal demeanour will win you over. Its favourite occupation is to spend time with its owner. What more could you want after a hard week? Unlike other very sociable breeds such as the golden retriever, the King Charles is petite and doesn't need a half-marathon every morning to be happy; it's usually content with a modest stroll. Forget to comb its luscious hair, though, and you'll have one grumpy pooch on your hands.

4. **Bichon frise:** If this nipper looks like it's just walked out of the salon, that's because it probably has. The bichon frise is the chic madame of the canine world. It can be a fussy eater (with a proclivity for podginess) and needs regular, often professional, grooming. But among the breed's many virtues are a playful, verging on comic, disposition and a compact stature perfect for apartment-dwellers. Exercise is a must, of course, but a 30-minute walk each day is sufficient. And did we mention how adorable it is?

5. **Basenji:** This African breed is the ideal city dog. Slim, graceful and independent (you might come home to find it playing poker with pals), the basenji is as fastidiously clean as a cat. It enjoys stretching its legs (but not as much as a boxer), and its short, suede-like coat is easier to care for than that of a terrier. Taciturn households, rejoice: the basenji doesn't bark, instead emitting melodious little chortles. That should keep the neighbours' noise complaints at bay.

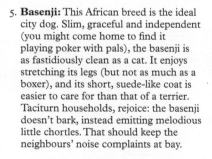

Water
Dive straight in

In cities, places to swim serve an important social function. They're like urban pressure valves: diving into and lolling around a cool blue rectangle of water acts as a distraction and a diffuser of daily tensions.

An urban swimming pool or city beach is an oasis in a concrete landscape and has a purpose far beyond fitness. These are places to gather, chat and soak up some vitamin D. Well-managed lidos, in fact, are like model communities, with their own rules and social mores. Packed together on our towels, we're happy, so long as we have the option of a cooling dip. Often we choose to recline, lathered in sun cream, and not take the plunge at all – it's enough to know that the water is close by.

Given all this, it seems odd that municipal leaders in coastal cities often choose art galleries and museums as catalysts for regeneration. While visually splendid – and located at the water's edge – these architectural feats overlook the very important human urge to dip a toe in.

Many cities, however, are beginning to refurbish old pools, build new ones and clean up urban rivers and lakes. It's dawning that swimming in the city provides a cool, calming antidote to the stresses and inequalities of urban life.

1.
Rivers and lakes, Global
Ripples of change

For decades, polluted urban rivers and canals were no-go areas for swimmers. But that's changing as city mayors reclaim towpaths, riverbanks and lakeside beaches and set ambitious plans to improve water quality.

The free swimming facilities in Paris's Bassin de la Villette (*pictured*) have enjoyed unprecedented success after the man-made Napoleonic lake was deemed clean enough to swim in 2017. City hall has also promised to cut upstream industrial pollution in the Seine and says the water quality will be good enough for swimming in by 2024 (when the city hosts the Olympic Games).

Decades ahead of the curve, Munich started to clean its River Isar in 1995. It now hosts swimmers, paddlers and surfers and is a wild, vital focus for the city. In Boston there's a campaign to build a new "swim park" on Charles River and in Los Angeles there's a big-budget drive to regenerate the river, which has regressed into a concrete storm drain.

Many Swiss cities never lost a grip on their urban beaches. In Zürich, residents can frolic in *Strandbad* during the summer. The cool water is a tonic and the ritual of bathing is seen as a powerful social tool.

2.
Swimming pools and baths, Global
Making a splash

The 1920s saw a lido building frenzy but many art deco pools fell foul to 1980s austerity. Recently, a recognition of their role as city stress-relievers has inspired a drive to restore them and build new ones. In the UK, fundraising and community action has revamped lidos from Reading to Penzance; in London the done-up London Fields Lido now sees some 200,000 visitors a year. Once threatened, pools are now being venerated as architectural treasures.

Lidos are also key to re-peopling a city's waterfront: Helsinki's Allas Sea Pool, a wooden structure abutting Market Square that opened in 2016, is one of the many new basins that have perched on seafronts across Nordic cities. Sørenga fjord pool in Norway – which opened in 2015 surrounded by grassy lawns and decks – has also been a hit with the public.

But pools also keep us fit. Seaside, walled-off baths can tame a crashing swell and provide inviting turquoise waters for laps. Despite having stunning beaches, Sydney has a plethora of outdoor swimming pools. From Andrew (Boy) Charlton Pool in Woolloomooloo Bay to the North Sydney Olympic Pool, these sites are a reliable spot for sporty types who don't want to dive into unpredictable waves. The city is also building on its stock with projects such as the Prince Alfred Park Pool, which features a structure with a green roof planted with native grasses.

Yet many lidos are much more than just places to launch into breaststroke. From Reykjavík's hot tubs to Budapest's Széchenyi thermal baths, these are places for the kind of pottering and conversation that only a long soak in warm water can encourage.

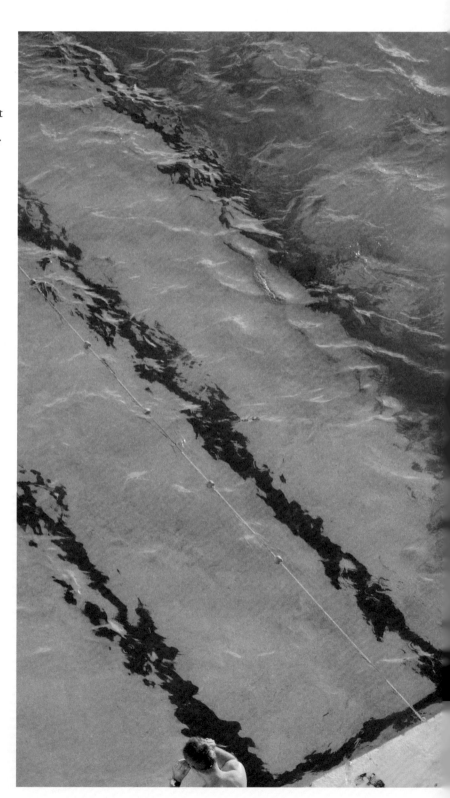

Ice ice baby: Bondi Icebergs Club was first built in 1929 and takes its name from the swimmers who brave the cold winter waters. To become a member, prospectives must compete three Sundays out of four for five years, even when the water temperature drops to single digits – now that's determination

3.
City beaches, Global
Built on sand

Picture Rio without Copacabana or
Los Angeles without Venice. Beaches
define a waterside city. They are a crucial
space for kicking back, cooling off and
retreating from the noise and pace of the
metropolis. In many cases, a well-tended
promenade is all that's needed to link
residents to the sea. This pedestrian-
ruled space has an important cushioning
role (and affords strollers the luxury of
people-watching without getting their
feet wet).

Beirut's Corniche is exemplary.
Wide enough to accommodate a cycle
lane, benches, palm trees and room
for pedestrians to stroll, this most
quintessential of esplanades is also
dotted with diving platforms and craggy
rocks from which to leap. It has become
perhaps this city's most recognisable
and joyful of visual icons. Barcelona's
reinvention is also arguably down to
the creation of its urban beach in 1992.
Many port cities would do well to follow
its lead, reconnect to the sea and give
residents the right to swim.

Landlocked cities too have realised
the importance of flaunting a sandy
patch and have started pioneering the
concept of the urban beach. From
Warsaw to Vienna, city authorities have
set up expanses complete with deck
chairs and beach bars to bring a slice of
the coast to hot inner-city summers.

These spaces usher in a change of
pace; the very idea of a "beach" is a cue
to relax. What is it about a stretch of
sand (as opposed to a grassy field) that
makes us comfortable with donning a
bikini, grabbing a volleyball and cracking
open a cool beer? Urban beaches may
sometimes be a little artificial – they can,
at times, feel like seaside theme parks –
yet they remain incredibly popular. And
for those who don't have the luxury to
spend their summer on the coast, they're
a democratic way of bringing the holiday
spirit into the urban centre.

Life's a beach: Looking for the best beach in central Europe? Try landlocked Warsaw. Come summer, the banks of the Vistula River give this city a whole new identity that's diametrically opposed to the wintry grey starkness of its socialist-era boulevards

Sport and fitness
Break a sweat

A windowless room crammed with weights and treadmills may yield results for those looking to build muscle mass but no gym – regardless of how well-equipped – can compete with an outdoor space when it comes to keeping residents happy as well as fit. Joggers fortunate enough to live next to a park can head to a green space to get their daily dose of endorphins, while cities blessed with a beach are a haven for surfers and swimmers. But built-up neighbourhoods with narrow pavements need not renounce sporty intentions.

Smart municipal governments know that building open-air projects where their residents can work out for free helps with the healthcare bill. Citizens who have desk jobs, extended working hours and a lengthy commute need to be encouraged to head outdoors to exercise. And that's even more true in the case of older residents who need to combat loneliness as well as stiff joints.

The best solutions are those that allow people to convene around a shared interest, where sport mixes with conversation in a space that feels secluded from the city chaos. Sometimes that means taking to the court and playing a game of tennis, football or baseball; other times, taking a seat in a stadium and cheering on a city's team, which can make for powerful social glue.

I.
Running tracks, Japan
High speed

Runners who would rather not get stuck on a treadmill often have to scout for roaming ground among their city's streets. Away from traffic-ridden lanes and packed pavements, green fields and tended-to paths may at first seem all that's needed to attract sporty types. Yet parks that invest in a few thoughtful additions such as marked-up tracks prove that small details can make all the difference in turning a regular green space into a runner's favourite – just look at Bangkok's Lumpini and its 2.5km loop of neatly marked shaded paths.

Some dense urban neighbourhoods, though, don't have the luxury of a space large enough for athletes to properly stretch their legs and need to turn elsewhere. In Japan some of the city's best workout spots are now found on rooftops. Property owners realised that empty, sky-high lots were the perfect solution to this dense city's lack of open space.

Raised above a crowded urban neighbourhood, Osaka's 300-metre-long Air Track (*pictured*) hovers over the shopping centre below. The site was formerly a baseball stadium and when Tokyu Fudosan Holdings Group took over the spacious plot to turn it into a mall, the developer decided to retain a sporting function. Other than the grass-green running track, this shopping centre houses two raised futsal courts, a climbing wall, changing rooms and showers, and a private fitness club with a swimming pool. Four-time Olympic sprinter Nobuharu Asahara helped to choose the track's artificial turf, while engineers at construction company Takenaka were tasked with building a structure stable enough to withstand earthquakes and the vibrations of a crowd of runners. The track is free to use and open until late in the evening, so there's never a shortage of feet pounding the ground here.

2.
Outdoor gyms, Miami
A breath of fresh air

Building an outdoor gym is a smart move for any metropolis: alfresco workout spots can serve many more purposes than meet the eye. Executed correctly, they have the potential to bring together a wide cross-section of society – beyond those obsessed with pumping iron – and, crucially, to create a space where people can stay healthy for free.

Outdoor fitness success stories abound, from Gordon Beach in Tel Aviv to the petite pea-green gyms built across the UK by the Great Outdoor Gym Company. Some, though, still miss the mark. At Muscle Beach in Venice, California, people gather not so much to take part but to ogle. Tourists stop to pose for photos alongside members of the largely male clique of gym bunnies. But an outdoor gym can, and should, be about much more than this.

Italian workout equipment brand MyEquilibria, founded in 2015, understands this well and has been working with a growing number of city halls who also get it. Collaborating with designers, sociologists and psychologists, the company aims to create apparatuses that not only look good but are also engineered to maximise morale-boosting properties. "It's not just about physical health but a sense of community," says Raquel Rodriguez, co-founder and director of MyEquilibria's partner Metalco Active USA. The three structures the company has brought to market include the "Leopard Tree", which claims to be the world's first outdoor fitness system to encourage instinctive movements (making it more accessible to people intimidated by traditional gyms). The company's other structures are the more intense, training-orientated MyBeast and MyIsle.

The first two units have been integrated into the new outdoor gym at Lummus Park in Miami's South Beach (*pictured*), which says a lot about the city's policy to encourage beachside activities beyond bronzing. It's not just staying in shape that matters; creating spaces for strangers to interact and share facilities is equally important. And if there's some sunshine to help with those bench presses, so much the better.

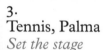

3.
Tennis, Palma
Set the stage

Outdoor training grounds make for great urban features by virtue of how easily accessible (and ever busy) they are. But slightly more secluded spaces in which to practise your serve are also precious in a city's stock of fitness facilities.

Sports clubs such as the Palma Sport & Tennis Club, a few blocks away from the seafront in Mallorca's biggest city, help to foster a sense of quiet and privacy for sporty pursuits – without ever renouncing a commitment to openness. First built in 1964 inside a low-slung, lattice-concrete structure designed by Catalan architect Francesc Mitjans, this handsome establishment was recently refurbished by Swedish owners Johanna and Mikael Landström (also behind the island's impeccable hotels Portixol and Esplendido).

The pair's previous experience is felt in the hospitable touch that they bring to proceedings; their revamp has returned an architectural gem to the community and has made this club the focal point of the neighbourhood. Many punters may swing by its glass-fronted doors to grab lunch at the handsome restaurant but most are later enticed to dive into the pool for a few laps or to step onto one of its five clay courts.

4.
Stadiums, Global
Set the stage

Colossal stadiums have occupied cities since the days of Ancient Greece. And while the arenas themselves might look different and the games are, thankfully, less grisly, their role hasn't changed. They're emblematic of the cities they inhabit and they facilitate a cohesion that's only possible when thousands gather in anticipation of a shared victory.

Sport stadiums often act as great levellers: there aren't many other spaces where all members of society are housed in identical seats in crowded stands, often in identical shirts. Sandwiched between the Mangueira favela and some of the city's middle-class neighbourhoods, Rio de Janeiro's Estádio Jornalista Mário Filho (known as the Maracanã) has often been considered a point of contact for different demographics in this polarised city. Opened in 1950 when Brazil hosted the World Cup, it hosted the tournament again in 2014 and was used in the 2016 Olympic Games. The stadium may have seen a degree of decline but its symbolic power persists. Importantly, many of the city's football teams share the pitch: Flamengo, Botafogo, Fluminense and Vasco de Gama all take to the grounds here, so the Maracanã (like Inter Milan and AC Milan's San Siro) feels like the city's stadium rather than a team's.

Like many other arenas, Maracanã has doubled up as a concert venue, hosting the likes of Madonna and the Rolling Stones. Given how expensive it is to build and maintain these places, ensuring that they serve the communities beyond match fixtures is key. At Sankt Jakob-Park in Basel, home to FC Basel, the complex adjoining the stadium has been opened up to residents (and visitors who wouldn't normally stomp these grounds) with a shopping precinct as well as apartments for the elderly. A well-used stadium is a telling sign of a city hall that is on top of its game.

Name of the game: While football can be divisive, stadiums should bring the city together as places of spectacle, not of partisan animosity. Milan's stadium, though commonly called San Siro, is appropriately named after Giuseppe Meazza, who played for both AC Milan and Inter Milan

Senior sports
Golden oldies

Medicine's progress means people are living longer but a tech-driven lifestyle often doesn't encourage exercise – particularly for senior citizens who spend most of their time indoors. The right infrastructure, though, can help to entice the silver set out.

1. **Senior playgrounds, Barcelona:** The term "playgrounds" may sound patronising but the initiative's heart is in the right place. Barcelona has installed 300 such public workout parks where seniors can enjoy light resistance and balance training in the fresh air, and where their grandchildren can join in too. Cities from London to Copenhagen are following suit.

2. **Surf clubs, Adelaide:** Since 2017 a smattering of South Australian surf clubs in Adelaide and Port Noarlunga have been inviting folk who are 55 and older to group surf sessions. A chance to pick up a new skill, engage with peers and spend time in stunning natural surroundings.

3. **Swimming, Hong Kong:** The waters off Kennedy Town in west Hong Kong are home to some serious chop but many of the city's adventurous seniors (the youngest of them in their 50s) are not easily dissuaded. Come to the Sai Wan swimming shed on any morning and you'll see many diving off the wooden pier.

4. **Hiking, Seoul:** With mountains making up 70 per cent of South Korea's landmass, it's only natural that hiking has become this country's national pastime. The elderly are heavily involved and a widespread penchant for investing in fancy hiking gear has further bolstered the regalia around the sport.

5. **Curling, Winnipeg:** In the chilly climes of Manitoba and New Brunswick, where heading outside for a jog can be dauntingly demanding, curling clubs have become a haven for the silver-haired. Many clubs, such as the Fort Rouge Curling Club in Winnipeg and the Riverside Curling Club in Rothesay, have leagues dedicated specifically to seniors.

Nightlife
Stay up late

Nightclubs, dive bars and music venues are the fundamental anchors of a packed calendar of urban goings-on. The languor of sundown encourages people to get up close and personal and leave the day's inhibitions behind: letting loose on a dance floor is an exercise that shouldn't be left off any resident's routine. A city's nocturnal life might sometimes show a naughty side but it should by no means be the preserve of the partygoer. There's plenty of connection-building (and fun) to be had after dusk.

There's something reassuring about a city that ramps up the revelry when the sun goes down. Places that don't put the brakes on frivolity are usually friendlier and more invested in having fun. Delve a little deeper into the wild nights of Berlin and Beirut and you'll discover that the cities with the most raucous nightlife – from Madrid and Miami to Buenos Aires and Tel Aviv – also have a compelling reason to dance away their woes.

Berlin's gritty underground club scene bloomed in a capital both devastated and divided by foreign power play. Lingering memories of regional conflict launch revellers in Beirut and Tel Aviv into clubs to live every night like their last. When four decades of Spain's straight-laced fascist dictatorship ended in 1975, Madrileños celebrated with a laissez-faire free-for-all, which even inspired the city's unofficial slogan, *Madrid me mata* (Madrid kills me). Miami, the tongue-in-cheek capital of Latin America, has become a playground for expats shaking off the conservative mores of their homelands.

The smartest city mayors recognise the value in letting loose. Small-scale benefits may be hard to quantify but they often underwrite the lifeblood of social connectivity. Bars and clubs nurture music culture, fashion trends and chance meetings that can often fuel creative collaborations. In a screen-enamoured world that seems to rely more on algorithms than a good old-fashioned frolic to find a life partner, the time-tested formula of actual face-time on the dance floor is still hard to beat.

On a macro level, the dividends are also hard to ignore. When Amsterdam elected Mirik Milan as the first night mayor in 2012, it didn't take long for cities such as London, Berlin, New York, and Zürich (yes, even Zürich) to follow suit. The argument – that a city doesn't go to sleep just because its politicians have gone to bed – was persuasive enough but the logic of putting a top-level voice at the government table tasked with improving safety, social cohesion and the night-time economy helped the idea gain traction around the world. The popularity of the post also highlights the inner party animal in all of us. Who wants to live under a regime that constantly wags its finger and throws the administrative wet blanket over the dance floor?

Cities aren't meant to be giant factories by day and dormitories by night. If they start preoccupying themselves with the pointless pursuit of nocturnal silence, they become the ultimate buzzkill. The best places to live are those that emulate the inclusive attitude of a laid-back party-planner: invite everyone to the jam, let the music move people to mingle and don't end the festivities until the dance floor empties of its own accord.

The nightwatch: 10 top tips
Never too late

Ideas for ensuring a healthy, happy city nightlife.

1. **Room to breathe:** A dive bar has its charms but after a couple of hours dancing, a rooftop or garden is an oxygen lifeline.

2. **Late-night grub:** Day-round stands such as Vienna's wurst-kiosks keep streets populated and munchies amply satisfied.

3. **Loud and proud:** Open your clubs on the seafront (or riverfront, as in Turin) and no one will complain if you keep the volume up after the watershed.

4. **Night direction:** A smart city mayor knows that there are plenty of business opportunities after conventional hours.

5. **Quick hop:** London's decision to open parts of its Underground at night was a defining moment for the city's nightlife but no night-time transport system is complete without affordable taxis.

6. **Light up:** Neon lights have amazing potential to brand a metropolis after dark. Hong Kong's streets would be unrecognisable without their forest of signs.

7. **Safe hands:** Policing needs to maintain a gentle touch when it's dealing with keeping the unruliest side of revelling in check. Security doesn't have to mean surveillance.

8. **Outside the club:** There's more to after-dinner activities than dancing: late museum and gallery openings and a solid schedule of gigs mean nights in the city aren't just the reserve of revellers.

9. **Open doors:** Chucking people out mid-boogie is a buzzkill. Nothing beats dancing when you've overdone the drinks.

10. **Aperitivo alfresco:** Watch your outdoor drinking laws (there's a reason Sydney is reprimanded for being uptight). Let your citizens pop the cork outside on a balmy evening and trust that most know when it's time to call it a night.

Few things have as obvious and direct an impact on citizens' quality of life as mobility. The ease with which we get from A to B, whether in a vast Asian metropolis or a small town in central Europe, and whether via public transport or under our own steam, has a huge influence on our feelings about a city. Do we feel that we're in good hands or is each day a mini battle to get around? Mobility is also of vital importance for city economies: done well, it can increase productivity; done badly, citizens waste frustrating hours in traffic and waiting on platforms.

Yet the challenge for transit authorities around the world today is immense. As urban populations boom, the need for fast and reliable mass transport is growing apace. To avoid sprawl, mobility needs to become a central part of a smart, dense urban plan. At the same time, new technologies are bringing with them their own issues that have to be solved: electric cars and scooters will need more charging points and bike-sharing systems more docks; ride-sharing apps are contributing in some cities to fewer people riding the metro and sitting more often in cars; and driverless vehicles, if and when they arrive, will require different infrastructure, such as expanded drop-off bays.

Some of the investment required may come from the private sector. Yet too much of this money is being poured into pie-in-the-sky fantasies, such as drones that carry passengers above our streets. Instead urban-planners need to understand how mobility fits into their wider vision for the city, from high-speed rail links right down to the famous "last mile" of a citizen's journey.

As this chapter illustrates, mobility doesn't have to be complicated. A few simple and well-designed fixes can go a long way and safeguard our cities for the future.

4.

ON THE MOVE

Walking
Something's afoot

When it comes to transport and mobility, one method is frequently ignored: walking. Whereas large-scale infrastructure projects are eye-catching and "leave a legacy", pushing citizens to make their way on foot is often more about working under the radar. Yes, there are a handful of signature schemes (New York's High Line and Seoul's elevated park, Seoullo 7017, are two examples) but, by and large, getting people on their feet is about smaller nudges: better wayfinding, cleaner pavements, more greenery.

Today cities are looking at how to encourage and promote this slowest form of transport – for the sake of their citizens' health. One of the most ambitious projects in recent years was attempted in Oklahoma City. During his tenure as mayor from 2004 to 2018, Mick Cornett decided to redesign his city around walking in an effort to reduce the city's concerning obesity rate. He asked citizens to back a tax rise to fund the creation of parks, pavements and paths, and his ambition was rewarded with stronger long-term health indicators. On a more focused level, the refurbishment of Tel Aviv's central beach promenade holds lessons for anyone hoping to design and build a walkable district.

Getting a city back on its feet
Tel Aviv

A vast refurbishment project transformed Tel Aviv's previously neglected coastal promenade into a vibrant new space for the city. Architects at Mayslits Kassif turned a retaining wall into terraces, stairs and seats, and there's also a new path at beach level, outdoor gyms, new shading elements and upgraded street furniture. Some of the café's rooftops have been converted into areas in which to sit and linger in the sea breeze. The project has also made the beach accessible to wheelchair users, buggies and the elderly.

Five more inspired ideas
Walk this way

1. **Legible London, London:** This pedestrian wayfinding system was commissioned by Transport for London in 2004 and designed by Applied Wayfinding and Lacock Gullam. There are more than 1,300 signs in total: stainless-steel totems with panels illustrating the local area and estimating walking times to landmarks. Before this, there were 32 separate signage systems in the city centre – Legible London has decluttered the streets and created cohesion.

2. **Outdoor staircases, Stuttgart:** Stuttgart's central districts sit at the bottom and on the slopes of a valley so pedestrians get about using more than 400 stairways that add up to about 20km. These *Stäffele* date from the early 19th century but in recent years Stuttgart has been rediscovering their significance for its transport infrastructure, with a healthy sum made available in budgets for maintenance and repairs.

3. **Pedestrian footbridges, Tokyo:** At its busiest, Omotesando in Tokyo can be a seething mass of people. The speediest way to cross is the pedestrian footbridge that runs from the police box on one side to the Gyre building on the other. Such overpasses can be found all over Japanese cities and they provide a thoughtful way of allowing those on foot to navigate their city and beat the traffic.

4. **Minhocão Park, São Paulo:** "Park" is perhaps a misleading name for this elevated stretch of highway in São Paulo, as it has no grass, play areas or proper seating. Yet every weekend since 2015, the roughly 3km-long stretch of flyover has been taken over by walkers, runners, cyclists and skateboarders. It's a healthier and more valuable use of what is, in most people's view, something of an eyesore.

5. **Tanderrum Bridge, Melbourne:** The city's surging population has led to congestion problems but one of the city's top firms, John Wardle Architects, has a solution. The Tanderrum Bridge is a striking walkway that balances looks and functionality, connecting the CBD to a nearby sports precinct.

Cycling
Pedal pushing

If there's such a thing as a universally accepted truth in urbanism, it might be that cycling should be encouraged as the best form of mobility. It has numerous advantages: it's healthy; it's clean and green, releasing no emissions and taking polluting cars off the road; and it promotes equality (if a city is more easily navigable by bike then job opportunities, for example, are also more accessible).

Yet as more city halls push people to get on their bikes, a greater strain will be put on cycling infrastructure. This will only intensify as cities launch bike-sharing schemes and, in some cases, open up the bike-sharing market to the private sector. Such projects promise to make cycling even more affordable by taking the cost of buying a bike out of the equation but they increase demand for infrastructure, from docking stations to cycle paths.

Cities have to be ambitious and match the growth of cycling with investment. This means more than simply taking space off cars to create bike lanes, which can cause increased vehicle congestion and pollution. Instead municipalities, such as Groningen in the Netherlands, need to come up with long-term plans to create sustainably cycle-friendly cities. Here are some of the best practices worldwide.

Two-wheeled city
Groningen, the Netherlands

Groningen is a cycle city. It adopted a radical urban plan in the 1970s that sidelined cars in favour of cyclists and today there are more bikes than people.

In 2015, however, it became clear that the cycling infrastructure was buckling. Groningen was one of the fastest-growing economic hubs in the country and its booming population was causing a problem: bikes were battling for space with pedestrians and buses on the centre's narrow medieval roads.

That year city hall launched an €85m 10-year strategy. Interventions ranged from the obvious – more bike parking – to the bold: four "smart routes" were built to provide paths to more than 20,000 cyclists a day. Meanwhile, innovative traffic systems were installed at previously deadly crossroads to reduce accidents.

Most cities are keen to get citizens cycling – and they should be. But this shows that investment has to increase in tandem with ridership and that a policy must be able to adapt if it's to be truly visionary.

Lighting the way
Auckland

Auckland modelled itself in the 20th century on US cities such as Los Angeles: it pulled up its tram lines in the 1950s and allowed its road network to sprawl. But the city's planners are now hard at work to reverse that trend, reducing citizens' car dependency and getting them back on their feet – and their bikes.

The Nelson Street cycleway is a former motorway off-ramp converted into a cycle path. The NZ$18m (€10.6m) project is part of the council's proposed network of 120km of cycle paths. The "The Lightpath" section of the cycleway was painted bright pink and fitted with 300 programmable LED lights, which create interactive displays when people walk or cycle along it. After all, if you're going to do something bold, why not let people know it's there?

What's in store?
Japan

Kochi-based engineering firm Giken has come up with several bike-parking solutions for Japanese cities short on pavement space. The ingenious Eco Cycle is an underground storage park for bikes. Bicycles are drawn into a small cradle, moved down into a parking slot and hidden away from view. A swipe of a smart card and in seconds your bike pops out at ground level. The system has been installed at locations across Japan, including Shinagawa, a busy station in Tokyo where there is space for more than 1,000 bikes.

Buses
Workhorse power

Buses are a rather unloved part of the urban transport mix – perhaps because they are not as elegant as trams, as efficient as light rail or as innovative as ride-hailing apps. Yet in most cities, buses are the true workhorses, covering routes that wouldn't be economically viable for rail or tram and – particularly in developing nations – providing affordable public transport to the masses.

They're relatively cheap for transit authorities too. Bus shelters cost a fraction of the price of railway lines, stations and platforms. And their routes are flexible, making them highly versatile. If the population in a particular part of town starts growing fast, a bus route can be set up to serve those residents faster than any other form of transport.

The bus is nonetheless still dogged by visions of a cumbersome vehicle sitting in static traffic, belching out toxic fumes. In reality, many cities, such as Madrid, are employing smaller electric-powered buses that can nip around with greater ease and fewer emissions. At the same time, cities around the world are investing in Bus Rapid Transit (BRT) systems, which are capable of moving almost as many people as a rail line. There is, indeed, much to praise about the humble bus.

Minibuses
Madrid

In 2008, Madrid's transport authority EMT bought 20 battery-powered microbuses and trialled them in the city centre with the aim of better navigating the narrow streets. Judging by the passengers who hop aboard each morning (old folk, young parents and schoolchildren), it's clear that the little buses – now a permanent fixture – have been a fine addition. The fleet has been expanding too: by January 2018, line 76 was the first fully electric bus route in Spain, and the number of electric buses and minibuses is expected to rise to 93 by 2020.

The Madrid Metro has also been expanding and burrowing a network of tunnels yet growth has been slow and expensive: €32m for every kilometre. Up above, the little microbus is not only cheaper (€220,000 per vehicle) but it's also more nimble. While they make up just a fraction of Madrid's 2,000-strong bus fleet, these little vehicles show that the bus will continue to play a vital role in our cities.

Technology companies that are improving our cities
Life in the fast lane

1. **Eluminocity, Munich:** Those who have lived next to a blindingly bright lamppost will welcome this invention with open arms. The company creates smart lampposts that detect the presence of a car up to 150 metres away. If there is traffic, the lights are turned up; if not, they're dimmed to conserve energy. These lampposts also double up as charging points for electric cars and their tracking data can be used to study and manage traffic flow. They've already proven popular (not least among investors – BMW was the first) and can be found in cities from Seattle to Singapore.

2. **Gogoro, Taipei:** The Taiwanese company has created sleek, battery-powered scooters as the next step on from the ubiquitous bike-sharing scheme. Not only do the scooters actually look good (meaning that riders needn't feel abashed when they pull up next to a Triumph) but they're also calibrated specifically for navigating cities; for example, they have enough power to get you going uphill (we're looking at you, Lisbon). The batteries can be recharged or swapped for fresh ones at stations around the city that are open 24 hours a day. Gogoro made a foray into Europe just two years after launching at home in 2015 and its fans have already saved more than six million litres of petrol by opting for this smart mode of transport.

3. **EO Charging, Suffolk, UK:** When it comes to electric cars, it's not all about the vehicle. That's what EO Charging – which operates out of a former farm in rural Suffolk – is trying to show the world. It produces efficient charging sockets that reduce the stress on the national grid. The sockets can be installed in the workplace or at home, and can even be connected to feed off solar panels rather than state-provided (and therefore fossil fuel-derived) electricity. EO is inventing for the future: it's anticipating the day when electric cars become universal and require sophisticated charging technology that can handle millions of Priuses or Teslas simultaneously demanding juice.

Trams
Back on track

The tram is enjoying an unlikely comeback. In the US, many cities that long devoted themselves to the automobile have reversed the trend and are using trams (or "streetcars") to get citizens out of their cars. Detroit is the most oft-cited example, with urbanists rehearsing the tale of how a new vibrant urban core has emerged from the ashes of Motor City. An important new chapter was written in 2017 when, 61 years after they were ditched, Detroit brought back its trams.

But Detroit isn't alone. Streetcars used to carry people in El Paso, Texas, around downtown and even across the Mexican border until they were dumped in the desert near the city airport in 1974 and left to rust. Now the city is spending close to $100m (€85.8m) to bring its trams back.

Even places that once modelled themselves on US cities are rethinking. Planners in Auckland, New Zealand, have long lamented the abandonment of their city's "tramways" in the 1950s and now they're promising to open new lines in the 2020s. Any municipality considering such a move should look to Zürich. The Swiss city has had tramlines since the 1880s and, sensibly, never dug them up, making it a perfect illustration of why they work.

Trolley dash
Zürich

If there's one sound Zürchers associate with their city, it's the cheerful "Ding!" of an approaching tram. Of the people who get to work by public transport, more than 60 per cent travel by them.

The tram sets the tempo of this surprisingly unhurried city. A metro can get you into town more quickly but a Zürich tram encourages you to gaze out at the buildings and landscape. It's also democratic; you can easily spot TV stars rubbing shoulders with business leaders and public servants on the Monday morning Line 2 through Seefeld.

The network, which is split across 15 lines, covers almost all of the city, with a total of 123km of track. It's configured in a classic hub-and-spoke formation: lines converge in the city centre before travelling back out into the suburbs. The City of Zürich has invested in major tram projects to tackle the bottlenecks that this can sometimes cause. One of these was the extension of Line 8 to Hardbrücke Station and on towards Escher-Wyss-Platz, which was completed in 2017. The recently completed Line 12, known as Glattalbahn, is named after the valley it passes through north of the city centre.

The tram isn't suited to every city, of course. Alone they wouldn't be able to carry the 1.5 million people who commute into Manhattan each day, for instance. But for a mid-sized city such as Zürich, the tram is perfect: egalitarian, pleasant and fast. Well, fast enough.

On the move (clockwise from left): About 60 per cent of Zürchers who commute by public transport rely on trams; Lisbon's historic trams evoke a nostalgia that's part of the city's brand; Hong Kong's trams look skyward to accommodate more passengers

Three transport projects to keep an eye on
Watch this space

1. **Going car-free, Helsinki:** The majority of Helsinki's residents already opt for public transportation over private – in fact, Helsinki City Transport estimated in 2017 that cars spend only 4 per cent of their lives in use. The municipal government is aiming to make Helsinki car-free by 2025 through the use of carefully built incentives. Many city streets are being transformed to accommodate high-speed trams and slower speed limits for cars. More finessed approaches include the creation of public transport-hailing apps – residents can hail minibuses, much like the Uber lift service. The first such app, Kutsuplus, was cancelled in late 2015 due to high subsidy costs but the government is determined to continue the experiment.

2. **The trams are back in town, Auckland:** "We are wasting our time stuck in traffic," says New Zealand's prime minister Jacinda Ardern. The Labour chief promises to shake up Auckland's inefficient, private-reliant transport system by reintroducing trams, which were scrapped in the 1950s. Back then they were hugely popular, transporting about 100 million passengers a year, despite the city's population of just 400,000. The goal is to streamline transport between key areas such as the CBD and the airport but also to serve lower-income Aucklanders who struggle to afford private transport.

3. **Crossrail, London:** Once completed in December 2019, Crossrail – London's flagship £14.8bn (€16.5bn) metro line – will revolutionise the city's overcrowded tube network, which hasn't welcomed a new route since the Jubilee Line in 1979. The Elizabeth Line, as it's formally called, will seamlessly connect financial districts such as Liverpool Street and Canary Wharf to Heathrow Airport, as well as provide speedy links to formerly isolated, working-class neighbourhoods in east and west London. What's more, many of the major tube stops will exist beneath large, mixed-use properties that will be destinations in their own right.

Rail
Doing the locomotive

New cathedrals
Arnhem, the Netherlands

Gone are the days when train stations were unloved buildings in seedier parts of town; the modern equivalents are architecturally spectacular and act as the beating hearts of vibrant city districts. In the Netherlands, the government has implemented a long-term plan to turn six vital stations into "cathedrals of a new era" and Arnhem Central in the country's east is a prime example.

When the plan for the new station was drawn up in 1996, the architects at the Amsterdam-based UNStudio knew that they wanted to create a new meeting point for the city. So they added commercial spaces, a conference centre, a big bus station and walkable links to a plaza with offices, shops and a cinema complex.

When it was finally completed in 2015, after several stages of construction, Arnhem Central was a destination in its own right; global companies have since taken up the office space and passenger numbers are set to be double what they were in 2009 by 2020. It's a perfect example of what modern rail stations should be: prime locations; multi-modal hubs integrating bus, tram and bike; new economic engines; and catalysts for urban renewal.

There are countless reasons why a rail network is the jewel in the crown of any public-transport system. When it comes to moving us around a city, no method of transport offers greater speeds, higher capacities and more reliability than light rail and its underground cousin, the metro. When it comes to connecting cities, rail also offers convenience, comfort and centre-to-centre travel.

The catch? Well, rail's main drawback has always been its high cost. In the past the way most cities made it economically viable was to generate revenues from retail spaces built into stations. Yet with large-format retail – from department stores to shopping malls – struggling all over the world, this may not be a suitable business model for long.

Instead, planners should look to cities that have tried something different. In Hong Kong, for instance, rail stations are used as platforms for residential property development and the transit operator is a rare thing: profitable. Rotterdam station is productive in a different way: 130,000 photovoltaic cells spread across its roof create valuable energy. Meanwhile, the central station of Arnhem has been placed at the heart of a new development and is an economic engine for the city.

Companies building the future of mobility
Leaders of the pack

1. **Bombardier:** The Canadian aerospace and transportation company Bombardier is a market leader in automated trains and metros. One of its most impressive driverless projects is the Downtown Line in Singapore, the longest fully automated underground metro line in the world. The company supplied Singapore with 264 unmanned Movia metro vehicles, which can travel at 90 km/h.

2. **ThyssenKrupp Elevator:** As the number of tall buildings under construction increases, so our need for smart ways of getting up and down them grows too. The German manufacturer ThyssenKrupp Elevator (*see page 114*) is creating the technology to achieve just that. The Multi – the world's first rope-free lift system – allows more people to travel higher within a building without lift shafts taking up too great a portion of the floor plan.

3. **Audi:** All big car brands are hurrying to adapt to the changes in the automotive industry but Audi has taken great strides. The German marque is developing technologies that will transform the mass-produced private automobile more dramatically than anything in its 109-year history. From autonomous technology that will be able to take over from the driver to longer-lasting batteries that will make electric vehicles more viable, the legacy player is across key developments in a sector that is now moving at great speed.

Ferries
Float your boats

Many of the greatest metropolises owe their success to one simple fact: their proximity to water. Today, however, getting citizens across vast bodies of water can be a challenge. Digging below ground is costly and bridges get congested. Ferries may seem a bit "old tech" but they can provide a refreshingly straightforward mobility solution.

At the same time, the demands of modern shipping (deeper water, bigger docks) have seen city-centre ports decommissioned, forcing planners to think how to repurpose them. Redevelopment projects from Hamburg and Seoul to Chicago and Liverpool have tackled this challenge and here, again, ferries can help, taking citizens, tourists and, crucially, their money right into the heart of a waterfront district.

It must be said that ferries are in many cities simply tourist vessels, seen as too ponderous and crowded to work for locals. But in Seattle and Istanbul, that's far from the case. These cities show how ferries can be a key piece of the mobility puzzle.

How to design a ferry terminal
Brisbane

In 2011, two-storey-high flood waters swept across Brisbane, causing at least AU$440m (€280m) of damage. A third of the city's public ferry terminals were lost and an international competition to design the new terminals was won by Australia's Cox Architecture and engineering company Aurecon.

Their sleek black-and-orange piers offer good visibility on rainy days, while the streamlined shape of the terminals lessens the potential for debris to lodge. A smart system also allows the gangway to unlatch and float away during extremely high torrents, reducing potential damage. With climate change likely to create more natural disasters in coastal cities, Brisbane can provide valuable lessons.

The old-fashioned way
Istanbul

First-timers to Istanbul often make a fatal error. To get to "the Asian side", they opt for a cab and join one of the world's most unforgiving rat races. An hour later they've missed their meetings and they're still crawling along the Bosphorus Bridge in a haze of diesel.

Thankfully, Istanbul also has a more pleasant, time-honoured way of crossing between continents. More than 200 official ferries, run by five big operators, ply the Bosphorus every day carrying some 250,000 passengers. The boats are an essential commuter link between European and Anatolian Istanbul, a feeder for trams and trains and a blast of fresh air.

In 2015, Istanbullus angrily rejected a new design for the state-run ferries. It was more streamlined and sleek but it sealed passengers off in an air-conditioned cabin. The designers were sent back to the drawing board to come up with a vessel that was less sea-bus and more in keeping with the steamboat-shaped vessels that have plied these waters for a century.

Tokyo is starting to see the potential of ferries and New York's Brooklyn-to-Manhattan route is a much-praised alternative to the subway (and has a bar on board). Traffic-clogged cities should take note of Istanbul's simple work-around. The UAE, for instance, wants a Hyperloop to zip from Abu Dhabi to Dubai in minutes but it's still a work in progress. So opt instead for a chugging ferry, preferably *en plein air*, and enjoy a more pleasant perch from which to watch the world go by.

Dream commute
Seattle, USA

The city of Seattle is surrounded by three bodies of water, the biggest being Elliott Bay, which is part of the much larger Puget Sound Main Basin. It's a stunning landscape that feels a million miles away from town. If, like me, you happen to live on one of its many islands or peninsulas and work in Seattle, you also happen to have one of the world's best commutes.

I begin my day by driving my electric car to a ferry terminal on Bainbridge Island where I park, stop for an espresso and walk to the Washington State ferry. Believe it or not, WSF operates the largest ferry fleet in the US and one of the five largest in the world; some 6.5 million people travelled my route alone last year.

Once aboard, I walk to one of two unmarked "quiet rooms" on the upper deck. Although there are no signs dictating recommended behaviours, it becomes immediately obvious that talking is verboten. More importantly, no one is screaming into their mobile phones. In the collective silence, people read, listen to podcasts or music through headphones, sleep, eat, work or stare out at the ships and the orcas passing by. Occasionally, Mount Rainier breaks through the clouds, accented by the sunrise or sunset. It can be remarkable. I usually spend the 35-minute trip drawing ideas for architecture projects.

Once in Seattle, I walk off the ferry, put on the bike helmet that's clipped to my backpack and hop on one of Seattle's three bike-share systems to Olson Kundig's Pioneer Square office. Seattle was the first US city to try "dockless" bike shares, a system that has transformed commuter transportation around the world in recent years. As for my return commute? It's the same, in reverse. Except that the sun is usually setting over the Olympic mountain range, beer and wine are sold on the boat and there are final emails that need answering.

It always surprises me that people assume the ferry must make for an unusual hardship for those of us living in suburban communities outside Seattle. I restrain from telling them it's about as hard as going on holiday twice a day.

Alan Maskin
Alan Maskin is principal and owner of Seattle-based design practice Olson Kundig. For more than two decades, he has pursued unconventional design challenges in public places. He is currently leading the Century Project for the Space Needle, a historic renovation of Seattle's most iconic landmark.

Taxis
Road warriors

The canary-yellow taxi is synonymous with New York and the bulbous black cab is as much a London hallmark as the red double-decker bus. But if you've ever taken one of these taxis, you'll know that the experience often leaves a little to be desired. Rude service and a lack of ambience are common. In both cases, this is a huge missed opportunity.

As Tokyo demonstrates, taxis can become a powerful part of a city's brand, beyond a simple visual cue. Like so many experiences in Japan, a ride in a Tokyo taxi is elevated above the ordinary by the small touches: the politeness of the driver; the pristine interiors; the door automatically swinging (or sliding) open to welcome you; the comfy upholstery.

Yet taxis around the world, including in Tokyo, are facing huge challenges. Partly this comes courtesy of the ride-hailing apps that have spread across the globe. While it's true that they have in many cities made mobility safer (particularly for women) and more affordable, these apps often have little to no connection to the cities in which they operate. How to survive as a traditional taxi? Again, Tokyo may have the answers: focus on service, upgrade your vehicles and don't forget to celebrate your traditional models.

How taxis can boost your city's brand
Tokyo

Tokyo is home to some 48,000 taxis, roughly one-fifth of all the taxis in Japan (for perspective, the city represents 11 per cent of the country's population). These taxis carry more than 300 million passengers a year and close to 900,000 every day. Yet the reason the fleet is exemplary has little to do with scale.

First there is the hardware. Regular visitors to the city will recognise the most common taxi type, the Toyota Crown, a robust boxy saloon that's as much a feature of the city as Tokyo Tower. Toyota has been making taxis for Japan since 1936 and is behind the new JPN Taxi, a more accessible, fuel-efficient hybrid vehicle that the city began rolling out ahead of the 2020 Tokyo Olympics. There will soon be 10,000 on the streets.

But it's the software that makes Tokyo's taxis special, from the service to the neat and tidy interiors. And the city is investing in these smaller details further. Thousands of drivers are being trained in handling wheelchairs and helping elderly and disabled passengers. The JPN Taxi is more spacious and has heated seats.

However, these are challenging times for Tokyo taxis. Numbers have declined since the glory days (2008 was the high point and it's been steadily dropping ever since). Although ride-hailing app Uber has made little headway so far in Japan, where taxis are tightly regulated, the industry is bracing itself for the inevitable attack to come. One of the country's biggest taxi companies, Nihon Kotsu, is pre-empting the unavoidable by developing its own ride-hailing app through its subsidiary, JapanTaxi Co.

How else do you future-proof your taxis? Here, too, Tokyo shows the way. Every year, 5 August is Taxi Day, which commemorates the date in 1912 when the first six taxis in Japan went into service in Yurakucho; it's also a day when the industry celebrates good service. And what business in Japan would be without a mascot? For Tokyo Taxi Association it's Takkun, the cheeky cartoon taxi. All this helps to ensure that locals and tourists appreciate the taxi – and guarantees that they'll thrive even in a challenged market.

What to do with car parks
Global

Car parks could well be a thing of the past in the not-too-distant future. Even if driverless cars aren't going to take over our streets, the prevalence of ride-hailing apps already means that automobiles are on the go more in city centres and are less likely to sit for hours on end in a car park. So what should we do with all these spaces that have for decades been given over to stationary four-wheeled vehicles?

1. **Space for retail:** If you live in Berlin or London, you may be getting tired of seeing shipping containers converted into quirky retail spaces. Still, if you have a flat unused expanse of concrete, this might be the simplest way of offering entrepreneurs a home. In Cleveland's Warehouse District, converted containers were put on a former car park and handed to young retailers. A sensible way of bringing life back to a wasted space.

2. **Pocket parks:** Cities are increasingly coming round to the idea of turning underused spaces into miniature parks. They increase the amount of greenery, soak up carbon dioxide and offer a moment to breathe in sometimes barren urban environments. A good example is the Converting Roads to Parks scheme in Yarra City, a Melbourne suburb, which transforms car parks into public green spaces and play areas for children.

3. **Planters:** Simple planters can easily be placed on individual parking spaces to add a bit of greenery to the streetscape and shield pedestrians from pollution. Norwegian street-furniture manufacturer Vestre offers Parklets, which consist of six modules that are the same dimensions as a standard parking space and combine plants and seating. They extend the pavement and bring a bit more greenery onto the street.

4. **Multistorey redevelopment:** Southeast London is home to Peckham Levels, a £3.53m (€3.95m) redevelopment of a seven-storey car park that launched in December 2017. The social enterprise behind it, Make Shift, gutted the building and brought it back to life with a multitude of different local businesses, shared workspaces, design and art studios, restaurants, shops and a yoga studio.

5. **Apartments:** Multistorey car parks are often seen as an eyesore but they're being reimagined all over the world. In Zürich, a sleek residential development called Schlotterbeck-Areal has been created inside the shell of a former multistorey garage, while in the US, students at the Savannah College of Art and Design created a micro community on the fourth level of an Atlanta car park with three micro homes and a small garden.

Airports
Perfect landings

Terminal 3, Narita International Airport
Tokyo

When officials at Tokyo's Narita International Airport announced that they wanted to build a new terminal for low-cost airlines at more than half the construction cost of the other terminals, few believed it was feasible. But shortly after the Terminal 3 building opened its doors in 2015, the ¥15bn (€115m) project became a global benchmark for good design on a shoestring.

Built by Nikken Sekkei – the architecture firm behind the Tokyo Sky Tree – and with design direction from Naoki Ito of Japanese creative agency Party, the terminal has nine gates that can accommodate up to 7.5 million passengers a year. The key to attracting low-cost carriers was to keep landing fees low, which had not been a strong point previously for Narita. But over three years Nikken Sekkei and Ito managed to stick to a tight budget, partly by replacing expensive features with cheaper yet equally appealing equivalents (painted signs and icons instead of illuminated ones, for instance).

Despite the budgetary constraints, or perhaps because of them, the designers employed some smart innovations. The original plan called for a no drop-off zone for cars and no railway station, so getting to the terminal would mean a 1.5km walk from another terminal. But the team turned this ordeal into a playful attraction by mimicking a sports track to make the walk more fun. For the colour scheme, Ito suggested blue, to represent the sky, for departures, and an earthy red for arrivals.

A city cannot claim to have mastered mobility until it has an airport. Yet what kind of airport should one have? Anyone who has flown into Toronto's Billy Bishop or Taipei's Songshan will appreciate the virtues of landing close to the city centre, where you swoop in alongside the towers and the sights and can be part of it just 20 minutes after landing.

A grand international hub that's 50km away from the centre makes a bolder statement and has greater capacity. But beware: you'll need a well-designed link to the city to prevent arriving passengers from feeling instantly disconnected. Indeed, design plays a central role in the making of an airport where we love to land – and it needn't cost the Earth, as Narita Terminal 3 demonstrates.

Chocks away (clockwise from top): The UP Express is designed to feel part of the airport, not an afterthought; Haneda Airport has ample information points; Narita's Terminal 3 will double in size by 2022

Going to town
Airport transport links to emulate

Even if you get the airport right, the journey from arrivals lounge to city centre can undo a lot of that good work. Here are some great examples of cities that have got the journey from tarmac to town spot on.

1. **UP Express, Toronto:** This is the air-rail link that opened in 2015 connecting Union Station in Toronto's downtown with Pearson International Airport. The passenger experience is coherent throughout, from the branding (by MONOCLE's sister company Winkreative) and the staff uniforms (created by local clothier Matt Robinson) to the terminus at Union Station (designed by Zeidler Partnership Architects).

2. **Yamate Tunnel, Tokyo:** Tokyo is home to the perfect case study of what a well-placed piece of tunnel engineering can do for a city. Constructed in three phases over two decades and completed in 2015, the 18.2km Yamate Tunnel is Japan's longest road tunnel. Built by a Japanese consortium, it involved burrowing up to 30 metres beneath city streets and a riverbed at a cost of ¥1.8trn (€14bn). It has cut the journey time to and from Haneda Airport roughly in half.

3. **Arlanda Express, Stockholm:** Stockholm has pulled off the feat of making the journey from airport to city centre actually pleasant. The city's air-rail link, the Arlanda Express, underwent a redesign in 2010. Since then soothing sound installations have been added, along with "contemplation" rooms at the station. And if that's not enough, the walk from carriage to the cab rank at Central Station is well signposted and takes a mere 15 seconds.

4. **Flughafen Zürich, Zürich:** Zurich has an embarrassment of riches when it comes to transport options from airport to centre. The train station is within the airport, so you don't have to get a bus or shuttle first, and it takes just 10 to 15 minutes. A taxi will take you in 15 while the Number 10 tram drops you at Zürich Hauptbahnhof in 35 minutes.

We tend to judge cities by their appearances. The assumption is that smooth streets, well-manicured parks, punctual trains and bustling high streets can tell you a lot about a city hall's managerial chops: if the place is looking its best, the authorities must know what they're doing.

While this is often the case, it's important to acknowledge that bureaucrats don't always have all the answers. There's nothing more frustrating than seeing a city that's struggling due to a lack of fresh ideas. It takes just one passionate patron or clear-sighted business owner to start turning a city's fortunes around – be it a conservationist encouraging rare birds back into Singapore's urban jungle, an architect campaigning for decades to preserve a slice of Beirut's heritage or a trio trying to inject culture into Christchurch's city centre post earthquake. There are many inspiring people worldwide who have taken it upon themselves to better their cities.

There's also another resource that shouldn't be overlooked: volunteers. Getting citizens involved isn't just a way for cities to save money; it's also an opportunity to build a more tight-knit community. In Tokyo, community leaders mobilise citizens – from school children to seniors – to pick up litter. Salarymen, housewives and shopkeepers can also sign up for the neighbourhood *shobodan* fire brigade, which supports the regular firefighting corps and specialises in prevention and response.

Other cities take this concept even further: in Santiago, Chile, all firefighters are volunteers. For more than 150 years, Chilean doctors, corporate executives and high-level public officials have joined the Cuerpo de Bomberos de Santiago, the city's fire corps. Santiago pays for new fire trucks and receives some funding from the federal government but private donations cover the largest share and dues from firefighters themselves help keep firehouses running.

There's no guarantee that what works in one locale will solve the problems anywhere else. And it can take years of testing and tweaking to get results – as the stories of the individuals over the following few pages show. But that's no excuse not to try. Let's meet some of the urban fixers fighting to help out cities in a bind.

5.

URBAN HEROES

I.
Mona El Hallak
Architect and heritage activist, Beirut

When Lebanon's 15-year civil war ended in 1990, Mona El Hallak was a young architect living in Beirut. Looking at the devastation left by the bullets and bombs, her ambition was to rebuild the city. But much of it wasn't being developed in a way that was respectful of its past, with many Ottoman mansions being replaced with skyscrapers. Then El Hallak discovered the old Barakat building.

Built in the 1920s and 1930s, it was used as a stronghold by militia during the war. When the building came in the crosshairs for development, El Hallak campaigned for almost 25 years to save the plot from being levelled and built upon.

After securing a €15.6m grant from the Lebanese government and advice from the French authorities, El Hallak was able to turn it into a war museum: Beit Beirut, also known as The House of Beirut. An archive and exhibition space, the building is an exhibit in itself. The architecture offers a glimpse of prewar Beirut, while bullet holes and graffiti tell the story of the war.

2.
Theaster Gates
Artist and founder of the Rebuild Foundation, Chicago

Theaster Gates is an artist of international repute whose work has been displayed everywhere from London's White Cube to the Whitney in New York. After studying in Iowa and returning to his native Chicago in 2006, he has made it his business to invest in the people – and buildings – of the South Side, an impoverished part of town afflicted with social problems and gun violence.

In 2009, Gates founded the Rebuild Foundation to transform neglected neighbourhoods through affordable artist studios, accommodation and cultural institutions. At the centre of these projects is the Stony Island Arts Bank, which he bought from the city of Chicago for $1 in 2013. He has since spent $4.5m (€3.9m) – from fundraising, loans and his own pocket – turning it into a community exhibition centre and library that contains everything from a vinyl collection to books and magazines donated by Johnson Publishing.

"It's the accumulation of a simple commitment to a place," says Gates. "And it's a gesture that the federal government takes note of."

3.
Michelle Senayah
Urban developer and co-founder of The Laneway Project, Toronto

Toronto has about 300km of alleyways – or laneways – running through it that often feature nothing but skips and discarded furniture. Urban developer Michelle Senayah reasoned that if they could be cleaned up they would present a social, cultural and economic uplift for the city. "Laneways have been treated as if they're mono-functional," she says. "The city's population is growing and we need more space so it makes sense to reconsider their use."

In 2014 Senayah co-founded The Laneway Project to get more out of the alleyways. So far it has incorporated design-led lighting installations into previously under-lit streets; piloted the idea of transforming laneways into cycle paths; initiated conversations about the development of housing in laneways; and researched the idea of building the city's first laneway public market.

Crucially, city hall is taking note. "We aren't seen as this novel community group any more," says Senayah. "Now we're actually seen as a viable part in shaping how our city develops."

4.
Ali Akbar
Newspaper seller, Paris

From the gilt awnings of Les Deux Magots to the canteen of the local university, there isn't an address in Saint-Germain-des-Prés where Ali Akbar isn't welcome. Born into a large family in Pakistan, he's one of the few *vendeurs à la criée* left in Paris: newspaper men who call out the headlines and sell direct to patrons, going café to café.

Akbar's presence helps to keep people reading in Parisian cafés rather than gazing at smartphones. Coupled with a network of well-stocked kiosks, he's intrinsic to the neighbourhood's media economy and brings authenticity to the grand cafés.

"The secret is humour," says Akbar, who has sold papers for more than four decades, as he stands by Café Louise on Boulevard Saint-Germain holding a stack of *Le Monde*. "I always play on the headlines," he says. "*C'est officiel!* Ali has the Prix Goncourt!" Other jokes are a little more barbed, taking aim at politicians and riffing on rumours making the rounds in Paris. Akbar's wit may be risqué but he is a much-loved fixture of the 6th arrondissement.

5.
Taku Hibino
Architect and CEO of Hibino Sekkei, Tokyo

Children who grow up in big Japanese cities are used to cramped quarters. But the lack of space has become a concern for educators in cities across Japan: could this be why local youngsters were becoming idle and overweight? Since the mid-2000s, Taku Hibino's firm, Hibino Sekkei, has been designing kindergartens and nurseries that put these worries to rest.

For a kindergarten in Atsugi, Hibino created a climbing wall; at others in Kumamoto, Kagoshima and Nagasaki he dreamed up indoor slides, monkey bars,

swings and poles. "We want to make it fun for children to get exercise as they move around the building," he says.

Hibino, whose father started the firm in Atsugi in 1972, picked up some of his ideas on trips to Europe but he was also influenced by his own upbringing. As a child, he was encouraged to bounce around the house and climb a large bush in the backyard. He often came away with scratches and bumps. "Children learn by trying things on their own," he says. "When done right, buildings can foster that."

6.
Fernando Ortiz Monasterio
Architect and founder of VerdeVertical, Mexico City

Finding parkland in Mexico City can be tricky but one thing it's not short of is tall concrete walls. Recognising his hometown's need for more greenery to purify the smoggy air, architect Fernando Ortiz Monasterio chose to plant up rather than out.

In 2007 he established architecture firm VerdeVertical to plant vertical gardens across the capital. He set out to cover some of the estimated 168 sq km of bare façades and today his gardens grow across more than 40,000 sq m of the city, from building exteriors to restaurant courtyards. In 2016 he proposed covering 1,000 support pillars on the main highway. Completed in late 2018, this stretch of greenery now filters more than 27,000 tonnes of noxious gases every year.

Through the conspicuousness of his leafy designs, Monasterio hopes to show Mexicans that improving the capital's air quality should be a grassroots effort. He says that the growing population will need 40 million sq m of green space by 2030 to meet World Health Organization standards. "Both citizens and the authorities must take responsibility and seize every bit of space possible," he says.

7.
Lena Chan
Conservationist and director of the National Biodiversity Centre, Singapore

"I'm not really a tree-hugger," says Dr Lena Chan, director of Singapore's National Biodiversity Centre and often dubbed the city's "mother nature". "I look at the practical side of things and the science." Singapore is one of the world's greenest cities, with verdant public spaces and a surprising abundance of plants and animals for such a dense urban environment.

Since 2009, Chan's efforts to restore the greenery and habitats once lost to the city sprawl has seen endangered species from otters to hornbills frolic and flit freely once again. And for a metropolis only half the size of London, Singapore packs a punch with more species of native plants and birds than Germany.

Chan also consults private developers and architects on what kind of foliage to use when adding greenery to their structures, and advises policymakers on conservation. In 2010 she co-authored a UN-endorsed manual for benchmarking biodiversity in urban areas. But she still makes time to get out in the field and is often found with a pair of binoculars, spotting birds among the skyscrapers.

8.
Martin Thim
Entrepreneur and co-founder of Friends of The Coal Bridge, Aarhus

As a child, Martin Thim was fascinated with derelict relics of heavy industry and the military. "It was something that I first discovered when my parents and I explored a disused submarine in Estonia," he says. So when the entrepreneur began working on the old coal bridge in Aarhus's Sydhavnen in 2014 (as part of a redevelopment of the South Harbour area), he knew it had potential.

An ex-industrial area, Sydhavnen was being gentrified as artists and entrepreneurs began moving in. However, Thim felt that unimaginative office blocks and executive homes would not be in keeping with the area. Beneath the bridge stood an old car park, inhabited mostly by rough sleepers and drug users who would huddle in grotty shelters and, though Thim wanted to improve the area, he didn't want to drive anyone out.

The initiative now gives the car park's inhabitants better shelters and access to toilets. By working with occupants around the coal bridge rather than forcing them away, Thim hopes to avoid the more toxic side-effects of gentrification in the area and to turn the bridge into a mini High Line.

9.
Yto Barrada
Artist and co-founder of Cinémathèque de Tanger, Tangier

Tangier was once Morocco's capital of Arab cinema and at night the streets lit up with the playbills of the Vox, the Ciné-Americano and the Mauritania. But after the 1960s, the city developed a seedy reputation and, as its glamour faded, one by one the picture houses closed down. "The city centre was almost abandoned," says Yto Barrada, who returned in 2003 after living in France and New York.

Three years later, Barrada completed the restoration of the 1938 Cinema Rif on Tangier's Grand Socco and founded Cinémathèque de Tanger there – the only arthouse cinema in North Africa at the time, with a café and a bar. "We decided that people needed a grand space to watch films but also somewhere for the things that happen on the side: meeting and working together, falling in love, planning other projects in the city."

Investment has now returned to the Grand Socco and other places have opened to cater to the Cinémathèque crowd. Barrada is modest about her role in Tangier's revival but she certainly set things in motion.

10.
Coralie Winn, Ryan Reynolds and Andrew Just
Founders of Gap Filler, Christchurch

Build a dance space in the middle of a city, with music powered by an old coin-operated washing machine, and people will come. That's what the three founders of Gap Filler discovered in 2011 while Christchurch was recovering from major earthquakes.

Dr Ryan Reynolds and Coralie Winn, who have arts backgrounds, together with Andrew Just, an architectural designer, invited the community to help bring life back to vacant sites and remedy a post-quake dearth of culture. The intention

was to do "a project or two", says Reynolds – something offbeat, creative and fun, blending performance and temporary architecture.

Gap Filler has since facilitated more than 70 highly visible projects in Christchurch, including a cycle-powered cinema, a venue constructed from shipping pallets and a giant outdoor arcade game. Early on the founders made their first and strongest policy decision: not to repeat themselves. They haven't run out of ideas yet.

II.
Karanja Njoroge
Chairman and founder of Friends of Karura Forest, Nairobi

Karura Forest, a 1,000-hectare woodland area in Nairobi, used to be a no-go zone. "It was viewed as a den of thieves," says Karanja Njoroge. "A place where criminals took their victims and left them for dead." Though this belief wasn't altogether untrue, it also played into the hands of those who wanted to cut down the trees and build on the land. After all, if people feared the forest they wouldn't fight to protect it.

After discovering an illicit deal to develop the land, Njoroge began a movement to save the forest – and suffered a beating by some heavies hired by a vested interest. A public outcry resulted in the deal being reversed and, in 2009, Njoroge founded Friends of Karura Forest under a 2005 law that allowed the formation of community organisations to safeguard forests.

"In 2010 we started fencing the forest," he says. The change was immediate. Karura registered 300 visitors in its first month and now more than 28,000 people a month come to walk, run or cycle the forest paths. "It's transformed people's lives," says Njoroge. "They value the serenity."

12.
Firefighters
Fire and Ambulance Services Academy, Hong Kong

Being a firefighter in any city is challenging but few present as difficult a landscape for battling flames as Hong Kong. Here, a 9,500-strong fire department responds to as many as 38,000 calls a year. Meeting the demands of this cityscape – from tackling blazes in high-rises to ensuring oil rig workers' safety in the South China Sea – has called for the formation of specialist teams, including the Urban Search and Rescue Team and the Mountain Search and Rescue Team.

The training of new recruits and existing firefighters takes place at the city's Fire and Ambulance Services Academy, which opened in 2016 at a cost of HK$3.6bn (€393m). Teams of firefighters and paramedics run drills on state-of-the-art training facilities tailored to Hong Kong's unique terrain; mock sets include an aeroplane, a container ship and an underground metro station.

The existing landscape isn't the only challenge: the rate of new skyscrapers breaking ground is unlikely to slow. But thanks to the academy, firefighters will be prepared to help keep Hong Kong safe for decades to come.

Citizen volunteers
Just for the love of it

For a city and its services to run smoothly, it's imperative to have a forward-thinking government willing to invest in smart healthcare and law enforcement programmes. Development from the private sector can also play a part in transforming pockets of rundown areas into bustling and friendly neighbourhoods. Yet the buck doesn't stop there. As citizens we must ask what we can do for ourselves and our communities. Here we take a look at the volunteers helping to improve their cities, from saving lives to collecting litter.

1.
Cuerpo de Bomberos
Santiago

In the Chilean capital, firefighting is farmed out to volunteers. The Cuerpo de Bomberos de Santiago is mostly funded by private donations and, while the drivers, cleaners and office workers are paid, firefighters do the job for free. Volunteers work nights at firehouses, enjoying a tradition-rich environment between emergency calls.

2.
GoodGym
UK

GoodGym's programme is as heartwarming as it is healthy. Volunteers combine exercise with efforts to help the community, capping off 5km sprints with visits to a pensioner's house to help with the gardening. The programme kicked off in 2009, when founder Ivo Gormley began doing odd jobs for a pensioner after his own jogs.

3.
Emergency Response Team
Wellington

New Zealand's capital city is precariously positioned near two tectonic plates and surrounded by ocean. Each week, groups of volunteers train in casualty welfare and search and rescue. Started by residents in 1971, the Wellington Emergency Response Team, funded by the city council, is part of the first line of response in a disaster.

4.
Green Bird
Tokyo

Alongside the Goth-Lolis, Forest Girls and other fashion tribes that parade around Omotesando there's a group in green bibs, holding metal tongs and plastic bags. These are the Green Bird volunteers, a litter-collecting non-profit set up in 2003. The initiative has spread across Japan and further afield to Paris, Boston and Singapore.

5.
Sidewalk Talk
San Francisco

It's a Friday evening and two rows of chairs are facing each other in a square in the Financial District. What looks like a speed-dating event is in fact an outpost for Sidewalk Talk. In 2014, two therapists gathered 26 colleagues to provide free one-on-one listening sessions. By 2018 the project had 700 volunteers in 19 cities worldwide.

6.
Surf Life Saving Australia
Sydney

Helping professional lifeguards patrol 21 Sydney beaches is a brigade of volunteers from the Surf Life Saving Club, which was founded in 1907. The lifesavers in their iconic yellow-and-red caps help to keep the beaches safe and dedicate their Saturdays to training the next generation of lifesavers.

7.
White Hat Volunteers
Calgary

Whether you're returning home or visiting a place for the first time, the airport is often your welcome to a city. Calgary's White Hat Volunteers, a group of cowboy hat-clad seniors who traipse through the airport offering directions, not only provide a valuable service but are also the perfect ambassadors for the city.

8.
Joy 94.9
Melbourne

Independent radio station Joy 94.9 has built a solid reputation while being run almost exclusively by volunteers. Its success is down to its identity as a true representative of its listeners: the LGBT+ community. Melbourne has long been known as a progressive city and Joy has been a big part of that since hitting the airwaves in 1993.

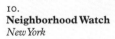

9.
Paseo Nocturno
Mexico City

Every Wednesday since 1998, cyclists have been gathering at 21.00 at Mexico City's El Angel de la Independencia monument to pedal around the city. The Paseo Nocturno (Nocturnal Promenade) encourages cycling in a traffic-choked city. Its volunteers fill in as mechanics and ushers to make sure no one gets lost along the way.

10.
Neighborhood Watch
New York

This community-driven watchdog was founded in the wake of a murder in Queens in the 1960s. Residents and shop owners are the eyes and the ears of a neighbourhood and report any suspicious behaviour to local law enforcement. It's proven an effective means to reduce crime and has since gone global.

As more people move to our cities there's one problem that planners have to face up to: where are they going to put everyone? The lack of affordable accommodation is the single most pressing issue facing cities from London to San Francisco, and it's tough to see how even wealthy places such as these will cope. Because, even if the problem is universal, there's no cookie-cutter solution.

It's not enough to simply throw up tall towers and lure us into ever-smaller apartments. Our homes can define us and shape our futures – and those of our families – so we need to build places that trigger a sense of community and a feeling that we're not alone in the vast metropolis. Well, the good news is that even if the problem may seem monumental, there are people determined to have a go – and also projects from the past that offer lessons for the future.

Over the following pages we visit property developers and architects – from Andreas Martin-Löf and Alejandro Aravena to Small Giants in Melbourne – who are offering thoughtful, resourceful ideas that don't sacrifice the softer design features that improve residents' quality of life. We also check in with those living in the most modern of accommodation spaces: mini apartments in Tokyo and Hong Kong high-rises.

If this is the future of inner-city living, what exactly does it look and feel like? And will we all fit in?

These compact spaces are often home to the young and ambitious, people who are part of the booming rental economy and who are less interested in owning suburban houses than previous generations. Too often, though, developers and architects focus only on catering to these city slickers and neglect both the worlds of the student and the retired. They may not be as sexy as a Tokyo tower but apartment complexes that provide lively environments for seniors or light-filled digs for university students deserve attention. And, on that note, so too do trailblazing projects that integrate different generations and encourage sporadic social encounters in communal spaces. In today's world, housing in cities should foster interaction between all sorts of people.

6.

HOW TO LIVE

Affordable housing
Smart moves

A lack of affordable accommodation is the most urgent issue facing cities today. We need clever thinking, new materials and a wise use of technology if we're going to create a new tier of both accessible and handsome housing. Here we look at architects and developers coming up with schemes that deliver both.

I.
RipollTizon, Mallorca
Social but individual

Years after a debilitating construction bubble forced Spain's regional governments to focus on the creation of smaller social-housing developments, many architectural studios continue to rise to the design challenge – not least on the island of Mallorca.

"We were drawn to social housing because it was less about selling real estate and more about the architecture's social legacy," says Juan Miguel Tizón, who, with Pep Ripoll, owns architecture firm RipollTizon in the island's capital, Palma. The pair's development in Sa Pobla, a village in the north of Mallorca, has placed interaction between residents at the top of its agenda.

The aim has been to put the "social" back into social housing. The 19 dwellings surround a plaza, with passages and walkways ensuring that residents can crisscross easily within the development. The tenants range from farmers working the nearby potato fields to immigrant workers and retirees.

Economic disadvantage is the common denominator but cheap rents and a smarter use of light, with solar heating for water, afford them a greater possibility of financial stability. The high cost of land has tempered the scale of developments on the island but Tizón believes that this is a positive: "The smaller the edifice, the easier it is to encourage more social interaction."

Back in Palma, an increase in urban density has seen the Pere Garau neighbourhood evolve from single blocks of units into more condensed housing. In place of three rundown buildings, a more compact structure of 18 apartments was erected in 2013 – RipollTizon's latest social-housing project (*pictured, above and right*). Its white façade is perforated by unevenly dispersed balconies that hint at the idiosyncrasies inside: like Sa Pobla, the design encourages unique interiors.

"We wanted to create versatile spaces and it's been interesting to see how each tenant has put their own personal stamp on their living quarters," says Tizón. "It's important that they see this as their home rather than just temporary accommodation."

2.
Peabody, London
Lofty ideals

Located in Bethnal Green, the Mint Street complex was designed by Pitman Tozer. Its 67 apartments are surrounded by industrial units, scrapyards and railway arches, with a noisy train line as a direct neighbour. The architect's solution to the noise was to triple-glaze some units and add "winter gardens" to others. These enclosed, glazed balconies are such good sound buffers that the train noise is reduced to a gentle purr.

This take on the traditional mansion block was made possible by Peabody, an organisation that has been commissioning, building and maintaining much of London's best social housing for 150-plus years. It's a fine example of Peabody's speciality: good-quality, well-designed housing combining affordable rents, shared ownership, market rent and private sale.

Set up in 1862 and now merged with fellow housing association Family Mosaic, Peabody provides homes for more than 111,000 people and has announced plans to deliver 2,500 new homes a year by 2021. Its reputation for thoughtful schemes is down to a commitment to quality and good architecture. The company works with a roster of innovative studios such as CF Møller, Orms, Níall McLaughlin, Haworth Tompkins and Hawkins\Brown.

In stark contrast to some shared-ownership schemes, the architects are expected to apply the same quality to their affordable and private-sale properties, and Peabody retains its architects right up to the end of the technical design so that the original details don't get diluted. If only all developers had such lofty aspirations.

Q&A with Alejandro Aravena
Santiago, Chile

Pritzker Prize-winning architect Alejandro Aravena, executive director of Santiago firm Elemental, is best known for his work in affordable housing. His projects include the rebuilding of Constitución, a Chilean seaside town wiped out by a tsunami, and Quinta Monroy, which saw him create accommodation on a shoestring budget for 100 families in the slums of Iquique.

What are the major issues architects have to face today?
I'll name one: inequality. Every day people travel from third-world countries to the first world. They work, study, perhaps have fun, and then return home. Some people feel that they don't belong to the same society. But change doesn't happen under normal circumstances: you need crises and we're witnessing many. Maybe it's a chance to improve quality of life.

Would you say that your Quinta Monroy project in Chile sums up this problem?
Yes. Our approach was to try to make better use of scarce resources. We had $7,500 per house. So if that allows for 30 to 40 sq m, and a reasonable middle-class house is about 80 sq m, we saw it as a chance to build half a great house rather than a small, average house.

Is it true you were disillusioned after architecture school?
I was disappointed not by architecture but by certain clients using it for profiteering. What I'm trying to build is some public common good. It's our responsibility as architects to recognise a chance to test our capacities, to turn the forces at play into something concrete.

3.
Andreas Martin-Löf, Knivsta, Sweden
Prefab sprouting

Is it possible to build more than 100 low-cost, high-quality homes in just six months? Absolutely, according to architect Andreas Martin-Löf, property development firm Junior Living and financier Sam Bonnier. Their prefab modular homes in Knivsta near Uppsala were completed in 2014 and are one of the standout developments being used to alleviate the housing shortage in Sweden.

Martin-Löf's Stockholm-based team of 12 architects set out to develop a housing concept that could be built quickly and economically – and be architecturally interesting too. "In Stockholm too many new houses look the same," says Martin-Löf. "It's like the big construction companies think that they've found the recipe. Here I got the chance to work with people who wanted something else."

The result is based on prefabricated modules, one side with a grid of balconies and the others clad in semi-transparent panels with an irregular window pattern. Each of the 124 units is 33 sq m and includes a kitchen, bathroom, living room and sleeping alcove. While their budget is light years from the high-end spaces that Martin-Löf often designs, the homes do resemble his other work, with clean interiors and floor-to-ceiling windows.

Construction finished in mid-2014 and the first homeowners, having paid between €55,000 and €87,000, moved in shortly after. "These are dignified homes for young people, real homes, not 10 sq m cabins like some of the solutions that have been presented," says Martin-Löf, who has continued collaborating with Junior Living on affordable housing. Supported by Svenska Bostäder, Sweden's biggest public-housing developer, they plan to build 1,000 more homes. The first 280 – in a smart block in Västberga, near Stockholm – were unveiled in 2016.

Intergenerational housing
All together now

Is there a new way of building old people's homes?
Should they even *be* just for old people? In the
Copenhagen district of Nørrebro those questions are
driving a rethink about how the elderly are housed.
Danish architecture firm CF Møller is working on a
project called Future Sølund, a beautiful complex of
buildings where old people live alongside young families.
Yes, there will still be nursing-home units to care for
the infirm but there will also be hundreds of houses,
a nursery, a barber shop and leafy squares and parks,
with a lake a stone's throw away. Under vaulted wooden
structures, seniors and youngsters will meet to exchange
stories. Wheelchair-bound residents can share pavement
space with buggies; young and old can nurture rooftop
gardens side by side.

Slated for completion in 2022, the
project sounds like a utopian vision.
But faced with a rapidly ageing global
population, this type of city planning
shouldn't feel novel and nor should it
be the exception. Rather it's a crucial
response to the pressing, unrelenting
reality that faces most western countries.

The principle behind old people's
homes is benevolent. Long-term
residential care for the elderly came
about during the 19th century as a
philanthropic housing alternative to
infirmaries, almshouses or, worse, the
workhouse, where "aged paupers" were
set to task in gender-segregated wards.

The postwar era and the advent of
welfare in many countries saw the state
step in to provide organised residential
care. By the 1970s the model for "homes
for the elderly" had become a lifestyle
option as well as a medical necessity.
Meanwhile, private care homes became

the norm. But the siphoning off of
seniors, be it to a purpose-built gated
community in sunny Sarasota or a
countryside care home, is a model
that has limited scope.

Creating ghettos for elders is a
segregation that most societies won't be
able to afford or sustain. What's more,
it's clear that mixing the young and old
can reap rewards for all. At one south-
London care home, a new purpose-built
nursery wing hosts 30 toddlers aged
between two and four – the first in the
UK. The rambunctious energy of the
little ones is a tonic for elderly residents.

Another project in Seattle combines
a rehabilitation and care home with
an intergenerational learning centre
catering for 125 children aged between
six weeks and five years. Throughout
the day, babies visit assisted-living
residents and toddlers sing along with
senior citizens.

This type of multigenerational mingling doesn't have to be staged and supervised. Designers, architects and planners can choreograph our communities so that young and old run into each other for casual chinwags. Thoughtful use of communal space can break down barriers and prevent the emergence of both urban youth-club-style zones and sleepy retirement settlements that are social cul-de-sacs.

By changing the configuration of our homes just slightly, architects can alter the social dynamics. "It's about making use of the threshold space in between apartments," says Mads Mandrup Hansen, project leader for the Future Sølund project, where every detail is geared towards breaking down barriers. "It's about creating halls and corridors that act as social hubs where people can stop and form relationships."

The blending of the very young and very old makes perfect sense. After all, retired seniors are often the only ones who have time to engage with little children when everyone else is at work.

There's a growing understanding that our societies need to adopt a plural approach to age, not just for the benefit of the old but for everyone. Matthias Hollwich is the co-founder of New York architecture firm HWKN and a proponent of what he calls "new ageing". He insists that there's an urgent need to reinvent architecture to respond to longevity and his firm has come up with a prototype. The Skyler tower provides 1,000 residents with social spaces (gyms, business centres and shared transport) where they can "collide".

"What we're looking at is promoting health and happiness," says Hollwich, explaining how the Skyler will place an emphasis on lively communality while also offering residents an inbuilt "stealthcare" system to care for the infirm in their adaptable homes. "It's a building that will serve occupants at every stage of life."

Even though Hollwich's plans look futuristic, he insists that the pursuit of modernity in this sector has hindered rather than helped the progress of new ageing. "There is a belief that we can solve everything through technology by providing special services," he says. "What we've forgotten is something much more humble: community. Intergenerational living used to be family-based. Now we have to find new ways in an active, modern society to create these relationships."

Indeed, many societies might have to look to old models of co-existence to deal with their ageing, imbalanced demographics. Take South Korea. According to the OECD, by 2050 more than a third of South Koreans will be over the age of 65. Perhaps this modern workaholic nation will have to look back to the traditional *hanok* home in areas such as Seoul's Bukchon for inspiration. The single-storey *hanok* always functioned as a multigenerational homestead for families; its courtyard typology provided a highly adaptable space for the old, young and everyone in between. Yet rapid modernisation saw high-rise apartments become the norm and, alas, many *hanoks* were demolished to make way for them.

Similarly, in China we have seen the systematic demolition of the traditional *siheyuan*, once a symbol of Beijing. It's a thing of the past yet Chinese architects and town-planners may have to draw from this older structure to solve a very modern social crisis.

Back in Copenhagen, Mandrup Hansen is confident that Future Sølund will alter the way in which Denmark approaches urban planning. "It's a model set-up," he says. "We want to show how an old people's care home can serve as an urban generator in a city rather than be a drain on its resources. We're seeing strong support from a wide range of political parties and there's a feeling that if we can nail this it will be an example to follow." Let's hope he's right.

Sophie Grove is Monocle's senior correspondent, based in Paris.

197

Students and seniors
How to do digs

Intergenerational living may be the ideal but it won't always be practical. It's still important that cities provide thoughtful housing for those people at either end of the age spectrum. Here are three ventures for students, and three for seniors, that are getting it right.

1.
4th May College, Copenhagen
Built in 1951 to honour Denmark's Nazi-resistance movement during the Second World War, this complex by Hans Hansen was renovated in 2017. Today the U-shaped structure is home to some 60 students, all descendants of the resistance fighters.

The renovation was led by Copenhagen's Bertelsen & Scheving Arkitekter, which focused on restoring the original colour scheme. Most of the rooms and bathrooms are shared – that's the way the students asked for it to be kept. It provides a cheery environment and costs a quarter of the average rent in Copenhagen.

2.
Bombarda House, Lisbon
There's a dearth of purpose-built student housing in Portugal, which is where Bombarda House comes in. Completed in 2016 by architect Tomaz D'Eça Leal, Bombarda has done away with the usual small rooms and dingy corridors. Here you'll find large, bright bedrooms and communal spaces for studying – and partying.

3.
Chapter, London
Halls of residence are big business in the UK: institutional investors spent £4.68bn (€5.2bn) on student digs in 2017. Chapter has set out to attract a chunk of the almost 450,000 international students who come to the UK each year. At its London properties the feel is more Soho House than student dorm, with black-and-white floor mosaics snaking between ping-pong tables and plush banquettes.

Coming of age (clockwise from top left): The reading rooms at 4th May College; The Werner Friedmann Foundation supports retired Munich artists (*left and right*); the Viktualienmarkt building is owned by The Werner Friedmann Foundation; 4th May College room painted in Hansen's original colour scheme; the living room at 4th May College

1.
The Werner Friedmann Foundation, Munich

This foundation was established by Anneliese Friedmann in 1969 in honour of her husband Werner, founder of the daily newspaper *Abendzeitung*. Ever since, it has been supporting retired artists, journalists, actors and singers in Munich. It helps to pay for their overseas trips to see friends and visits to exhibitions and, most importantly, it subsidises their rent.

There are more than 30 retired creatives, most aged 70-plus, living in subsidised apartments across town. Many of them occupy a 14-unit building at Viktualienmarkt, an enviable address. The foundation also provides everything from electric bikes to art supplies.

2.
Setagaya, Tokyo

Japan is a world leader when it comes to looking after the elderly and firms such as Community Net have created remarkable nursing homes in rural areas. Yamazaki Kentaro Design Workshop paves the way in inner-city accommodation. One of its projects is a nursing home in central Tokyo, built into the forested hillside of Kokubunji-gaisen; it boasts vast windows, vaulted ceilings and fountains.

3.
Andritz, Graz, Austria

This retirement home by Dietger Wissounig Architekten, completed in 2015, shows the value of hands-on care. Buildings are divided into areas that house 15 residents and one carer, with a shared space. There's also a café, hairdresser and "village square".

Community housing
Good neighbours

I.
Bretagne Building, São Paulo
Join the club

Perhaps it really is the impact of the sharing economy, or maybe it's simply that so many of us spend the day staring at a back-lit screen. Either way, developers have latched onto the concept of co-living and are frantically promoting it wherever you turn. Yet the heart of the issue is surely this: how do we all get to live in places where there are neighbours you can count on and where residents can come together? Here we look at successful examples of using design to build a community, from a more innovative take on co-living in Zürich to a modernist matchmaker in São Paulo.

The Bretagne Building in São Paulo's Higienópolis neighbourhood was conceived by ambitious businessman and architect João Artacho Jurado. When it was built in 1958, the Bretagne was the only development in the city to have a pool and a playground. Add to that a games room, gym and sauna, a mezzanine for parties, a tearoom, bar and residents' deck, and it looks like an exercise in residential largesse.

For all its glitz, Jurado's scheme has nurtured a real sense of community. Elderly groups gather in the bar to play cards, mothers take turns looking after each other's children and 30-somethings catch up on the rooftop garden among the greenery.

2.
Kalkbreite, Zürich
Communal experiment

Kalkbreite came about when Swiss architecture firm Müller Sigrist built 97 apartments, as well as office and retail spaces, in a desolate part of Zürich's Kreis 3 that's dominated by the tram depot. The lively development is an exercise in community living and funding.

It was completed in 2014 in collaboration with the Genossenschaft Kalkbreite, a union dedicated to creating affordable and sustainable housing. The majority of floors are dedicated to communal apartments similar to university dormitories: most are inhabited by about 10 people, who share a kitchen and living room. The foyer is at the heart of the development, next door to the café where residents gather for their morning catch-ups, and there's also an in-house hostel and office spaces for rent.

As one of the world's most expensive cities, reasonably priced apartments in Zürich are rare and the Kalkbreite development (named after the street on which it sits) was built specifically to remedy this in an innovative way.

3.
Barbican Estate, London
Concrete benefits

With light-sapping concrete, arrowholes and turrets, and an almost impenetrable pedestrian system, the Barbican Estate can look aggressive from outside. But to those who live in its 2,000 units, the Barbican – which was designed by Chamberlin, Powell & Bon and opened in 1982 – is a cohesive inner-city community. Gardens, lakes, tennis courts, secret passages: all in the centre of London.

Homes here don't come cheap but the variety of scale, from studio flats to four-bedroom houses, has fostered a dynamic community. There are grandmothers who have lived here since the 1960s, families with teenage kids, architects and City boys. It's not social housing and it never was – but inside its walls is a society whose uniqueness is magnified as London's housing situation deteriorates. And, even now, it offers some lessons for community building.

Skyscraper lifestyles
Shoebox chic

As people continue to leave small towns and flock to sprawling metropolises, residential blocks grow ever-taller and the apartments within them shrink. For many millions of people, living small – and tall – is the reality when calling a city home.

1.
Living small
Tokyo

I was born and raised in a rural town on Japan's Kyushu Island and moved to Tokyo in 2011, when I joined MONOCLE. The space in Japan's capital is limited: more than nine million people live here. Although there are large apartments and mansions, for most people living in Tokyo this means inhabiting a pint-sized apartment. The first place I lived in was shared accommodation in Otsuka and all I had to myself was a coffin-sized bedroom. Like many other young people in this city, I started with a cheap, cubby hole-sized place and spent most of my waking life outside. Soon, however, I began to crave my own space.

By chance I secured a spot in Nakagin Capsule Tower near Ginza, designed by Kisho Kurokawa. Built in 1972 during Japan's period of economic growth, each of its 140 capsules was designed as a second base for salarymen who spent their weekends at their homes outside Tokyo. Each cube had a built-in bed, TV, radio, desk, sink, cupboard and bathroom. They may have been small but there was a big idea behind them.

My room no longer had the original bed, so I ordered one from Muji. I remember the deliverymen stepping into the fridge-sized lift, shuffling down the corridor and depositing the bed in a perfectly synchronised move. Companies such as Muji have invented suitably small products for compact living, from

Junichi Toyofuku is Monocle's associate bureau chief in Tokyo.

a one-slice toaster to a two-litre washing machine. And estate agents have become creative at selling petite flats. If the room is tiny, they trumpet its natural light, its view or the fact that you can stretch your legs on the rooftop.

In recent years, small living has become more popular. Magazines such as *Casa Brutus* run smart-storage specials while books on *danshari* (decluttering) fly off the shelves. People lead simplified lives as a result. Extreme minimalists, it's said, should be able to fit their life possessions into one suitcase.

Today I live in a larger space (at least compared to where I started) near Yoyogi Park. One day I had a conversation with a fellow resident, who asked how big my apartment was. "It's 30 sq m. A bit small," I said. "May I ask if you live with someone?" he asked politely. I shook my head. "Ah, that's enough then. Why would you need more space?"

He had a point. Apartments in Tokyo may be small but they're proportionate to the size of the inhabitants, the furniture and the streets. Only when I stay at my friend's apartment in Berlin do I realise that my room is the size of her bathroom. But it's OK. I could always look for a bigger space but is it really necessary? My current priority is to master creating a home that I want to spend time in – however small it might be. So far, I'm enjoying the challenge.

Small business
Making money out of less space

The downsizing of the domestic sphere means activities that used to take place in the home will be transferred to other spaces. It also means that household items will need to be redesigned to make them more compact. Here are three innovative businesses turning the shrinking home to their advantage.

Problem 1:
Storing winter clothes
Blue Crates, Chicago
The Walker brothers were living in one-bedroom apartments in Chicago and moving winter clothes into storage to make more room was "a pain in the ass", says co-founder Michael Walker. So in 2016 they launched Blue Crates. It's pitched as a "limitless closet"; the company provides sturdy crates for packing goods and then picks them up and stores them in nearby warehouses (you can recall your crates once a month for free).

Problem 2:
Fitting in domestic appliances
Wasbar, Antwerp/Ghent
Wasbar is a smart reinvention of the traditional launderette business that attracts young city-dwellers who don't own a washing machine. The space features a well-appointed café where patrons can wait for their washing. It was founded in Ghent by Dries Henau and Yuri Vandenbogaerde in 2012 and was quick to take off, with further outposts now in Ghent and Antwerp.

Problem 3:
Parking your bike
Vello Bike, Vienna
Storing a bike can be impossible in a tiny apartment and foldable bikes are a bit too functional to be cool. This was the problem that designer Valentin Vodev set out to fix when he founded his foldable-bike brand Vello Bike in 2014 with partner Valerie Wolff. High-quality materials (including leather saddles) give the bikes a less functional feel but practicality is still a key promise. "We needed to think of a product with full flexibility," says Vodev. "One that's fast on the road but can be stored in the wardrobe or under the desk."

2.
Living tall
Hong Kong

The population explosion coupled with the ever-decreasing amount of land available is leading to an inevitable, ahem, rise in high-density skyscraper living. The future of housing looks like Hong Kong: millions of people stacked on top of each other in high-rises. That may sound dystopian but not even small, faraway places will be able to escape it.

Take Auckland. In the 1960s, New Zealand's largest city, home to just 1.4 million people compared with Hong Kong's 7.3 million, adopted a single-occupancy, single-storey housing plan serviced by scant public transport. It needs to change, so the city is supporting higher-density housing like Hong Kong's, albeit not quite so sky-scraping.

Given that more of us are going to be living in high-rises, what's it actually like to live in a tower in Hong Kong? It's very normal. Everyone does it.

What's odd, after canvassing the opinions of other Hong Kong high-rise residents, is how our positive experiences are a world away from the countless academic papers that decry high-rise living. "You can't categorically say that high-rise living is either good or bad for you," says Layla McCay, founder of the Centre for Urban Design and Mental Health in London. "It's more about what it does to your quality of life." Basically, housing happiness depends on your ability to choose your place of abode. Being stuck with an option you didn't actively choose is when dissatisfaction comes in.

McCay does point out that being suspended in mid-air heightens the risk of loneliness and the removal from a feeling of place; thoughtful design is therefore needed to encourage interaction with nature and other people. Sadly Hong Kong property prices, coupled with a land shortage, has seen developers cram as many apartments as possible onto one plot, with thinner walls, fewer shared spaces and even smaller floor plans. The city already has building height restrictions and now there are calls for a minimum apartment size.

Mayors and urban-planners should look to Hong Kong's active seniors for inspiration: for example, the elderly folk doing tai chi in groups every morning. "Even in an incredibly dense city such as Hong Kong you have this space-sharing that you don't see quite so much in some other cities," says McCay. "As more public space is being consumed for private use, a big question we face is how can we make more of it available to people."

James Chambers is Monocle's Hong Kong bureau chief.

Developers
Raising the roof

There's a new generation of independent property developers who have a genuine passion for placemaking and creating buildings that they're proud to have their names on. The following developers are rethinking the way in which we live, and play, in our cities.

1.
Infill
Oslo

Parkveien 5B-C is tucked between two 19th-century houses in central Oslo. It was once an empty plot; now nine flats are nestled here.

"We're filling in the gaps, building a little bit taller and a little bit tighter," says Sverre Landmark of Aspelin Ramm, whose subsidiary, Infill, specialises in developing petite plots. The building, designed by Kima Arkitektur, is a perfect example of how developers can make use of near-invisible spaces.

Oslo is one of the fastest-growing cities in Europe, set to expand from 670,000 people to 815,000 in 2040. Densification often means cramming apartments into towers but city hall's strategy makes use of gaps between buildings and redevelops industrial sites. This has allowed Oslo to protect its natural landscape, defending inner-city green spaces while keeping the centre alive for residents and businesses.

2.
Project
Portland, Oregon

"Development is a draconian business at times, often very volume driven," says Tom Cody, the managing partner of property developer Project, based in Portland, Oregon. "We want to create new spaces that make a contribution to their cities."

The Union Way arcade of shops and cafés is typical of Project's focus on designs that fuse nature and civic life. Developing retail, apartments, university housing and offices, Project works to redefine places; Union Way punched through a bland building to create an inviting wood-panelled passage.

"We try to operate with a curiosity that's rare in other developers," says Cody. Take Hayashi, Japanese-inspired low-profile townhouses on Portland's north side, which broke away from the pattern in the area. Or Framework, a 12-storey tower that will be the US's first high-rise to use cross-laminated timber.

Building a case (clockwise from top left): Pumpkin Hole 36 development in Oslo by Infill; interior of the 10 Star Home in rural Victoria by Small Giants; exterior of the 10 Star Home; The Commons development in Melbourne by Small Giants; Vøyensvingen 10 project in Oslo by Infill; Project's Union Way arcade in Portland, Oregon

3.
Small Giants
Melbourne

Since launching Small Giants in 2007, founders Danny Almagor and Berry Liberman have partnered with brands that want to create a positive social and environmental impact. One project is The Commons in Brunswick. With an energy-efficiency rating that's off the scale, it's a benchmark for green building; its concrete design eschews air-conditioning and there are no car-park spaces.

The Commons marked a turning point in Small Giants' business model: while it maintains a diverse investment portfolio, it has focused on community building by forming the Impact Investment Group. Some 200 investors pool as much as AU$200m (€126.5m) to inject into projects of social and economic value. "We can't change much on our own – we're just a drop in the ocean," says Almagor. "But if there are 10,000 drops you can fill the bucket."

Zürich co-operatives
DIY development

In most western cities, building places for working, living and leisure has been left predominantly to commercial developers. But since about 2000, Zürich has seen the revival of the old model of co-operative building (in Switzerland these groups are called *genossenschafts*). Co-ops are now responsible for generating not only community-focused affordable housing but also great mixed-use spaces for the city – and increasingly they're proving themselves to be an excellent alternative funding model.

In Zürich, examples of co-op-backed projects include mixed-use developments Kalkbreite, Hunziker Areal and Zwicky Areal. Kalkbreite transformed a dilapidated tram depot into a lively hub (*see page 201*). The members of the *genossenschaft* banded together to bid for the building rights and fund the construction, and the co-op now rents out the 97 apartments and manages the commercial and retail tenancies.

Co-ops are more viable than many idealistic suggestions for alternative forms of development. They're pragmatic, rejecting a purely profit-driven model and lofty ideals that end in underfunded, underplanned mediocrity. By functioning sensibly in a market-driven contemporary city, they can achieve social aims in tandem with operating effectively as financial ventures for themselves, residents and entrepreneurs.

Suburban living
Tapiola, Finland

Suburbs evolve in different ways. Some, such as Levittown on New York's Long Island, are mass-produced experiments in affordable housing. Others are random urban overspill, like outside many Chinese cities. There are exclusive but boring gated communities; low-income, densely populated housing projects on the periphery; and simply the nondescript, interstitial zones that the Pet Shop Boys sang about in the 1980s hit "Suburbia". Most get a bad rap.

Suburbs continue to be built because some people like being close to the city but also want space and greenery – and urban pontificators need to get over their prejudices. Some suburbs do have character and offer a special quality of life. Take Tapiola on the outskirts of Espoo (near Helsinki) in Finland. This leafy, bustling hub shows that the best suburbs are more than just residential areas near town centres.

At your service: Tapiola is self-sufficient when it comes to services. It has schools of all levels and is located next to Finland's highest ranked university, Aalto. It also has a well-stocked library, a public health clinic and both public and private daycare offerings. Plus there are sports facilities ranging from arenas and gyms to public swimming pools

Let's get together: Tapiola's strong sense of community is rooted in its history as an internationally lauded example of urban planning. Many of its residents are keen to uphold this community atmosphere. Common areas such as the central pool and the cultural centre that hosts ballroom dancing bring people together

Sea change: Some parts of Tapiola overlook the sea and others are located just a few minutes away. Residents sunbathe on the rocks or go for seaside runs and some have their boats docked in Otsolahti harbour. The nearest sandy beach is just a short walk away in Westend

Home comforts: While some of the new apartment blocks have given in to demands for more compact urban living, most of Tapiola consists of low-density housing. The residential blocks are also low-rise so as not to stand out and, in addition to these buildings, there are terrace houses and modernist villas

Tapiola's residents don't need to make the 10-minute metro journey to downtown Helsinki in order to eat in a great restaurant, find a decent coffee, check out an art exhibition or catch the latest films in a cinema.

Tapiola was designed in the 1950s and 1960s as a verdant garden city by Finland's leading postwar architects Aarne Ervi, Alvar Aalto and Kaija Siren; it was hailed internationally as a leading example of mid-century modernist town planning. Much of that original ethos still remains and is reflected in Tapiola's low-density housing, low-rise architecture and its expansive green areas such as the Silkkiniitty park.

That's not to say that Tapiola is stuck in its past glory. It's constantly being updated to meet modern demands for better retail, more versatile transport infrastructure and smart housing. While not all of its original residents are happy about the pace of modernisation, Tapiola continues to attract new residents and is widely regarded as one of the most attractive suburbs in the Helsinki metropolitan area.

Tapiola has a strong sense of community that's partly thanks to the way in which it has been planned – emphasising spacious communal areas and pedestrian zones. In summer, residents gather around the public pool and watch films together at the alfresco amphitheatre. In winter, the outdoor ice-skating rink becomes a meeting place for families from all walks of life. The local library has a wide selection of books and magazines, and many residents linger in its reading rooms instead of their own living rooms.

One area in which even the best of suburbs often fall short is culture. Understandably, museums are built and events organised in city centres in order to maximize accessibility and visitor numbers. But, fortunately for its residents, Tapiola seems to buck the trend. Its music and cinema festivals are popular annual events, while the Espoo Museum of Modern Art (Emma) is considered among the best of its kind in Finland. The Tapiola cultural centre, meanwhile, designed by the prominent Finnish architect Arto Sipinen, houses a concert hall, a theatre and a gallery space. It even has its own symphony orchestra – not something every suburb can boast about.

Due to its location at the crossroads of Helsinki and Espoo, Finland's two biggest cities, Tapiola's cultural events attract visitors from other parts of the capital city region too.

Being close to the sea also has its benefits. The air is fresh and the nearest beach is never far away if you fancy a dip in the chilly Baltic Sea. The residents of the Otsolahti bay area of Tapiola are known to keep canoes and kayaks inside their apartments in order to sneak out for a pleasant early-morning or late-evening row. And if they join the local fishing club, Tapiolan Kalakerho, they can even catch their own dinner.

Five more fine suburbs

1. **Oak Park, Chicago**
   Few suburbs attract architects like Oak Park in Chicago's west. Frank Lloyd Wright spent the first 20 years of his career here and completed 25 projects in the area.

2. **Hampstead Garden, London**
   The rows of ivy-covered houses here are often cited as pinnacles of early 20th-century domestic architecture.

3. **Echo Park, Los Angeles**
   Before the US film industry moved to Hollywood it used to reside in Echo Park, which has become one of the stars in a city that's almost entirely suburban.

4. **Ladugårdsgärdet, Stockholm**
   A chic suburb built in the late 1930s by Swedish modernists. Functionalist apartments are set around the green vistas of the central Tessinparken.

5. **Wannsee, Berlin**
   A green oasis accessed by crossing Berlin's Glienicke Bridge, Wannsee contains a mix of flat-roofed modernist houses, grand manors and old farmhouses. Its residents gather at the lake, whether sunbathing on the white sand or catching up at the sailing club.

Green fingers: Originally built as a garden city, lush parks still cover large parts of Tapiola. Most of the apartment buildings are surrounded by patches of trees and greenery instead of concrete, creating a calm and serene living environment

Retail therapy: Recent developments have upgraded Tapiola's retail scene. There are good cafés and restaurants, boutiques and high-quality fruit-and-vegetable shops. Some famous Helsinki restaurants have also opened their first suburban outposts here

On the move: With frequent subway and bus connections, residents can be in downtown Helsinki in about 10 minutes. Tapiola is located at the intersection of two main roads, so car-owners are within easy reach of various destinations, and there are good cycling paths that lead to other parts of Espoo and Helsinki

Culture vultures: This is perhaps Tapiola's greatest feature and one that really distinguishes it from other suburbs. It plays host to one of Finland's most famous modern art museums, as well as jazz and cinema festivals, a symphony orchestra and a concert venue

How we earn our money, how we do our jobs and even the technology we use have always shaped the cities in which we live. But now as the world of work changes at breakneck speeds it's forcing planners, developers and even café owners to think equally fast about what they build, who will use their spaces and how to future-proof what gets erected.

If you can run your whole work life from a laptop and a mobile phone, perhaps you don't even need an office. Years ago there was a fear that this freedom to roam would see people fleeing the cities for rural idylls but what's transpired is something very different. The contemporary nomadic worker is still very much an urban beast who frequents the members' clubs, bars and hotel lobbies that now go all out to court this shifting herd. It seems that when we're let off the lead we don't go that far because we still crave the juicier life in the city (great food, people to look at, interesting goings-on).

But these workers are reshaping restaurants and hotel lobbies, even challenging their engineering (sockets and more sockets). They also, in the long term, question the need to build traditional small offices let alone to have an old-school commercial core.

Alongside these workers are the shared-space devotees, a category that has swollen as fast as a dead whale on a beach in the sunshine. In every city, quick-off-the-mark developers are carving buildings into grim cubicles and renaming kitchens as "collaboration zones". Yet despite all the profiteers,

there are some genuine pioneers out to engineer more creative work spots. Again it's a shift and one that sees the office merge with hospitality and often private forms of green space.

There will always be big businesses but even how they slot their HQs into our cities is adapting to a new sensibility. Today many aim to be more open to the public and definitely try to appear more cool than corporate in their bids to lure the best talent (think state-of-the-art bike parks, green roofs, running tracks). And it's not just the tech players who are creating campuses as part of this process.

Across this chapter we look at some of the moves taking place, from a renaissance of headquarters to the future of shared spaces, and meet some of the people affecting where we make a living. It's hard work but someone's got to do it.

7.

WHERE WE WORK

Central business districts
The heart of it all

A mark of a great city used to be its CBD, or central business district, packed with gleaming towers and besuited men and women. It was the era of the briefcase, the commute and end-of-day boozing for the traders, bankers and wheeler-dealers who populated these architecturally muscular backdrops. But after last orders these neighbourhoods would empty out, and remain forlorn at weekends, because the restaurants and services simply shut shop when the office set went home to their suburban pads.

Then the world of work began to change and many CBDs started looking badly hungover. The men in suits with a craving for a corner office were gone, replaced by both men and women with laptops who could work from home two days a week. Fewer people heading into the CBD threatened the health of the whole ecosystem. Something had to be done.

So wise city leaders remade CBDs as places where you might want to hang out. Where bars were open on a Saturday night. Today, from Sydney to Los Angeles, there have been good attempts at breaking down the invisible walls that surrounded these areas. And many new developments are getting it right from the get-go.

1.
Rising to the challenge
Tokyo

When property developer Mitsui Fudosan got its hands on a sizable site in Hibiya in central Tokyo, expectations were high. Over the past two decades, rival developer Mitsubishi has transformed neighbouring Marunouchi from a soulless business district into somewhere people flock to in the evenings and at the weekend. Mitsui Fudosan had the added pressure that its project involved demolishing a much-loved pre-war structure that had seen better days but still held a place in the city's architectural biography.

The company's answer was Tokyo Midtown Hibiya. Centred on a 35-storey skyscraper, it has 60 shops and restaurants on the lower floors, with offices occupying the higher levels. The outlook is spectacular: a sprawling green vista that includes leafy Hibiya Park and the grounds of the Imperial Palace. At lunchtime, crowds pile in for the restaurants; others come for the shopping, which is a mix of fashion, fitness and cosmetics.

Hibiya Central Market is a beautiful section that includes an old-school Tokyo barbershop, a gin bar and a retro Showa-era style coffee kiosk. A garden on the sixth floor offers views over Hibiya Park and somewhere to sit when you're escaping from your office. The shops are open until 21.00 and a state-of-the-art Toho cinema multiplex brings in visitors from morning to night. Mitsui Fudosan also installed some classy tenants such as Star Bar, one of Ginza's most highly rated bars. And the office area has its own gym, showers and nap rooms.

The developer has worked with the local community and hosts events in the atrium. The basement arcade is a nod to the old Sanshin Building that once stood there and the new plaza in front of the development has perked up the surrounding buildings and brought new life to the area as a whole.

2.
New life on the streets
Sydney

Melbourne's CBD has long been celebrated for its laneway bars and bustling crowds. Sydney's equivalent, by comparison, always seemed moribund – especially as most of the workers fled to the suburbs come 18.00. But that's all changing.

Over the next decade, it's predicted that the population of Sydney could expand by as much as one million. To help prepare for the influx, in 2007 the City of Sydney hired the Danish urban-planner Jan Gehl. Back then Sydney had "low priority for pedestrians", according to Henriette Vamberg, partner and managing director of Gehl Copenhagen. The city suffered from "inadequate walking space, long waiting times for pedestrians at traffic lights, obstacles on footpaths, underdeveloped bicycle infrastructure and low-quality public spaces for recreation".

To combat this, Gehl recommended transforming the historical George Street back into the CBD's "key spine". Pedestrianisation and a AU$2.1bn (€1.3bn) new light rail are now underway. The erection of Sydney Metro, meanwhile, will increase train services entering the CBD by 60 per cent.

Paul Stoller, managing director of environmental design consultant Atelier Ten's Australian office, notes that one success is Sydney's lush green spaces, including Hyde Park and the Royal Botanic Garden, where office workers eat lunch and families picnic. But critically, he says, Sydney is turning its attention to "not just the parks but the everyday trees; the ones you walk past on the way to the bus." He adds, "If you make the walk a lot nicer, you don't get in your car. These little investments have multiple benefits." Other wins include the introduction of the small bar license in 2013, which has allowed the blossoming of myriad cocktail and whiskey spots, as well as renewed cultural investment.

3.
Ripe for resurrection
Naples

Back in the 1980s, Naples wanted to build a mighty new business district. Yet what made this example so exciting and risky was that it would follow a masterplan by Japan's Kenzo Tange. What could possibly go wrong?

True, as your high-speed train pulls into Naples, those modern and post-modernist glass towers in the distance look impressive, and yes, there's a whiff of teched-up Osaka in their demeanour. But when you get closer to Centro Direzionale di Napoli (CDN) you realise that you're staring at a white elephant, albeit a rather handsome one.

Tange, with his penchant for the monolithic, planned a district of towers that would sit atop what's effectively a vast concrete slab some three levels deep. Down inside the slab today, the access roads and car parks that service the CDN operate in a darkened underworld. And above ground things aren't much brighter: many offices sit vacant and foot traffic is thin.

So how do you turn around a project that's too expensive to bulldoze and too big to dress up with some nice plants? Well, there is a shot of optimism. The area is being better linked to the subway system, new co-working spaces have opened and people are increasingly valuing the residential properties here. But there's a lot to do if this area is to ever realise its potential and truly be an emblem for a modern Naples.

4.
Rust Belt reinvention
USA

The US model hasn't always been conducive to vibrant CBDs. Thanks to the automobile, coupled with social and economic factors such as "white flight" in the 1950s, your average US city has often felt like a set of sprawling, dispersed communities. That's meant that central areas have often been left to decay – and middle-class people haven't cared because, although they might work there, they live in nice suburbs.

But there's been a resurgence of late. We've seen it in places such as Los Angeles (where Downtown LA was once off-limits at night and now buzzes with busy bars and restaurants), Miami's Brickell development and San Diego, where residential skyscrapers have been shooting up.

But it's perhaps some of the US's one-time blue-collar, industrial towns that have been showing what reinvention really means. Arguably it was started by the formerly bankrupt city of Detroit, whose central core revitalisation was anchored by the likes of Shinola and aided by Ford moving to Corktown, as well as newer up-starts such as furniture-maker Floyd.

Pittsburgh is another success story, a champion of green energy despite its sooty past, and a new home to a slew of tech companies east of downtown that are redefining what city living means and redrawing the limits of the CBD. Cities such as Cleveland and Buffalo are also paying close attention.

Micro-hubs
Arresting developments

Take a disused site, add a handful of diverse businesses and a sprinkling of food and drink options, and allow to stand: the micro-hub is a real recipe for success.

Twenty years ago a fledgling business would often have found itself stuck in a shoddy, less-than-cheap office. Today all that's changed. One of the trends responsible is the "micro-hub", a small development housing a group of businesses of the same ilk (art, fashion or tech) alongside a nice spot for food and coffee (usually for outside consumers too, not just tenants). These are places where you can grow a business without worrying about rickety stairs or the landlord's failure to fix the boiler.

"Can you believe this was almost knocked down?" asks Belgian entrepreneur Stefan Bostoen. He's in a quiet, cobbled, car-free piazza at the heart of Pakt, a regeneration project in Antwerp. Formerly a construction yard between new real-estate project Het Groen Kwartier (the Green Quarter) and Antwerp's historic Jewish neighbourhood, its beautifully renovated

buildings have housed independent businesses since 2017.

Bostoen is one of the driving forces behind Pakt, along with Yusuf and Ismaïl Yaman, the two owners of the project. Bostoen guided the brothers after they bought the site in 2007. "Initially their idea was to create lofts to sell and rent out," says Bostoen. But the city's building regulations prevented this and, for a while, nothing much happened. Then, in 2014, they had the idea of using the site as a hub for creative businesses.

It took some time to determine the concept and two years working with Belgian architect Roel Vermeesch to transform the warehouses without interfering with the essence of the place. Building restrictions again forced a rethink but the trio fought to keep as many original features as possible.

Some additions were made, including an old bridge that hangs over the

courtyard. The rooftops are home to sizeable herb and vegetable patches, with 200 sq m of greenhouses – the second-largest of their kind in Belgium. Farmer and agriculture expert Bram Stessel and urban greenery specialist Maarten Weemaes helped design the gardens, using aquaponics and rain-collection systems. Some tomatoes in the greenhouse get compost from waste produced by fish in tanks below. One section of the roof is reserved for restaurant The Jane, which grows herbs and edible flowers for its kitchen, and Antwerp chefs buy fresh produce from Stessel.

Claudio Minnai owns fashion agency Ulla Models and is a tenant in the workspaces below. "We used to be in Brussels but in 2016 I decided I'd had enough of the capital; it has deteriorated in terms of quality of life and work," he says. The concept behind Pakt immediately attracted him. "You need more than one person or one business to create something unique. Pakt is a combination of interesting and creative businesses, different in background but with the same mindset."

He's right: there is a wonderful sense of coexistence among the businesses here. The gym (the oldest tenant) has a training exercise that involves carrying bags of coffee beans up to the roaster of on-site café Caffènation; the coffee-bean husks are then used as organic fertiliser for the rooftop garden. Likewise, heat from pizza restaurant Standard's huge oven is used to keep the greenhouses warm in winter.

"Pakt is a never-ending story," says Bostoen. "We want this project to evolve organically and inspire people in an unpretentious way. There's always room to improve but that's the charm and the challenge of a venture like this."

Sustainable workplaces
Building for the future

"We will see a revolution over the next five to 10 years," says Andrew Waugh, director at Waugh Thistleton Architects, when discussing the future of sustainable workplaces. Waugh Thistleton uses only cross-laminated timber (CLT) in its office developments and is looking forward to seeing the material spring up across cities. "We have an unhealthy obsession with concrete and steel in our cities," says Waugh. "The production of those materials accounts for 15 to 20 per cent of all greenhouse gas emissions, and the ecological devastation caused by the use of sand in concrete is vast." By comparison, building with CLT is quiet, dust-free, requires fewer delivery trucks and takes, on average, half as long.

While CLT is the sustainable building material of choice, within the workplace there needs to be more natural ventilation. Fresh air gently blowing through an open window across the office should no longer be the privilege of small studios. Global architecture practice Foster + Partners has developed the world's most sustainable office building, which includes natural ventilation across deep floor plates.

Bloomberg HQ in the City of London has been awarded the highest ever sustainability score of 98.5 per cent by Breeam, the environmental assessment method for buildings – and it includes natural ventilation. "The façade can open, allowing natural air to pass along deep-span floors," says Michael Jones, senior partner at Foster + Partners and project architect for Bloomberg. "There are about 700 people on each floor and the air can pass through, up and out of the roof, using the physics of hot air rising."

Alongside natural ventilation, there ought to be a more liberal use of plants, water and wood to create a healthier and more enjoyable working environment. City halls need to push harder for sustainability in the workplace in its broadest sense, related not only to energy and carbon but also to the wellbeing of the people who use the building.

Headquarters
Motherships with a mission

Gone are the days when the headquarters of a big business were like a Bond villain's lair. Nowadays, they can be welcome – and welcoming – additions to the city community.

I.
BETC Building
Paris

Moving your office from the heart of the city to the suburbs may seem like career suicide but to Rémi Babinet, founder of Parisian advertising agency BETC, it was an opportunity to breathe life into a neglected part of the capital. The company took over a 1930s former grain warehouse in Pantin, just northeast of Paris's main ring road, and rather than keep the vast building to themselves, they transformed it into a mixed-use public space with the help of architect Frédéric Jung.

Unveiled in September 2016, the goal is to create an exciting cultural agenda and social hub, and to promote Greater Paris as a destination in its own right. "Our vision is to convey another image of the suburbs, beyond the usual 'it's dodgy' reputation," says Babinet. "Greater Paris has almost 1,200 cultural venues, 300 concert halls, parks larger than Central Park and thousands of bars and restaurants. We want to actively participate in changing mentalities."

To reflect the HQ's multipurpose, democratic nature, BETC called it Les Magasins Généraux (The General Stores). The ground floor is entirely open to the public: there's a concert venue and restaurant; an organic food hall called Le Pantin (it fills a big demand as most delis and fresh-produce shops stick exclusively to central Paris); and an exhibition space with a regular and varied cultural itinerary – one multimedia show, whose title

translates as "For the Love of the Game 1998 – 2018", focused on football in contemporary art. The rooftops and terraces, meanwhile, are home to verdant public gardens, apiaries and birdhouses.

In order to spur local creatives, the building was restored with other professional media in mind. Almost a tenth of the space is purpose-built for radio, film and music production. So if there's a young film-maker in Pantin who can't afford their own studio, they can head here. There are ateliers for artists-in-residence too, as well as dedicated workspaces for companies partnered with BETC. The space needed by such enterprises differs, of course, so Babinet worked with various designers – such as T&P Work Unit and Unifor – to create bespoke furniture and room fittings that foresee every use, whether you're after an enormous conference desk or a reprography room.

All this was done with respect for the building, which is a cherished cultural site among residents. Its formerly abandoned walls were covered in intricate graffiti by some of Paris's best artists. To preserve this patrimony, BETC created an online catalogue of every illustration present before renovations began, along with detailed histories of their respective artists.

The company's efforts to change the conversation about Greater Paris doesn't end here. In February 2018, to further encourage people to explore Paris *extra muros*, BETC launched a cultural travel guide to the metropolitan area: *Le Guide des Grands Parisiens*. And with the completion of the Grand Paris Express, which will connect the centre to suburban areas such as Pantin, slated for 2023, the nifty travel guide is sure to come in handy and Les Magasins Généraux will doubtless see plenty of footfall.

In and out: BETC's lively agenda isn't confined to its HQ. The quay along the canal hosts everything from football matches to food markets and generally creates an environment where Pantin's residents can get together for a good time

2.
Pasona
Tokyo

On the 13th floor of its headquarters in central Tokyo, Pasona Group keeps pigs, cows, goats and silkie chickens. Raising livestock in an office building has helped to draw attention to the sharp decline in Japan's dairy farms: 10,510 at last count, just a 20th of the number four decades ago. Since planting a rice paddy in the basement of a Tokyo office tower in 2005, the Japanese recruitment firm has experimented with urban farming in the hope of getting young Japanese interested in agriculture.

It's an urgent task given that two-thirds of the country's 1.9 million farmers are 65 or older. Pasona now operates a small farm in western Japan for training programmes and business seminars, and places thousands of interns with family-run farms and agricultural co-operatives around the country. It's a model that's worthy of praise, a reminder for city-dwellers about the vital and often underappreciated role of food producers in the countryside.

3.
RDC-S111
Long Beach, California

"Our mission is repairing cities and invigorating downtowns," says Michael Bohn, a senior principal at Studio One Eleven, an architecture, landscape and urban design firm. But its former office-tower HQ did little to reflect its values. So, in 2017, Studio One Eleven and partner firm Retail Design Collaborative (together RDC-S111) turned a vacant department store into a new HQ.

While once struggling businesses have gained from the arrival of 130 employees, the headquarters' clever design – including offices that have been donated to local non-profits – has also precipitated foot traffic. The building's corners were earmarked for restaurants. Nearby, a former service dock has been turned into an urban garden and hosts community gatherings, while an indoor gallery space also draws the public.

A flurry of new businesses has followed their move and, today, this once forgotten stretch of Long Beach has a new vibrancy at ground level.

4.
Mykita
Berlin

The Berlin-based eyewear brand Mykita defies the notion that manufacturing can only happen somewhere hours away from the city centre. Since the firm's inception, the company has kept all of its product making in the city core and it now generates more than €30m in annual revenue.

Moving from Mitte to Kreuzberg in 2014, the brand acquired a five-storey neoclassical building with a central courtyard and turned it into an HQ and factory known as Mykita Haus. It's home to 290 employees in more than 14 divisions and outputs 600 pairs of glasses a day. The company has also rented space to other fashion and design firms.

Companies such as this show how an HQ can be a place of making and how jobs in a city core can deliver easier lifestyles and more enjoyable commutes (perhaps even just a short walk). We need more businesses like Mykita – and less restrictive zoning laws too.

5.
Squire and Partners
London

Squire and Partners may be one of London's most prestigious architecture firms but its headquarters are in the energetic, socially diverse community of Brixton. While the inner-south-London district deals with the reality of gentrification, the practice has shown integration to be the smart option for arriving businesses.

Squire and Partners has implemented an "open doors" policy and filled the former department store with Brixton life. The public can enjoy a drink and dinner at the rooftop restaurant, while a basement event space has a lively calendar of free exhibitions.

By throwing open its doors, Squire and Partners is cementing the building's value within a community largely against gentrification. It's not easy being the new kid on the block but the firm hopes to provide a valuable community platform and to play its part in the ongoing story of this neighbourhood.

Shared spaces
All together now

Co-working spaces are drawing in an ever-more itinerant workforce. Are they the way of the future?

With huge latticework metal doors and a marble-and-stone vestibule, it's clear that the 1930s façade of 33 Rue La Fayette was built to impress. In a lobby almost the size of an Olympic swimming pool, workers huddle in discussion on tan-leather sofas, sheltered by an ornate geometric glass ceiling. Others sit at long wooden tables next to a winter garden, tapping away on laptops with the uniformity of a typing pool. A zinc-clad lift whisks anyone in need of a breath of fresh air up to a terrace overlooking the Sacré-Cœur.

This lavish set-up was once the HQ of France's largest nuclear power company, Areva, but in spring 2017 it became a co-working space, the first Parisian outpost of WeWork, a company founded in 2010 by Adam Neumann and Miguel McKelvey. "There's a real energy, a professional momentum," says Anthony Yazbeck, WeWork's deputy managing director, Europe. "We have pantries on every floor. In the afternoon we open the beer taps – and because it's France there's rosé too."

Pinot noir on tap? Shared offices have come a long way from the rough-and-ready creative co-ops that gave life to the concept of "co-working". Big names in commercial real estate have entered the game, assuming the fun-professional design vernacular and adding a Germanic twist to their branding (think "haus" rather than "house"). Even Regus, the grandfather of the serviced office, has turned its hand to hot desks.

The industry is no longer fringe. At its last round of investment, WeWork was deemed to be worth $20bn (€17.2bn). Its service model includes IT support, 24-hour access and a range of cultural events. And then there's the community, or "ecosystem". Every lime-infused watercooler moment has potential. "More than 50 per cent of our members have done some form of business with another member," says Yazbeck.

Propelled by technology, the "gig economy" is evolving rapidly. A survey by the McKinsey Global Institute found that 162 million people in the EU-15 and the US (that's 20 to 30 per cent of the working-age population) engage in some form of independent work. Since the financial crisis of 2008, swathes of the workforce have chosen (or been pushed towards) a more agile approach to earning a living. Andrew Scott, a professor of economics at the London

Chain reaction: The boom in shared workspaces throws up numerous issues for cities planning their futures – because if these fun, sleek, communal spaces are such a pull for entrepreneurs, cities must make sure that they're being provided. After all, if this breed of worker is truly mobile, they will go to where the living is good. Many of these projects are housed in remade spaces – those not built from scratch – so, again, city halls and developers need to look at their property portfolios with a fresh eye. The corporate takeover of the sector will scare some creatives away but it's clear that this trend will change the look and rhythm of our cities

Business School, says that though most of us still hold a conventional job, the trend towards more flexible work is clear – and it's having a fundamental effect. "What we're seeing is a reconfiguration of time and space," he says.

Are the co-working spaces that have sprung up a genuine attempt to grapple with the fundamental transformation of work in our cities as we know it, or opportunistic real-estate experiments? Indeed, some are so evangelical about the value of "ecosystems" that they smack of a hard-sell gym subscription. With rental prices high, some companies appear to be cashing in on a new fiscally vulnerable freelance demographic. Often they're simply selling desk space to sole operators who can't afford it and might just be lonely.

But there are companies that appear genuinely to offer their members this vibrant community. NeueHouse opened a co-working office a few blocks from New York's Madison Square Park five years ago and quickly amassed a member base drawn from the worlds of film, fashion, art and media. Its second venture was in the CBS Radio Building on Sunset Boulevard, Los Angeles, where members have access to repurposed sound stages and recording studios once used by the likes of Orson Welles.

Co-founder Joshua Abram insists that design is very important but also

that "the magic is in the mix". "The architect meets the journalist; the film-maker is in discussion with the scientist," he says. "Our vision was taken directly from a good dinner party presided over by an attentive host."

Meanwhile, others are seeking to build a meaningful social dimension into this burgeoning sector. Vancouver-based entrepreneur Ashley Proctor has rolled out a co-working health insurance plan that now covers all independent workers and small businesses in Canada. Meanwhile, Trehaus, situated on Singapore's Orchard Road, combines its co-working space with a nursery.

Communal workshops that give users access to hi-tech machines such as 3D printers, laser cutters and CNC machines (as well as the training to use them) are also changing the picture. "We're making tools available that were previously only accessed on the university campus," says Thomas Ermacora, a trained architect and urbanist who runs Machines Room in London's East End, one of an estimated 1,400 makerspaces globally.

Ermacora has helped to develop London's Vyner Street into an "informal cluster", with the shared workshop at its heart. He thinks big developers will have to start doing the same, factoring innovation space into their schemes alongside amenities such as public parks.

He argues that these spaces have social capital as forums for education and business development; here the much-touted ecosystem can have economic value. "When people have lost their jobs and come to us to use the space, they often find another job," he says.

But why stop there? Entrepreneurs can also live together and cook up business solutions while they cook dinner. Paris's Station F, which hosts 3,000 desks and 60 meeting rooms, making it the world's biggest "start-up campus", will provide 100 co-living apartments in the coming months. "We wanted an offer that's flexible, cost-effective and doesn't require a tonne of paperwork," says Roxanne Varza, Station F's director.

In many ways, co-working is a counter-cultural phenomenon come of age. The sector is now the subject of debate at big real-estate conferences, and property scions are seeking to replicate some of the most dynamic co-working projects that really did spring from an urge to collaborate (rather than just to make money). What's more, we're seeing increasing numbers of corporates such as KPMG and Santander moving groups of employees into independent "spring" spaces in the hope that the can-do spirit will rub off.

But rather like arts clubs that charge too much for real artists to afford the fees, the bottom could quickly fall out of creative ecosystems. Some people really do just want a quiet space to go and work, and there's an argument that this is what libraries should provide.

The issue of where we will all work in the future is far from certain; governments, architects and developers should start planning in earnest for the advent of a truly itinerant labour market. As NeueHouse's Joshua Abram says, "Change at an ever-accelerating pace is the new normal. The salary job – and the office that went with it – is dead. Only time will tell whether the global real-estate industry has read the memo."

Nomadic workers
Wherever you lay your laptop

Desks, reception areas, meeting rooms and corporate ringtones: all trademarks of the workplace traced back to Frank Lloyd Wright's Larkin Administration Building. A century-plus later the office has been through many guises and, when all you need to run a business is a laptop, the ideal place to work is changing too.

People are casting their nets ever wider to find the best spots in which to pen a report, pore over a drawing or get a start-up off the ground. These so-called third places aren't new. Starbucks was among the first to lure in customers not just with coffee but with comfy chairs and free wi-fi. In the UK it's expected that 50 per cent of workers will work remotely by 2020. "People want the flexibility to work and socialise on their own terms, to structure their day," says Nick Jones, founder of Soho House.

While business districts filled with offices may not disappear entirely, demand is sure to fade and neighbourhoods that now lie desolate on weekends will be more receptive to the ideas of architects and city-planners. But the long-term solution to the workplace conundrum may lie in the strategy of the city itself. Public charging points are springing up in the streets and, during one-off international events, entire cities re-engineer themselves to host mobile workers. The city becomes an office as people stop to work in places from small restaurants to furniture studios. If this becomes the status quo we can once more connect to our piazzas and the indoor office may face a gentle challenge.

We head out into London to meet the nomadic workers making use of two of the capital's hottest hangouts.

Jessica Skye (The Hoxton)
DJ and founder of Fat Buddha Yoga

"I'm constantly moving around the city so having a safe bet like this to stop and work in between meetings is a goldmine."

Sucheol Park (Ace Hotel)
Graphic designer

"I come here whenever I'm in London, especially in the morning when it's quiet. Being in a nice and well-lit space is inspiring."

Grace Haworth (The Hoxton)
Business development executive

"I have a full-time office but I prefer working remotely. It's relaxed here, with just the right amount of buzz and a great menu."

James Thompson (The Hoxton)
Freelance photographer

"I have days here when I just plug myself in and get on with it. Other times I chat to people and even host meetings."

Hanne Berulfsen (Ace Hotel)
Masters student studying special education

"I'm studying just outside London but I prefer working here. I really enjoy the buzz, music and being surrounded by people."

Niklas Jakobson (Ace Hotel)
General manger of brewery in Sweden

"I enjoy the general vibe here – and the coffee. It's important to start the day with a decent coffee and breakfast."

Jimmy MacDonald (Ace Hotel)
Director of London Design Fair

"This place is great for meeting up with regulars from the neighbourhood. The bacon-and-egg breakfast roll is also a highlight."

Noah Murphy-Reinhertz (Ace Hotel)
Sustainable design lead at Nike

"I like how worn everything is – these leather sofas are slightly collapsed. It feels like a comfy living room when friends are visiting."

Grace Zhu (The Hoxton)
Director

"I've made friends here, including the staff. In fact, they know what I like without having to ask – green tea with lemon."

Amber O'Rouke (Ace Hotel)
Lobby manager at Ace Hotel

"I'm here five days a week for work and I like how relaxed it is – especially with the long workers table."

The best cities are fine urban tapestries woven with threads from all walks of life, with ideas from all ages, and made up of all sorts of infrastructure. And not all of it needs to be Instagrammable. Sure, commissioning a beautiful building à la Sydney with its postcard-perfect Opera House and Harbour Bridge will help stamp a sense of identity on your city but it's a slow burn to design a place that's truly memorable. Take a look at Milan's main piazza, surrounded by architectural wonders from medieval and modernist eras alike: it's a mixture of styles but it provides a sense of place that's definitively Milanese.

A city's design should both surprise and inspire, allow us to see it from many different angles and traverse it via all modes of transport – it should never be static. Often it takes a city hall visionary to drive a city's design forward and be daring enough to take some unexpected turns. The millions of citizens who have enjoyed the High Line should salute former Mayor Michael Bloomberg and his team. It not only provided New Yorkers with a different way to enjoy the city, it also spurred urban-planners the world over to think about creating their own version. From London to Aarhus, this simple intervention is being employed with great success – and it started off with an abandoned rail line that many thought was anything but beautiful.

But mayors and town-planners should be equally thankful to us, because citizens design cities as much as architects do, adding human character to the bricks and mortar. Indeed,

getting the idea of the High Line off the ground was an uphill battle fought by a grass-roots organisation that saw the potential in the project long before Bloomberg did. Citizens brand our cities in countless ways. Lisbon's identity has been defined by its residents' loyalty to using rich blue azulejos on the façades of buildings. In the same way, a Swiss passion for shades and awnings has seen these simple cooling devices applied liberally to Zürich's homes and businesses. The result is a practical and chic look that's emphatically Zürich and a reflection of its outdoor-loving people.

With this mixture of factors in mind, we've distilled the essence of what makes a well-designed metropolis into a series of benchmarks. Our City Rules showcase the best interventions that both beautify a city and provide citizens with a worthy sense of place.

8.

CITY RULES

Guiding principles
Designs for life

Citizens, architects, urban-planners and anyone else who wants to improve a city, gather round. Despite what you may think, the city – with its steel, glass, concrete and tarmac – is not too cumbersome to upgrade or even too polished for us to tackle ingrained problems. And, in an era in which smoggy, congested urban centres are challenging the very future of the planet, it's an environment that must evolve and improve.

But while using better materials and thinking about sustainability are vital components of modern town planning, giving citizens a well-designed city that promotes both liveability and civic pride is equally pertinent. Here we've assembled the best design ideas, both old and new, and the smartest tucks and incisions that will give your city an urban facelift (without too much pain).

1.
Re-use when right
Copenhagen

Copenhagen has long been setting urban design standards and its recent redevelopment of the disused port district of Nordhavn is no exception. Reusing existing property allowed multiple Danish architects to get creative. The best effort came from Jaja Architects, which gave this multistorey car park a makeover, crowning it with a playground and applying a façade that turned an eyesore into a beauty.

2.
Be brutal
Takamatsu, Japan

Big, tough and bold –
brutalist buildings hark back
to the end of the modernist
era in the 1960s and 1970s.
For the most part, they don't
tend to mesh well with today's
architectural tastes yet the
socialist principles behind
many of these hefty structures
and the optimistic nature of
their design are well worth
taking note of.

   In Takamatsu – a remote
backwater in southwestern
Japan known for its udon
noodles, bonsai trees and
laid-back charm – architect
Kenzo Tange took design to
a new level with a collection
of brutalist buildings,
including this gymnasium.
Today the buildings are
attracting designers, architects
and tourists to a city whose
daring architectural character
is spurring a local renaissance
in the creative industries.

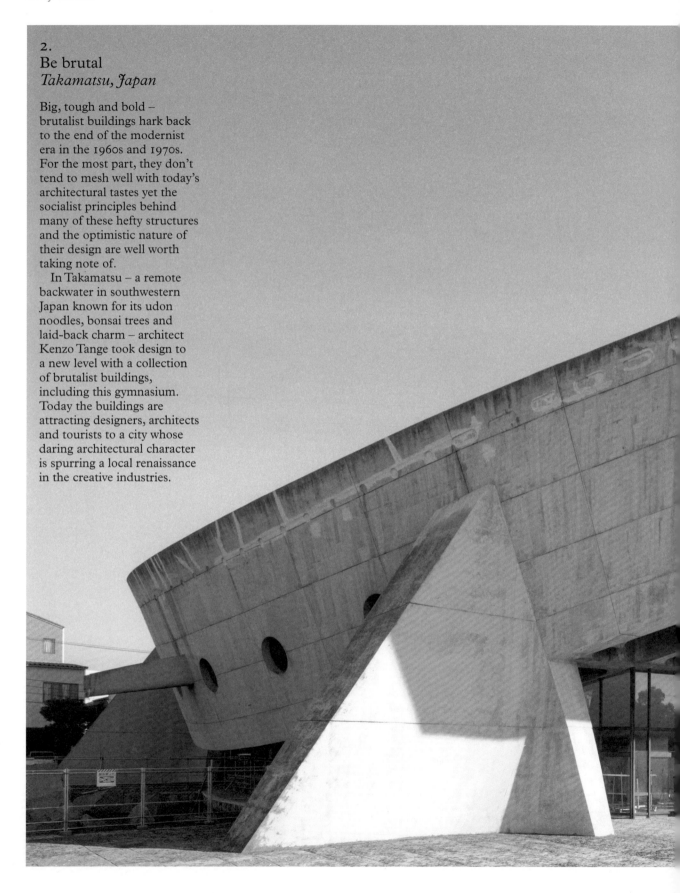

3.
Walk on air
London

Pedways are once again making headway in the UK capital. Impressed by the success of New York's High Line urban regeneration project, developers have chosen to reimagine the concept of the skywalk that first cropped up here in the 1960s.

Elevated walkways that weave above city streets have many benefits, not least the fact that they are pretty easy to set up. While New York's effort took over a defunct rail corridor, the new pedways in London can be built from scratch, connecting higher floors of buildings and enabling pedestrians to skip above the churn of traffic below.

But the factor we most appreciate is their ability to give us a new perspective on the city. The rumble of the streets a few floors below is apparent but softer, and rather than having to crane your neck skywards to appreciate the lofty architecture, you can stroll your way right through it.

4.
Turn to timber
Stockholm

As town-planners push for higher
sustainability standards, developers are
frequently turning to timber. This trusty
traditional building material has been
transformed thanks to new technology.

Cross-laminated timber is the
technical term but all you need to know
is that this reinforced wood doesn't
go up in flames when burnt and it's
strong enough to build skyscrapers. And
aside from its eco-friendly credentials,
handsome looks and good smell, it
allows for much quicker, and therefore
more cost effective, construction.

Sweden's Folkhem, which makes the
world's best-looking timber towers, is
hoping to construct 6,000 apartments
in Stockholm in the coming years.
Residents of Folkhem homes have
noted many benefits, including that
the natural properties of timber have
eased symptoms of traffic fume-fuelled
afflictions such as asthma.

5.
Go with the flow
Milan

Milan may not be Italy's most beautiful city but it has a well-earned reputation for being its most creative. Architecture firms blossom here in part due to the richness of the ever-evolving urban tapestry. Take this view of the city's main piazza: here, the 19th-century Galleria Vittorio Emanuele II looks out onto the neoclassical design of a 1920s palazzo. Standing tall in the hazy distance is the famous 1955 Torre Velasca, a modernist marvel that looked to both gothic architecture and more contemporary ideas about tall buildings in its high-rise design.

The result is a heady and imposing architectural celebration of Milan and a metaphor for the variety within the broader urban environment. It shows that when a city's form is allowed to progress organically its architectural creativity can be nurtured.

6.
Respect your elders
Los Angeles

Heritage buildings give character to a city but this can all too easily be forgotten in modern metropolises such as LA, which always seems to be in the midst of an infrastructure boom. The City of Angels may have never really cherished longevity (who needs sturdy buildings made from heavy materials when it's warm most of the year?) but luckily many of the city's diners and coffee shops have endured and give character and richness to the place.

The futuristic "Googie" architecture of LA's 1950s coffee shops harks back to an age of excitement, aspiration and exploration, and houses businesses that still catch the eye (and the dollar) more than half a century later. Alongside a waiter who knows your name and your order, there's something about these establishments that's undeniably rooted in a place (in this case, sun-kissed southern California). In today's identikit world, that's an idea we'll have to-go please (you can hold the fries).

Fine diner: Bob's Big Boy diner in Los Angeles was designed by architect Wayne McAllister and originally built in 1949.

7.
Show a united front
Lisbon

From the cloudless, indigo sky in
the height of summer to the moody
midnight of the Tagus River, blue is a
constant feature of Lisbon life. And
the shade has been translated from the
natural world into the city's architecture.

Here buildings covered in the
traditional blue-and-white azulejos,
often with intricate painterly designs,
are plentiful and conspicuous among
the pastel shades of painted façades.
Buildings ranging from modest homes
to palaces and churches are clad in the
same style.

Prescribing a uniform colour to your
city – particularly such a tasteful one
– gives it an identity and a smart base
tone for even the most colour-blind of
decorators to work from.

246

CERÂMICA
CONSTÂNCIA
→

8.
Stick to a signature style
Hamburg

Hamburg's penchant for brick dates back to the 1200s and this humble material is still widely used across the city today. The warm red correlates to a high iron content in the native soil and the legacy of the brick building is one that modern architects are happy to continue.

Hamburg's ubiquitous red bricks and "clinkers" – bricks fired so hot that they vitrify, forming dense blocks that clink when struck – have indelibly coloured the cityscape. Their maroon, rust and crimson hues adorn municipal buildings, neo-gothic warehouses, modernist housing projects and, now, even the luxury buildings in Hamburg's modern urban expansion.

This tradition not only creates a recognisable look and draws on a local material but also points to the city's belief in structures that are built to last.

9.
Throw shade on your city
Zürich

Strict building codes have ensured that Zürich's builders prioritise shade and breeze over air-conditioning – a cool idea that cities in similar climates could learn a thing or two from. Buildings across Zürich's neat streets and boulevards are given a much-needed cooling down on summer days thanks to smartly planned shading systems: shutters and awnings adorn façades and shield wide windows.

Another popular (and secure) option is the mechanised or manual blind, which is designed to roll out at a pleasing angle to bring in the breeze on a warm day. Trust the Swiss to ensure that their cities play it safe, keep cool and remain looking good year-round.

Cool cover: The success of this simple design tool is indicative of a Swiss penchant for detail, ingenuity and quality in construction – and it's something that cities with a similar climate can learn a lot from

10.
Take it to government
Aarhus

Danish architects Arne Jacobsen and Erik Møller's masterful Aarhus city hall was completed in 1941. From the council chamber decked with timber furniture designed by Hans Wegner to the cool marble exterior, creative thinking marks every corner.

While city halls may not be the all-powerful planning hubs that they once were (today's town-planners are more at the mercy of big property developers), a city's design still needs to be driven by its government. In Aarhus, Jacobsen's work has clearly influenced its governors. Here good architectural thinking and urban planning is applied in abundance, from a successful harbour regeneration to a new High Line re-use project.

II.
Put creativity at the centre
Toronto

Cities thrive on creativity. And while the
scent of freshly cut wood is increasingly
rare in urban centres, it hangs on the
air at the Junction Workshop, hidden
away in a former munitions factory in
Toronto's once industrial west side.

Enlivened by natural light and the
whirring of table saws, the workshop
was founded in 2016 by Heidi Earnshaw
and Carey Jerniga, just minutes away
from the city's subway lines and some
of its busiest thoroughfares. It provides
both professional designers and
budding woodworkers with the tools,
the space and, for those that need them,
the skills to craft furniture.

This model allows craftspeople
to remain downtown, in spite of
skyrocketing rents and ravenous
developers. When not instructing classes,
Peter Coolican – of the eponymous
Coolican & Company – crafts his mid-
century and Shaker-inspired stools and
chairs here. The continued existence of
makers and inner-city residents working
and living side by side ensures that
creativity remains woven into the city's
rapidly changing fabric.

12.
Make memorable memorials
Columbus, Indiana

One of the trickiest briefs for city-planners is the construction of memorials. Besides serving the purpose of remembering solemn occasions they also need to engage with the public and their setting.

War veterans receive a dignified remembrance via the limestone pillars in front of the Bartholomew County Courthouse in Columbus, Indiana (*pictured, left*). Engraved with the names of those who lost their lives, the pillars not only honour the fallen but also provide a shaded area in which to contemplate the past. The clean lines correspond to the city's other modernist memorials, including the nearby Cleo Rogers Memorial Library (*pictured, right*).

If a city is a body then its organs are full of culture, its heartbeat the sound of applause pouring from concert halls, gallery openings and cinema queues. Its skeletal structure might be supported by its newsstands and kiosks, delivering the media that allows a town to look at itself in the mirror; or its television, radio and newspapers that speak truth to power, politicians and bad restaurants.

Not long ago, a day at the museum was the preserve of the classics professor or the art student. No longer. These institutions have shaken the dust off, rearranged the furniture and retooled themselves as shining palaces of modernity that sell coffee and giftwrap as keenly as they curate exhibitions. But what happens when these places refuse to fit comfortably in a town's contemporary view of itself? Munich's Haus der Kunst comes complete with Nazi friezes that send shivers down your spine but the past can be addressed in these places – and better futures envisioned.

The travelling circus of the international art world, both the commercial and curatorial, can offer a city an injection of financial and social dynamism far more thrilling than the everyday satisfactions of a thriving high street. Art fairs and biennales have grown along with the appetite to host and attend them and everyone from framers to barmen and taxi drivers to hoteliers stand to start the retirement fund when the fair rolls into town.

Of course this circle of artistic commerce comes with its detractors and so we'd call back to the fact that art isn't made in a bubble: the best of these events happen in cities that sustain artists in sensibly priced studios under the guidance of galleries with a long-term view. And how do you know about any of this stuff anyway? The last spoke on the wheel of a smart city is good media whose writers, photographers, critics and reporters let you know if any of it's any good.

Let's begin our cultural journey with museums, the institutions that have the power to turn a wasteland into a blossoming neighbourhood. Welcome to the show.

9.

CULTURE CAPITALS

Museums
All together now

From unlikely beginnings, museums have become city glue, something similar to town squares with artwork: places to meet, greet, kiss once on each cheek. Those heavy, gilded doors of yore – once barriers, now thoroughfares – are open for business. Exhibitions are supported by cafés, shops and restaurants; programmers and curators push their museum brands far beyond their buildings' walls; events are everything.

At London's Tate Modern, late-night events turn galleries into parties. Why not? In Miami, the Pérez Art Museum helped regenerate a neighbourhood: where once there was wasteland, there is now public art, palm trees and places to rest. Museums know that when they create spaces for everyone, they're building a community. Come on, people like going out.

1.
Zeitz Mocaa
Cape Town

Historic grain siloes towering over Cape Town's harbour have been transformed by British designer Thomas Heatherwick into what art aficionados have dubbed "Africa's Tate Modern". Since it opened in 2017, the Zeitz Museum of Contemporary Art Africa (Mocaa) has cemented Cape Town's status as Africa's art capital, its nine floors home to works by stars of the continent's contemporary-art scene.

But the building is more than just a showcase for cutting-edge creativity. With an emphasis on providing a platform for marginalised voices, the museum's progressive programming – encompassing panel talks, workshops, performances and readings – seeks to promote tolerance and foster dialogue that's sorely needed in a city in which prejudice and persecution linger in spite of South Africa's admirably liberal constitution.

Zeitz Mocaa has also catalysed the development of the surrounding area, which for decades was a neglected brownfield site. Today it's a vibrant mixed-use precinct – the Silo District – where eco-friendly offices (which use seawater cooling systems, for example) rub shoulders with residential blocks, restaurants and two hotels. Commercial art-and-design galleries also give museum visitors cause to linger in the neighbourhood.

Without the arrival of the glittering-windowed art museum at its core, it's likely the district would have remained a windswept car park. The project also gives the city's brand a more polished creative halo.

Tate Modern
London

Frances Morris joined Tate as curator in 1987 and helped put together the opening displays at Tate Modern in 2000. She became director of the latter in 2016.

There's always been this feeling that national museums serve the nation but I think here, in this space, we really need to be embedded as a local museum. We're literally a space for everybody and we should reflect the demographic of the city in which we live and be a place that people feel is theirs.

Tate Modern had always been open to the north – the riverfront and the city of London – but in a way it had put its back to its local community. That changed with the opening of the Blavatnik Building in 2016, which created access to Southwark and beyond. We are literally a street connecting north and south London. The new building has also allowed us to slightly reinvent the museum in that we have created a space where the divisions and barriers between gallery and public spaces are much more porous.

I think the top-down model is disappearing and we want to enable people to access art in all sorts of different ways as participants, as collaborators, as makers but also in a more traditional sense, as observers. I think Tate will become a place where you encounter works of art but where you also hear stories and histories and experiences that you can relate to from all over the globe.

This will be the one place in the world where you can visit the whole world without a visa. No visas, no language qualifications, absolute equality – a truly civic space.

Pérez Art Museum Miami
Miami

After stints as a curator at the Menil Collection in Houston and the Los Angeles County Museum of Art, Franklin Sirmans became the director of the Pérez Art Museum Miami in 2015, engaging both the local community and the international art world through exhibitions by artists from Julio Le Parc to Ebony G Patterson.

Miami is incredibly diverse, with its foundations in Latin America and the Caribbean; I'm really interested in that space as an area for thinking. Today the city is also experiencing tremendous change, growth and opportunity – everything is so fresh. Being here at such a pivotal moment is exciting.

The Pérez Art Museum Miami's location at Biscayne Bay makes it particularly attractive to visitors, regardless of whether they're interested in the art. And the city's art spaces complement one another. We're modern and contemporary; the Bass has some amazing pieces that go way back; the ICA is super contemporary; and then you have university galleries and Locust Projects, which is a more gritty alternative. We each serve a different purpose.

Miami Art Week has helped the art scene grow. The city has galleries, museums and incredible private collections that people from all around the world come to see, mostly during that week; it shines a light on that and gives a sense of some of the art that's being made and collected here. It's also had economic repercussions; there are many more people in the city at that time.

MUSEO JUMEX

2.
Museo Jumex
Mexico City

The Museo Jumex is definitively of its city. David Chipperfield's calm, considered building in regional stone is all large windows that let the light in and expansive doorways that circulate the breeze; open spaces bring contemporary art into the public sphere; and high ceilings allow the museum's fine collection to breathe and sprawl.

The Museo is also a platform for art and events, accessible to everyone; this exemplary exercise in opening your arms to your public – potential visitors and city stakeholders, the lot of them – could be used by anyone building a city hall anytime in the next 100 years too.

Oh, and fear not for the art. Eugenio López Alonso, the collection's owner and heir to a Mexican fruit-juice fortune, has impeccable taste that's pitched some way above the greatest hits of the art market.

3.
Haus der Kunst
Munich

Munich's Haus der Kunst is a museum that has fearlessly looked its tricky history in the face. Adolf Hitler had the museum built in 1937 as a propaganda showcase and it was originally known as Haus der Deutschen Kunst. Until 1945, annual exhibitions showed government-approved images of German power and productivity (blonde nudes, sheaves of wheat and soldiers in action) while "degenerate" art by the likes of Kandinsky was confiscated.

Today the museum mounts diverse exhibitions by international contemporary artists such as Ai Weiwei. "Haus der Kunst has outlasted the years of its infamy," says Okwui Enwezor, the Nigeria-born curator who directed the Haus from 2011 to 2018, continuing the venue's postwar mission to rehabilitate German culture and take artistic risks.

The Haus's architecture and exhibitions narrate the story of the city instead of erasing a past that should not be forgotten. It was reimagined to showcase Munich as the open-minded, cosmopolitan city it is today.

Making, buying and selling art
Get the picture?

The ecosystem of a city's art world is fascinating to observe. It all starts with the art school, which weaves its influence through town like a warm breeze, lightly ruffling the hair of all it touches. Galleries bring some backbone to the scene, a focal point with four walls going out on a limb to put their money where an artist's mouth is.

And then the fair comes to town and there's a different pace to proceedings. Museums hitch up their skirts and show a little more leg, visitors descend, deals are done and you can see the ecosystem working in real time. It's bewitching.

I.
Art schools
Vienna

The art school is the foundation on which a city's creative pedigree is built. In these institutions the ripples from a single drop of paint permeate through everything else in town; art schools are a benign influence on a city. Their students provide a civic service of sorts: adding vibrancy to dowdy streets, transforming neighbourhoods, demanding cheap studios and bars, therefore creating an arts area all by themselves.

The Akademie der bildenden Künste (Academy of Fine Arts) in Vienna has been around for nearly 330 years and is a definitive part of the city's fabric; it could be considered a microcosm of Vienna itself. With the school's alumni including Egon Schiele and architect Otto Wagner, it could choose to rest on its laurels – but wouldn't dream of it. An interdisciplinary outlook, edgy curricula and a commitment to feeding the city's art scene keep the academy's focus on the present and future.

2.
Artist studios
Havana

All cities love the artistic vibe but often destroy it with high rents. As such the affordability of artists' studios is a good judge of cultural cachet. Young artists in Havana will often use their home as their studio before renting a flat or a house with other emerging artists to use as a studio. "We took advantage of a change in Cuban property law to buy a 1940s house in La

264

Sierra," says Frank Mujica, who moved in with two fellow graduates of Cuba's Instituto Superior de Arte. Artistic spaces and communities like these have the power to reinvigorate neighbourhoods all over the world.

3.
Galleries
Los Angeles

What use are all these art academies and affordable studios if a city doesn't have a rich cluster of local and international galleries?

In lieu of tiny spaces, entrenched institutions and extreme competition, artists in Los Angeles benefit from a plethora of huge studios, progressive academies and a big dollop of alone time. It's this kind of freedom that has not only given birth to some of the country's finest and most unconventional artists – such as John Baldessari, Mark Bradford and Catherine Opie – but also some of its most wildly experimental spaces, including Gallery1993, which kits out a Ford Crown Victoria with art shows that then roam the city's infamous traffic-choked streets.

LA's art district gave this sprawling city the unifying cultural hub it was missing and international galleries such as Hauser & Wirth haven't stopped flocking here. The icing on the blue-chip cake came in February 2018 when Frieze announced it would launch a fair here. For fair director Bettina Korek there seemed to be little question as to why: "There is so much going on here, but what the city needs is a galvanising moment that brings everything to the surface and puts the city of artists on display – for visitors and locals alike."

4.
Art fairs and biennials
Global

Art Basel was a game-changer for Miami. It brought collectors, artists, new galleries and museums to the city. Yet, according to gallerist Fredric Snitzer, the cultural evolution is still in its adolescence. "We have big museums and private collections but it's a work in progress," he says. "It reminds me of a kid in his late teens who says he's 25. You know that the moustache is painted on."

The most important fair for most in the business remains the Basel mothership in Switzerland. But international gallerist David Zwirner, who opened his latest space in Hong Kong in 2018, says, "I keep saying that without Art Basel Hong Kong we wouldn't be opening a gallery here." More proof if it were needed that art fairs really have the power to spur on a city's art market and boost the cultural scene.

Besides art fairs, the number of biennials and triennials has exploded. Since 2000, biennials have launched in Gothenburg and Bucharest, and triennials in Auckland and Yokohama, among others.

Cities have been keen to back the biennial bandwagon in an effort to lure cultural tourists. Adrian Ellis, director of AEA Consulting, says that, in an era of globalisation, "cities homogenise, they move from being brands to commodities, so establishing events such as biennials is one of the ways in which a city can re-assert its identity".

Public art
City as canvas

1.
Digital Orca
Vancouver

Douglas Coupland's "Digital Orca"
is one of Vancouver's 300-plus
public art installations. It's located
in the Jack Poole Plaza overlooking
the harbour and was built
in homage to the workers of
Burrard Inlet and Coal Harbour.
The aluminium sculpture has
a deep significance for the city:
the Canadian artist and novelist
turned a whale, frequently seen
in these waters, into a symbol
of Vancouver's past, present
and future. The pixelated form
represents the city's digital
ambitions, while the orca itself
stands for its natural resources.

What is the point of public
art? Should it be beautiful?
Need it be bold? Should
it memorialise or just
amuse? Public art has the
power to unite or divide a
city – as the debate about
Confederate statues in
the US showed us – and
it's why London's Fourth
Plinth in Trafalgar Square
draws crowds and excites
celebration and derision
in almost equal measure.
Done well, these works can
inspire neighbourhoods and
bring people together. Done
badly, they can still inspire
public dialogue – albeit in
a more fiery style.

Taste is subjective
but what public art can
objectively offer is a way
to see a city with fresh
eyes. Let's take a look at
three prime examples from
around the world.

2.
Crown Fountain
Chicago

The Windy City is well known for its public art (so much so that Anish Kapoor's elliptical "Cloud Gate" has become an emblem of the city) and allocates 1.33 per cent of its public-buildings budget to the cause. One interactive project is Jaume Plensa's "Crown Fountain". Plensa's goal was to turn a traditional fountain into a modern meeting place – and his installation along Michigan Avenue has done just that. He isn't the only Spanish sculptor to have contributed to the city either: Picasso designed a large-scale installation for Chicago in 1967.

3.
Myth of Tomorrow
Tokyo

Tokyo is a city of murals but few match the scale of Taro Okamoto's "Myth of Tomorrow" (1969), which depicts an A-bomb explosion and hangs in Shibuya Station. The mural, originally designated for Mexico City, was returned to Japan in 2005 after mysteriously disappearing. In the 1960s tiled murals were all the rage and many still exist in situ, such as Rokuro Taniuchi's rustic scene on the side of Sanyodo Books on Omotesando Crossing. Art can improve the dreariest highways and bring life to the most functional public building.

City media
In the know

Now, most media's made *in* a city but we want to focus on the stuff that's *about* that place while also managing a national and global outlook.

The daily media rhythm is a habit, a verse-and-chorus, a metabolism: the morning radio show that makes you dash, the newsprint on your fingers while you buy a coffee, the lunchtime bulletin. Not to mention the hits of online intelligence that amuse work hours, evening entertainment on your good old television (we *know*, online alternatives are available) and film, gig and restaurant reviews that define the after-hours offerings of a city.

Local publications and broadcasters shape a city's identity and sense of community – and put a place on the map now that they've moved online. Let's visit the institutions that are at the heart of their cities.

1.
Newspaper
Rome

Romans take daily rituals seriously – think morning espresso at the corner café – and one that many residents can't do without is a visit to their local *edicola* (newsagent) to pick up a fresh copy of *La Repubblica*.

Since it emerged on the scene in 1976, the newspaper has become a trusted source of information, keeping Romans up to speed with goings-on in the Eternal City. Today it has developed a loyal following of readers who stroll to their neighbourhood news kiosk each day to see which topics are making headlines.

The daily was founded in Rome by Eugenio Scalfari, a left-leaning atheist who sought to shake up the conservative world of Italian journalism with a new title that sported a more adversarial tone and looked to tackle head-on the hot-button issues of the day. The paper was unconventional from the get-go, adopting a Berliner format to counter the dowdy broadsheets of establishment dailies. It initially chose to forego a sports section and placed its cultural coverage at the heart of the paper.

Staffers in its newsroom are quick to mention the loyalty of local readers, many of whom have been buying the liberal-oriented paper since year one. "People have grown

up reading the newspaper and see us as an essential part of their day," says art director Angelo Rinaldi.

The paper stands out from the pack of Roman-based titles thanks to its offering of daily inserts, each addressing a different subject and packed with rich content. The Sunday edition comes bundled with *Robinson*, a graphic-savvy cultural insert that gives a rundown of the city's key exhibits and musical events. Thursday copies feature a food-themed supplement while Wednesdays come complete with a science-and-technology insert that schoolteachers often use as an aid in the classroom.

To stay current and competitive, *La Repubblica* continually invests in design. It looks at ways to make fonts more legible for older readers, commissions illustrators to create sketches and infographics, and attracts younger readers by creating graphic icons and more web-style layouts to draw their eyes to topics on the page.

2.
Radio
Paris

Parisians are showing no sign of falling out of love with the radio. The number of listeners has held up during the past decade, a testament to the high-quality programmes on offer. Transmitted out of the French capital are half a dozen stations with a strong focus on current affairs. Anyone taking a taxi during the morning rush-hour will be treated to one of the *matinale* talk shows offered by the likes of France Inter, RTL and RMC – and a lively political debate with the cabbie too.

The radio dial is also a reflection of the cultural diversity of Paris. Radio Soleil, Radio Orient and Beur FM cater to the Middle Eastern and North African communities while Radio Latina pumps out salsa and Spanish-language tunes.

Maison de la Radio's prime position on the banks of the Seine speaks volumes about the importance that radio has in Paris. The state radio headquarters looms over the city. And looming even larger is the Eiffel Tower – the most iconic transmission tower a radio station could ask for.

3.
Magazine
New York

It's perhaps not surprising that *New York* magazine originated from the same person who delivered the "I heart NY" logo to the world. Just like the ubiquitous design, *New York* magazine is part of the fabric of the city. It's everywhere and every New Yorker, from the neophyte to the born-and-bred native, feels a kinship with the title.

"Milton Glaser and Clay Felker [who co-founded the magazine] viewed New York as the centre of the Earth," says editor Adam Moss. "They wanted to cover it well but they also understood that New Yorkers were sophisticated people who were interested in the whole world." That lens continues to shape the magazine but the digital age has brought its content to a wider audience: today more than 80 per cent of online readership is outside the city. It has gone from being about New York as a place to being about the city's state of mind – fast-paced and evolving. *New York* magazine is simultaneously accessible, progressive and also reflective of the city.

The requisite at the magazine isn't to publish stories first; what's essential here is its voice. "Our lens is our product," says Moss. "The set of characteristics that we ascribe to, what we do when we tell stories through words or pictures, that point of view. Those characteristics are the ones that we associate with New Yorkers."

4.
Television
Sydney

While other programmes often occupy sets that are constructed in lonely studios in anonymous industrial areas, one of Australia's flagship morning programmes *Sunrise* greets its viewers live from a fishbowl studio in the city centre. Viewers wake up with the show on television before strolling past it in action as they step out of Martin Place Station on their way to the office. In Sydney, breakfast television is part of the daily rush.

Australians are in disagreement as to what to watch in the morning (Melburnians lean towards the Nine network's *Today* while Sydneysiders side with Seven's *Sunrise*). But whatever they're watching, there's one thing that they all seem to agree on: Sydney is a city that knows the meaning of good morning.

Bookshops and kiosks
Good reads

In the past decade, bookshops have been reconsidered – and rightly. The barn-dwelling, pile-'em-high merchants have gone (or gone online) and we're left with the good guys: booksellers that act as cultural stakeholders, bricks-and-mortar investors and taste-makers. Books and the people and places that sell them are back in the vanguard of making cities patient places that encourage the browse as well as the buy. There's something trusting about placing your best stock on a pavement to draw people in; there's a reason couples meet in bookshops (it's why those in Tokyo and Taipei stay open all night, *wink wink*).

The news kiosk, too, has had a time of it and is coming out with its headlines held high. While the news cycle has bent itself to meet the media that cheat it, the value of the digest, the long-read and the considered view have become paramount and premium.

City-planners worth their salt keep these totems of civility as smart as paint (in Paris, that's green). Your pavement needs lights and bins – and it also needs print.

In 1981 the Canadian prairie city of Winnipeg got its first large-scale bookshop: an independent outfit called McNally Robinson, opened by husband and wife Paul and Holly McNally. Twenty-three years later their daughter Sarah (*pictured*) founded her own bookshop 2,600km southeast in bustling New York. The two may appear to be on opposite poles of the Earth but their principles are in sync: to act as an anchor in their neighbourhoods.

Sarah's literary judgement, as well as her ability to hire passionate staff and host sought-after authors, has made McNally Jackson stand out in the retail monster that is Manhattan. It's become a place for people to meet and mingle, a serene living room in the swarming city.

In 2018 Sarah opened a second outpost in Williamsburg. Property developers here are keen on renting spaces to bookshops as they have the power to infuse new developments with life. They're also good for a surprise: who wants an algorithm to calculate book recommendations when you can have someone personally point you in the direction of your next read?

Back in Winnipeg, employee Chris Hall has been stocking the shelves since the shop opened. It wasn't always plain sailing but "Winnipeg rose to our support," says Hall. "We couldn't afford to restock after Christmas one year and I swear people were buying books they didn't want because they wanted this place to stay."

2.
Tsutaya Books
Tokyo

Ever since it opened in 2011, Tokyo's Tsutaya Books has paved the way for city bookshops. Few can match its selection of 140,000 titles – but it's not just about quantity. Tsutaya is a standout because it goes beyond being a repository for literature. It's a neighbourhood meeting place that stays open until 02.00; a lounge with out-of-print magazine archives that also serves martinis; a DVD and CD rental shop with obscure titles; and a refuge for children on a rainy day.

It acts as a community arts-and-culture centre; you can grab a flat white in the café and load up on stationery before attending a talk by a Japanese author, musician, film critic or photographer. Tsutaya reminds us of what a great bookshop can be: a stage for writers, a forum for new ideas, a public reading room, and a home from home for insomniacs and lonely newcomers to the city.

3.
Kiosks
Milan

Lilliputian huts of iron and glass cloistered on city pavements, Milan's newsstands are freestanding shrines to media. Headlines in Italian, dialect and a smattering of foreign languages broadcast the day's biggest news to pedestrians. Magazines deck the vitrine windows with a crowded riot of the latest styles, the latest scandals, the latest politicians' earnest or sinister faces.

Milan's first newsstand opened in 1859; in the postwar boom, they opened on every well-peopled corner. The five years preceding 2018 saw 30 per cent of their kin shuttered but the city's culled ranks endure, filling a niche that's become an immutable part of the physical and cultural fabric of Milan.

"People don't come to us for news anymore but the more curious, the more sophisticated readers, they come for what they can't find online," says Fabrizio Prestinari, who's been operating a legendary Brera-area newsstand (*pictured, top right*) since 1990. He's known to offer detailed suggestions to anyone he considers a worthy, open-minded reader, whether they be first-timers or his long-time faithful clients. Unlike most *giornalai*, as the stands' operators are known, Prestinari hasn't added extra knickknacks (subway tickets, phone refills, plastic gizmos for kids) to supplement the plummeting sales of dailies that used to prop up the newsstand business. Instead he's doubled down on his personally selected and much sought-after range of ambitious magazines, with newly inaugurated international

publications stockpiled next to iconic glossies. All of these are becoming evermore like books, he says, with literary-level writing, engaging design, long-term relevance and collectability aimed at the print-loving newsstand faithful of today.

Like other *giornalai*, Prestinari takes home a slim 18 per cent of his sales and is pitted against rising costs but bolstered by a newsstand's superlative visibility and the cheaper rent of public land. The local government is smartly seeking to turn Milan's newsstands into "service points for every neighbourhood," as the city's assessor for labor policy and commerce Cristina Tajani has termed the plan, with digital resources designed to draw in both locals and tourists. And unlike in other countries, where large, browsing-friendly magazine shops have become the norm, in Italy, kiosk operators such as Prestinari find that it's the old-fashioned human exchange and advice on the best reading in the stacks that still matters most.

Music
Beat goes on

Venues are a city's temperature gauge: who's having fun and how can you have it? They are the bright side of the dark hours and the places where you'll really see the fibres of a city's fabric. From classic jazz clubs to dive bars and grand old theatres repurposed for a new era of going out, we believe that, really, the night has it.

You can tell a lot about a city from how it treats its venues, clubs and nightspots. The trend, you'll know, is for rent hikes, noise complaints and closures from London and Madrid to Rio and Sydney. What are you thinking, cities? Venues are the first-movers in lending a city a good reputation; outliers in a well-structured, profitable night-time economy. They are the rose-tinted shades through which a city is seen at silly o'clock. And those first impressions are the last to leave.

These are not the concerns of well-planned bus routes or cleverly considered signposting. This is the stuff that dreams are made on, the fabric of a place and charge of a night that changes your life: everyone wished they had seen Janis Joplin and Jefferson Airplane at the original Fillmore in San Francisco so they lied about it. And these tall stories are still being told. This is a city's heartbeat, blood type, eye colour and shade of make-up.

The Echoplex in Los Angeles has fostered its own feeder-system via a dive bar and Mexican food scene while, a few miles away at the good old Hollywood Bowl, you can still get high in the cheap seats with relative ease. A night's end at Sometime in Tokyo always seems to lead to another beginning and Paradiso in Amsterdam is where seeing a band becomes a dance party – if you have the legs for the canalside

stagger after. ChaChá in Madrid is sophisticated fun playing a little dumb and maybe the best night out you'll ever not remember. Have you been to Clube dos Democráticos up the hill in Lapa, a cheap cab from Ipanema? Sure, it's changed a little but it's still worth changing your shirt for. A place that isn't is Camden's unreconstructed pub-rock paradise, The Dublin Castle, where every band seemed to play their first gig under that once-dripping ceiling. It's a rite of passage and not much bigger than one.

Just as those great old restaurants such as Le Grand Colbert defined for a time the very *idea* of dining in style in Paris, so the great music venues similarly focus the mind: *so, these four walls are where it happened*. And maybe the bathrooms too. There is folklore to these places; there is history to be absorbed but, really, who cares? The night is young and you look it too.

Festivals
Global

As we reach a certain age, the smell of slurry and the sight of faecal objects overflowing in the communals begin to porta-lose their charm, and summers spent burning, churning and gurning up the green belt fade with a sigh as the fourth decade of our lives passes us by. In all honesty, how many of us (apart from those brought up in the proverbial barn) really enjoyed the muck and schlep of a rural music festival anyway?

Nowadays, for those of us who still enjoy a bop to something new and loud, punctuated by a bit of a sit-down with a cold lager served in a (recycled) plastic pint, an urban setting makes much more sense. There is something to be said for growing old disgracefully, or at least every now and then. The odd white hair has its upsides. By now, we generally walk in with deeper pockets and have fostered the right contacts to ease the whole affair.

Case in point: Barcelona's annual Sónar dust-up that recently turned 25. Even the descriptor of "International Festival of Advanced Music and Congress of Technology and Creativity" sounds grown-up. It's now easy to book your Vueling with a little extra legroom, check into some upscale digs (a necessary haven from the hustle of the inevitable hangover) and dip in and out of the three-day festivities to refuel in the dim quiet of La Dama or opt instead for a few "chilled ones" at La Caseta on Montjuïc.

For us, the days of slipping and sliding around Somerset are done in favour of a more refined rave-up within the familiar urban embrace of the city limits.

City soundtrack
Every city has a song that's synonymous with its streets and spirit. Here are our picks.

1. **New York:** "I wanna wake up in a city that doesn't sleep ... I'll make a brand new start of it in old New York. If I can make it there, I'll make it anywhere." Frank Sinatra's definitive "New York, New York" is a song that many who move to the city live by. Then there's Lou Reed's "Walk on the Wild Side" – a tribute to the stars he hung with over at Andy Warhol's.

2. **Los Angeles:** LA's atmosphere is best captured in "Hotel California" by The Eagles, the title track of the US rock band's fifth studio album. The song is inspired by the legendary Beverly Hills Hotel and confronts the darker side of the City of Angels, where "some dance to remember, some dance to forget".

3. **London:** The UK capital has produced so many hits that it's almost impossible to choose one. Perhaps the most iconic is The Clash's "London Calling", the title of which comes from the BBC's opening broadcast during the Second World War.

4. **Tokyo:** Kyu Sakamoto's "Ue wo muite arukou (AKA Sukiyaki)" is a karaoke staple. What sounds like a ballad is in fact a song about the frustrations felt after a student demonstration in Tokyo to protest the postwar US military occupation. For something more upbeat, tune into Pizzicato Five's "Tokyo wa yoru no shichiji" – known in English as "The Night is Still Young".

5. **São Paulo:** Brazilian singer Caetano Veloso grew up in the country's northeastern state of Bahia and wrote "Sampa" (the city's nickname) during his first visit to São Paulo. Initially he's apprehensive of the concrete jungle but by the end of the song he's fallen in love with the city.

Film
Screen time

For a while, it seemed as though the sun had set on independent cinemas. But despite the arrival of streaming services and glitzy multiplex movie theatres (or, perhaps, in response to them), arthouse cinemas are experiencing a revival. In cities around the world, communities are giving these eclectic establishments a round of applause.

Cinemas
Global

Countless cities around the world have been immortalised in films but few more so than Los Angeles, which is synonymous with Hollywood. It's only natural then that the City of Angels has its fair share of cinemas, from the spectacular 1960s Cinerama Dome at the ArcLight on Sunset Boulevard to the historic neon-lit Nuart theatre with its art deco façade.

Across the pond in Athens – a city famous for its ancient amphitheatres – open-air cinemas carry on that great Greek tradition of coming together for entertainment. Cinema Filothei is one of many outdoor cinemas that pop up across the city in the summer. Holidays here are made for stargazing (of both sorts) and there's something about this very Greek phenomenon, watching films along with the rattle of the crickets, that makes going back to anything with a roof seem positively square.

That is, unless you're somewhere such as Cinema Oasis in Bangkok. Co-founded by film director Ing Kanjanavanit, Oasis doubles as a gallery. With the closure of Bangkok's storied Scala and Lido, it's one of the city's last two remaining independent cinemas. "I want to appeal to all the neighbours and the amazing thing is that I'm seeing that," says Kanjanavanit, who even asks her *som tam* (papaya salad) seller for feedback.

That's what cinemas should be about. They should celebrate the city, its counterculture and its many communities. Cinemas have the power to bring people from all walks of life together – and modern cities are desperately in need of that.

Years to remember
Full of nostalgia – the fashion, the music, the hair – some films define a decade in a city. Here are our picks.

1. **1950s Rome, 'Roman Holiday':** Audrey Hepburn's princess Ann and Gregory Peck's newspaper reporter Joe embark on a romance that ticks off the Eternal City's key charms over a swooning score and, of course, astride the saddle of that Vespa.

2. **1960s London, 'Alfie':** Michael Caine embodied more than just a handsome chap in NHS spectacles. Like the Rolling Stones and Terence Stamp, he embodied a city in happy flux in which a working-class lad did something unknown: kept his accent. Alfie himself is, of course, a bastard. Sean Connery ruled the fictional world as a spy but Caine ruled the one he was born into with aplomb.

3. **1970s New York, 'The French Connection':** After Edith Wharton but before Wall Street was the 1970s: drugs, gangs and civic bankruptcy, a bleak canvas for the vibrancy of disco. But it's the dark stuff that celluloid loved and *The French Connection*, along with *Taxi Driver* and *Mean Streets*, epitomised the struggle between not-so-good and evil.

4. **1980s Los Angeles, 'Beverly Hills Cop':** LA owned the 1980s with *Fast Times at Ridgemont High*, *Ferris Bueller's Day Off* and *The Karate Kid* enshrining that great US invention: the lifelong teenager. But it was Eddie Murphy's charming cop who ruled them with a winning smile and a cock of the pistol. The hills, dells and malls of LA star almost as much as Murphy.

5. **1990s Hong Kong, 'Chungking Express':** Watching Chinese cinema in the West at the end of the past century was to be offered the exotic, the historical, the romantic and the hilariously violent. Wong Kar-Wai fused it all together in *Chungking Express* – his love letter to Hong Kong. You can taste the chicken feet, smell the opium and crave the buzz.

Much of the cut and thrust of city life unfolds after the working day is done. Cities are places in which to shop, revel, dine, drink, delight and ideally linger a while.

Although it's been a tough decade for bricks-and-mortar retailers, there's been a fightback against faceless big-box malls that suck life from the streets and price out smaller independents. Our case studies focus on a Sydney side street that still hits the right note with shoppers by offering unique buys and experiences plus a pleasant place in which to meander. And in Bangkok we visit a retailer that's rethinking what the mall can be, with natural materials, thoughtful shops and an added dose of intimacy.

Luckily, planners and private investors are slowly recognising the power of these softer aspects of city life to tempt footfall, revive buildings and even change the face and fortunes of entire neighbourhoods. In Oslo, for example, the once down-at-heel Vulkan district was recharged by the seemly renovation of the Mathallen, a steel-and-brick former ironworks that has become a thriving food hall. It houses 32 budding restaurateurs and producers, and demonstrates the power of food and drink to improve city life and satisfy rumbling tums.

Restaurants can also be community hubs and neighbourhood staples that leave a lasting social impact. That's the case with Italian chef Massimo Bottura's Refettorio Felix in London, which provides fresh meals and the dignity of a dining table to the homeless and the displaced, and Save on Meats in Vancouver, which serves a galvanising sense of community and acts as a meeting point as much as a restaurant.

Hotels too have fundamentally rethought their civic purpose. No longer are they shut-off stopovers for the overnight set. Increasingly they're spaces that define their neighbourhood and invite nearby residents to mingle with guests.

Restaurants, markets, hotels and shops aren't just pleasant diversions or things to pencil into plans at the last minute; they offer sustenance of another kind to urban-dwellers. We meet the folk with innovative ideas to share from the kitchen, behind the reception desk and on the shop floor.

IO.

SHOP, EAT, STAY

The new high street
Tills still ringing

Bricks-and-mortar shops have been hit hard by online competitors but there's a growing unease about the compromise of all that screen-to-door convenience. Are more delivery vehicles on the road a good thing? What if you want a recommendation? What about losing that excitement of finding a shop you didn't know existed on a lane you might not otherwise have ventured down? What about the sad prospect of a future in which our streets sit shuttered and shopless?

A humming high street keeps a city vibrant, brings footfall, boosts employment and adds to the charm, patina and excitement of city life. Far from bemoaning the times or harking back to the days of yore, smart retailers are building new solutions to stage a concrete (and brick and wood) comeback. Some are rethinking the mall, others the future of department stores, others still pushing pop-ups or simply offering smaller spaces with flexible leases in which to let entrepreneurs tinker.

The trade-off of losing the independent retailers that give a city its character, in favour of samey fit-outs or big multinationals, isn't to the benefit of city life. So here's the deal. We meet the switched-on sellers rethinking, reviving and raising the retail game.

Streets ahead: William Street isn't an isolated example. Physical retail done well (with room for characterful owners and a few surprises) is an easy sell. Look at the independent shops thriving on Yong Siak Street in Singapore's once-dull Tiong Bahru or the traders uniting formerly down-at-heel Division Street in Portland, Oregon

Ten tips for a healthy high street
Shopping list

1. **Embrace variety:** Diversity is key. Planners need to design smaller spaces and entice entrepreneurs with a range of options to get their businesses past year one. (Many mid-market retailers who wanted giant shops are struggling.)

2. **Choose wisely:** A good developer-operator is a curator – picking the right line-up of retailers to create a cohesive and appealing street. You need reliable payers and fresh names that may carry a little risk.

3. **Provide pit-stops:** Good seating and ample shade create places in which to linger longer.

4. **Think transport:** Nobody wants to be dodging traffic as they cross the street but going pedestrian-only isn't always the solution either. You need the right mix of accessible and safe.

5. **Keep it clean:** A little civic pride goes a long way. Traders should plump for a lick of paint or break out a broom to keep their patch pristine.

6. **Respect the old:** Don't just build new. The character of a street and its buildings offers a point of difference from glass-and-steel shopping centres.

7. **Be flexible:** Pop-ups make use of space that would otherwise be empty but how about flexible leases that guarantee a month – or two or three?

8. **Love late nights:** Local governments shouldn't be too prohibitive about when places open and close. Life after dark is a must for vibrant cities.

9. **Dare to be different:** A little rust and patina add texture and the interplay of different styles throws light and shade. Cities should be a constant delight to discover.

10. **Break the rules:** Finally, it's impossible to commission the perfect high street. Success lies in layered living, common sense and community.

1.
William Street, Sydney
Road to success

High streets have been having a tough time of late – not least in Sydney. In 2003 a Westfield shopping centre opened in Bondi Junction, luring away larger brands with the promise of bigger spaces and greater foot traffic. "That basically sucked up all the retail," says Giovanni Paradiso, who owns a restaurant called 10 William Street and knows the area well. "There were 'for lease' signs everywhere."

But while the main thoroughfare of Oxford Street suffered, smaller and quirkier William Street has remained robust and resilient. One of the main reasons for its success is its unusual mix of start-up brands and family-owned shops, which have been here for decades, make the most of still-reasonable rents and offer passers-by unique experiences and take-homes.

"The spaces here are smaller," says Theodore English, who co-opened menswear shop Belancé near the southern tip of the street. "This helps small businesses that want to start out but have to be careful with costs and overheads. It allows them to try something new, get feedback and improve step by step." A breath of fresh air in a world of luxury developments.

Chapter 10
Shop, eat, stay
The new high street

2.
Grocery shops, Montréal
At your convenience

City-slickers have moved away from faceless supermarkets and opted to patronise smaller, local grocery shops. These nimble independents offer security, a friendly face and a community hub where people know your name and will take delivery of a parcel or keep a spare pair of keys to hand.

"Here, a customer is not a number. They're part of the family," says Maximilien Lalime, who's taking a break from making sandwiches at the Lalime *dépanneur* (convenience store) in Montréal, a city where a strong tradition of independent grocery shops is being buoyed by a new crop of openings.

Lalime was opened by Maximilien's grandfather in 1959 and is now owned by his uncle and managed by his father. Big supermarket chains are still present (Loblaw-Provigo, Sobeys and Metro have a 60 per cent market share) but smaller operations such as Vieille Europe, Fruiterie du Plateau and Milano are thriving thanks to their charmingly personal take on retail.

Three community-minded models around the globe
Shopping for good

1. **Canny co-operatives:** The Park Slope Food Coop started in Brooklyn in 1973 with a simple notion: to take control of what its founders saw as unfair mark-ups and opaque business practices imposed by larger food retailers. The venture is run by members, who support it with subscriptions and benefit from a more transparent route to market. A similar outfit sprang up in London's Bloomsbury in 2010, stressing environmentally friendly practices, lower food prices (for members) and community-minded events.

2. **Unbeatable meats:** People are eating less meat than in years past and some neighbourhood butcher's shops have felt the sharp edge of the trend. But others are thriving. Hill & Szrok on London's Broadway Market is a neighbourhood shop by day and a delightful diner by night. This is a model that can also be seen at Lennart & Bror in Stockholm's Vasastan, which sells less, but higher-quality, meat and "has a relationship with people over the counter", as co-founder Rasmus Ek puts it.

3. **Analogue alternatives:** There are questions about how digital delivery platforms might reshape our cities (the fear is more traffic on the roads and fewer shops on the corner). But food delivery hasn't yet sated our appetite for restaurants and delivery drivers haven't driven food shops off the high street. In fact, there's a lurch toward treating the food shop as a luxury and investing in it.

   That's the case in Paris with the Grande Épicerie, a vast food hall opened in 2017 by LVMH's Le Bon Marché Group. But it can also be seen in the rise in smart food retailers from Fukushimaya in Tokyo to Käfer in Munich.

3.
Lulu Dans Ma Rue, Paris
With a little help

The world of deliveries has made getting goods more convenient for city-dwellers but it hasn't had the same effect on chores and services – at least not yet. This is what the concierge-style service offered by Lulu Dans Ma Rue aims to address in Paris.

Charles-Edouard Vincent saw a gap in the market for residents who need shoes shined, shirts pressed and dogs walked. From a JCDecaux-designed kiosk, he and his colleagues recruit helpers (known as Lulus) from all over the city with various skillsets, while charging a fee of about 20 per cent for connecting them with customers. Their business is also a high-street reviver.

Every Lulu is local to their kiosk, from students in need of extra money to skilled retirees. A Lulu's time will set you back between €5 and €20 for 30 minutes of service. "Sometimes we focus on our own personal development and our own happiness," says Vincent. "Society can be selfish but Lulu's promise is beautiful." Hear, hear.

4.
Save on Meats, Vancouver
Building bridges

Downtown Eastside in Vancouver is Canada's poorest neighbourhood and Save on Meats has helped to respond to the area's challenges. The kitchen has provided some two million meals to those in need and employees are plucked from backgrounds that might make finding a job hard. But it's also about engaging the community. A token programme allows for meals to be donated and then redeemed.

"On one side of us, there are million-dollar apartments, and on the other there's social housing," says owner Mark Brand. But on Save on Meats' red-leather banquettes, residents of both find common ground over hamburgers and milkshakes (there's even a community radio station). "It's a place where you feel comfortable meeting people from different walks of life," he adds. While inequity remains a challenge for Vancouver, Brand's vision is an example of the role that private businesses can play in bridging communities without displacing them.

5.
Bal Harbour Shops, Miami
The anti-mall

For years there has been a backlash in the US against drab shopping malls. But Bal Harbour Shops in the Bal Harbour suburb of Miami is showing no sign of succumbing. When founder Stanley Whitman set up a retail outpost here in the mid-1960s, he defied the trend for air-conditioning and decided to celebrate rather than bemoan its balmy location.

Shops and restaurants overlook courtyards lined with fountains, palm trees and a fishpond. "Our local tenants refuse to use the word 'mall' when describing it, as it's unenclosed and lushly landscaped," says Matthew Whitman Lazenby, operating partner and grandson of the founder. "They've always considered us to be the anti-mall." The approach is paying off and 100 or so retailers still call it home, from organic gelato shop Bianco to Balenciaga.

Lazenby's lesson is that being different rather than staying the same is key to knitting multi-shop retail complexes into a community. Just don't, whatever you do, call them malls.

6.
Central Embassy, Bangkok
Making it big

Another retail development that shows how some malls (not the much-maligned, out-of-town sort) have a bright future and can take a very different form is Central Embassy. The flagship mall of Thai retail empire Central Group is located just off Ploenchit Road and lures visitors right into the heart of the city.

Despite its size and sleek finishes, the mall has achieved a degree of intimacy that's struck a chord with locals, expats and fly-by-night visitors alike. Foremost among it is Open House, designed by Tokyo-based Klein Dytham Architecture. The colossal mixed-use space is beset with welcoming wooden touches and an offering of more than 20,000 books.

It doesn't hurt that this deft combination of attractions (including 12 restaurants) brings a little humanity back to the mall model that can often feel outdated and unwanted. Physical retail, it seems, is still an easy sell when it's done right.

Food for thought
Consuming passion

Food draws visitors to cities and defines how we think about a place and its customs: what's more Roman than pasta in a piazza or more redolent of Melbourne than a smashed avo' with your eggs? But food also nourishes and reflects urban life in other ways. Neighbourhood restaurants (the independent, self-run, "the usual, sir?" sort) can anchor or revive communities and offer spaces in which life can unfold over a table or in the flicker of candlelight.

Meanwhile, markets – once hoary relics of times past – are proving powerful and popular regenerators of forgotten spaces and long-empty buildings. The "weekly shop" as an activity has passed its expiry date, with unsure-of-their-evening-plan urbanites now buying less (but better quality) food, often on the whims of what they fancy that evening. Cue the blossoming of a new branch of markets and food entrepreneurs.

So, forget the tasteless chain restaurants and flash-in-the-pan openings (they'll fizzle and fade) and join us on a tour of the food-focused businesses that are satisfying hungry tums and forging more fulfilling cities.

1.
Markets, Helsinki
Hallowed halls

New markets may have transformed once-fallow spaces into lively ones but there's also been a spate of fix-ups that have helped to take time-tested halls to hallowed new heights. In Helsinki a plan to renew the Finnish capital's fin-de-siècle markets breathed new life into the Hakaniemi, Hietalahti and Vanha Kauppahalli (*pictured*) halls. It's an expensive but worthwhile endeavour and the best ones keep room for older traders to continue alongside the up-and-comers.

2.
Grand Central Market,
Los Angeles
Downtown delight

The revival of this market, built in 1917, shows how much Los Angeles has changed. The city's downtown isn't the no-go zone it once was. From the vegetarian fare at Madcapra to the fish tacos and spicy ceviche at La Tostadería via the chop suey at China Café, the offerings at each stall reflect the wave of immigration that has shaped the city – and have encouraged punters back into the city's formerly forgotten heartland. Here, food is an ingredient for urban renewal.

3.
Kooperativet, Oslo
Fare traders

Cities can have a habit of making us feel a long way from the places in which our produce is grown but Kooperativet in Oslo has found favour by connecting farmers around the city with consumers within it, to the benefit of both growers and buyers. "We saw that the food market didn't satisfy either the consumer or the farmer," says Helene Austvoll, co-founder of Kooperativet, which works with some 20 farms around the Norwegian capital.

Established in 2013 to cater to Oslovians hungry for freshly grown goods, Kooperativet offers a biweekly subscription service for organic produce, which is delivered to the Mathallen food hall in the city's once-shabby Vulkan district. For €22, members receive a carrier bag (artfully branded and made from natural jute) brimming with locally sourced fruit and vegetables. One week it may include crisp lettuce or juicy red peppers, another sweet carrots or leeks. And what started at the revived brick-built food market is now available for collection at several points around the city.

It's very easy to see why Kooperativet works. What's harder to glean is why other cities haven't found such innovative ways to feed their city's desire for fresh produce, provided at a fair price.

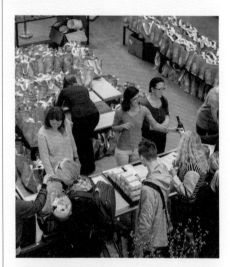

4.
Timbre+, Singapore
New tricks

Newer isn't always better and protecting a city's food culture can pay delicious dividends. Timbre+ was founded in 2016 by Edward Chia and Danny Loong, who went from running music venues to setting up a unique take on Singapore's traditional hawker centres (food halls).

The pair's space in the One North neighbourhood gathers businesses from across the generational divide to address the lack of young talent willing to join the oldsters. Alongside 14 restaurants and 21 hawkers, and a lively calendar of pop-ups and fairs, there is a restaurant and a stall that act as an incubator programme.

Timbre+ stepped in to develop a new food hall on the site of a demolished one but they didn't want to erase what came before. "What about the older guys?" says Chia. "There was no intention of kicking them out."

The success of the project, aside from being a beloved local lunch spot, has safeguarded a space in which both older traders and young talent can meet, mingle and share ideas over a square meal.

Take a stand: Timbre+ shows how food halls can safeguard a city's culinary heritage and include all ages. Elsewhere in Southeast Asia, the banning of street food has been considered on hygiene and safety grounds. Instead, follow this example and set aside spaces for it to thrive

6.
Gotham Greens, New York
Hit the roof

"Local" is a bothersome word when it's attached to a food product since everything is local to somewhere. But it's rightly become a rallying cry when it comes to limiting the distance food needs to travel. Cue a growing crop of entrepreneurs making more with less space.

Gotham Greens started in 2008 in a climate-controlled greenhouse on a two-storey building in Brooklyn's Greenpoint neighbourhood overlooking the East River; it now has two other spaces in the Big Apple and another in Chicago. The original site grows more than 120 tonnes of lettuce and herbs a year, which are sold to restaurants and supermarkets in the area. Co-founder Viraj Puri says that Gotham Greens uses 10 times less water and 20 times less land than a traditional farm, thanks to recycling and smart design choices.

"It was the first commercially viable urban farm on a rooftop in the country," says Puri. Luckily for city slickers, Gotham Greens isn't the only food-focused business eyeing up a hungry market on its doorstep.

5.
Refettorio Felix, London
Social ingredient

Eating well is often a privilege but one project run by star chef Massimo Bottura (*pictured*) proves that it doesn't just need to be for those who have the cash and cachet to afford it. Food for the Soul is an NGO set up by the Modena-based restaurateur in 2016. It provides meals for vulnerable adults, many of whom are homeless or suffer from mental health issues.

What started in Milan spread to Rio de Janeiro then London and Paris, with two more US outposts in the offing. The London incarnation, Refettorio Felix, sits next to a church in west London and offers an elevated and restaurant-like experience (for free) with dishes made by volunteer chefs from otherwise bin-bound produce. The space was kitted out pro bono by London-based Studioilse (with plenty of tactile touches, natural light and plants to humanise it).

Most importantly, it brings dignity and respect to the table for many who are denied it in day-to-day city life. Food can, after all, be an ingredient in social inclusion.

Restaurants as community hubs:
Gentrification is a word about which we're suspicious, and sometimes restaurants can be seen as agents of change rather than continuity, services for outsiders rather than locals. This is a mistake. There are plenty that unite neighbourhoods and serve as meeting points: for political debate, chance encounters and shared spaces. Think of how sitting and sipping in Paris's cafés became a sign of defiance after terrorist attacks in the city

Hotels that help the 'hood
Here to stay

Much more than a simple bed for a night, hotels (at their best) are windows onto their city and spaces where overnighters and locals can mingle to the benefit of both. They're integral to placemaking, keeping streets lively and ensuring that a steady flow of money is coming into town.

Recently, however, there has been much scaremongering about the future of hotels, particularly in light of the popularity of apartment-sharing apps and also the kickback against mass tourism in cities such as Barcelona. But a sense of balance, calm and purpose is re-emerging as the shoddier hotels suffer and the bright sparks shine all the more clearly.

So forget the sad start of finding the keys to your apartment – that looks nothing like the pictures – in a deposit box on a square. Join us instead on a tour of three of our favourite hotels, which offer a worthy and warm welcome to visitors and work hard for, reflect and embellish the community in which they're based.

1.
The Old Clare Hotel, Sydney
Barrel of laughs

If proof were needed that hotels can reignite the fortunes of a forgotten neighbourhood, look no further than The Old Clare in Chippendale, Sydney. The inner-city suburb became a grungy outlier that was famed for rough pubs and usually given a wide berth. But this spot, just west of Central Station, was where Singapore-based Unlisted Collection converted the old brewery into its first Australian stopover in 2015.

As well as safeguarding the 150-year-old architecture of the Carlton & United Breweries Administration Building, the development pedestrianised an adjoining street that's now home to three new restaurants. The success of the 62-key affair is partly down to architecture firm Tonkin Zulaikha Greer and obvious in the fact that you're as likely to spot a Chippendale local, or at least a Sydneysider, enjoying the space as you are a guest. Cue the influx of art galleries (White Rabbit is our favourite) and a revival in fortunes of this once down-at-heel 'hood.

2.
Magdas Hotel, Vienna
Warm welcome

Vienna has long been a nexus of political, artistic and economic clout but for the most part the city's hotels have been the preserve of the rich and powerful. Not so for the Magdas Hotel, which, under the control of charitable group Caritas, is on a mission to provide work and shelter for young refugees and to make itself a meeting point.

The former retirement home was built in the 1960s and renovated in 2015 by Vienna-based AllesWirdGut architects. The studio's name means "everything will be OK" and this is the sense you get in the lobby; it's also a restaurant, bar and living room, and has furniture that's spare and comforting yet mostly upcycled or donated. "Our philosophy is based on the work of Nobel Prize-winner Muhammad Yunus, who says that when all income in a business is reinvested, it can engender greater social change. So the hotel is self-funding, putting profits back into the business," says CEO Gabriela Sonnleitner. "Magdas is a place that brings people together."

Character studies: Vienna's tourism sector has a staff shortage and Magdas Hotel shows that people from a refugee background can help. They're motivated and hospitable and more than 20 languages are spoken by the 16 nationalities represented. Magdas also invites students from the nearby Academy of Fine Arts to contribute to the design of the space, which is forever changing

3.
The Drake Hotel, Toronto
Fit for a queen

Among the many regeneration success stories told in Toronto over the past decade or so is that of Queen Street West in the city's West End. Historically home to Toronto's artists' studios and many of the city's immigrant communities that arrived in the late 19th century – Irish, Portuguese and Jewish people once called the area home – it's now considered one of Toronto's most desirable neighbourhoods.

At the vanguard of the transformation was The Drake Hotel, opened in 2004 on Queen Street West by the Canadian technology entrepreneur Jeff Stober. The Drake is named after the former hotel that had occupied the 19th-century red-brick corner building (since the 1980s it was variously a flophouse and punk bar). "We started off as a bit of an oxymoron," says Stober. "We tried to create a hotel for locals as much as international travellers. We looked to the historic relationship between artists and hotels and knew there was an intrinsic value to creating a 'town square' for the community – somewhere that allowed for genuine hospitality."

When you look out across your city, what are the elements that catch your eye or help define your home as unique, even a touch odd? Is it a bombed-out cinema in Beirut or a brutalist elephant house in London? Or something more internationally iconic such as the Sydney Opera House?

We asked our editors and correspondents to share the elements that shape their hometowns and delve into the stories behind them. At times we get all historical on you, at others we yearn for modernity. But each story is a shortcut down the secret side streets of metropolitan life and an antidote to the idea that the world is blandly uniform.

Sure, a few mighty architects and global brands seem to shape too many places but our cities remain defiantly unique – layered with history, mistakes, design bravado, memories and more.

II.

TALL STORIES

I.
The Egg
Beirut

. . . .

The UFO-like Egg building was designed in the 1960s but never finished. Today it stands as a symbol of Beirut's unresolved history.

. . . .

If there's a single building that sums up Beirut it's the Egg. Perched like a spaceship two floors above ground level, it's also known as the Dome, the Bubble and the Soap. In a former life it was a cinema, part of the avant garde Beirut City Centre shopping and office complex designed by local architect Joseph Philippe Karam in the 1960s, slap-bang in the centre of town.

It was only half-finished when the Lebanese civil war broke out in 1975 and has remained that way ever since. Because it was on the frontline between east and west Beirut, it endured 15 years of fighting, gaining a mess of scars, cuts and gaping wounds in the process.

After the war, an adjoining tower (one of two that were supposed to be built) was torn down when a government ministry briefly considered setting up shop there. The plan fell through, leaving a giant pit exposing the empty

"The Egg has become symbolic to thousands of Lebanese who have watched their capital undergo traumatic waves of transformation over the past few decades"

subterranean car park that still exists. As the 1990s wore on, Beirutis began to reclaim the war relics of their city and the space was used as a nightclub, an exhibition space and a cultural platform. But all that ended when the valuable plot was sold first to an Emirati firm and then to a Saudi one by development company Solidere.

Controversially, Solidere was put in charge of redeveloping Beirut's beating heart, Downtown, in the wake of the civil war. Many feel that it's responsible for turning it into a Gulf-inspired playground. Unsurprisingly, Solidere does not agree.

Regardless, the fact remains that most of Beirut's historic buildings have been replaced with too-perfect golden sandstone, creating a sanitised architectural landscape that erases the city's past. With so few reminders left of Beirut's troubled recent history, the Egg has become symbolic to thousands of Lebanese who have watched their capital undergo traumatic waves of transformation over the past few decades.

For years there have been plans to turn the Egg into a hotel but, as of yet, nothing has happened. Civil society groups and architects argue that it should be renovated for public use, not privatised like so much else in Beirut.

At its core, the Egg is an uncomfortable, unanswered question. Is it a monument to Beirut's long-gone golden era? Or a necessary reminder of a war that took hundreds of thousands of lives? Or a space for something new? No one agrees but that's Beirut in a nutshell: a place whose past, present and future are picked over and disputed. Evocative, messy, unapologetic and ultimately unforgettable.

2.
Kaiserlinden
Vienna

. . . .

There's a reason you see so many linden trees in Austria – and it's not just because they look good.

. . . .

Most nations have a symbol of national pride and in Austria this role has been assigned to a tree – more specifically, the linden. Today you'll find the species across the country, standing tall in the middle of squares in cities, towns and villages.

In the past, these trees were often planted to honour the birthday of the emperor or empress. In the grounds of Vienna's imperial Schönbrunn Palace, many were raised in honour of the ruling Habsburg family. Known as Kaiserlinden, these trees are most likely the last living organisms to have been around in the late emperor Franz Joseph's day, in the 19th and early 20th century.

Giving trees as gifts in Austria turned into a veritable industry as emperor Franz Joseph celebrated anniversary after anniversary of his reign with yet more Kaiserlinden. And he's not the only monarch to have received arboreal presents: the 18th-century empress Maria Theresa was also the lucky recipient of a tree or two. Among those in her name is a Kaiserlinde that's now 300 years old, stretching skywards near the Gloriette at Schönbrunn.

The custom of planting saplings to commemorate Austrian statesmen has now come to an end but the Kaiserlinden will remain in place in Vienna for another few hundred years at least. And aside from providing pleasant greenery, each one is a reminder of what some Austrians still regard as the greatest period in their country's and capital's history.

"For Ponte City, the 1990s and early 2000s were the darkest hour. It became the world's tallest vertical slum, a crime-ridden behemoth full of brothels, drug dens and violent gangs"

3.
Ponte City
Johannesburg

From modernist dream to urban nightmare, Ponte City's fortunes have changed almost as much as South Africa's.

Few buildings have been both held up as a utopian vision and decried as a symbol of urban decay. Johannesburg's Ponte City, however, has been both in its almost 45-year existence.

When it was completed in the Hillbrow district in 1975, this 170-metre-high doughnut-shaped tower with its gaping central chasm was the tallest residential building in the southern hemisphere. It imposed itself on the low-slung, sprawling skyline, a 54-storey concrete celebration of high modernism.

Ponte City's developers sold it as the high watermark of urban liveability. And for a while, through to the early 1980s, it was just that: the pinnacle of chic metropolitan life. But only for the city's wealthy white minority – this was during South Africa's apartheid regime and Johannesburg was segregated along racial lines. Ponte City was a whites-only building.

While it started life on a wave of grand promises, Ponte City lost its way. By the mid-1980s, white wealthy residents had started fleeing inner-city districts such as Hillbrow for the leafy and supposedly safer northern suburbs. As they moved out, in came Johannesburg's poorer black residents and immigrants from neighbouring countries.

In 1994 the apartheid regime ended and Nelson Mandela ushered in a new era of hope and democracy in South Africa. But for Ponte City, the 1990s and early 2000s were the darkest hour. It became the world's tallest vertical slum, a crime-ridden behemoth full of brothels, drug dens and violent gangs. The doughnut's central shaft became a dumping ground for rubbish, which reached the windows of fourth-floor apartments. Ponte City, once the symbol of modern living, became a manifestation of Johannesburg's troubles, its inequality and deprivation.

But the tower's fortunes have shifted once again. While Hillbrow and Ponte City itself are still deprived and occasionally dangerous, things are heading in the right direction. An epic clean-up operation has taken place and there are now roughly 3,000 people living in the tower. Dlala Nje, a community organisation founded in 2012, has been organising initiatives to shift popular perceptions of Ponte City and its neighbourhood.

Few countries have seen more momentous change and upheaval over the past 40 years than South Africa – and Ponte City has been there to witness it all. In its journey from riches to rags to redemption, it has become something of a symbol, with its hollow core an empty vessel to hold the nation's shifting hopes and fears. Like South Africa itself, Ponte City has demonstrated an extraordinary resilience and capacity for reinvention.

4.

Santa Maria dello Spasimo
Palermo

. . . .

In its five centuries of existence, Palermo's Lo Spasimo has seen wars, earthquakes and fires. And, still, nobody has given it a roof.

. . . .

Santa Maria dello Spasimo in Palermo doesn't have a roof but that was never a problem. Despite the plans of the wealthy man who first willed its construction, this topless building wasn't really a church for very long at all.

The story begins in 1506 when widowed lawyer Giacomo Basilico donated his land so that a grand church could be erected in honour of his dead (and very rich) wife. Blueprints were drawn up and ground broken in 1509. Lo Spasimo was to have a bell tower, a cemetery, cloisters, a refectory, a dormitory and a vegetable garden.

Its name pays homage to the moment the Virgin Mary collapsed when she saw her son on the way to Calvary. Lo Spasimo translates as "the pang"; the breaking point. And indeed a breaking point came when predictions that all building work would be completed in six years proved ambitious. Come 1535, with an unfinished structure and fears of a Turkish invasion, Palermo had to make a choice: complete Lo Spasimo or invest in fortification. The city chose walls and ramparts over a roof.

One of the bastions for the city's defence was to be built next to the incomplete church so even parts of the complex that had already been made were sentenced to razing. Away with the cloisters and monks' rooms. Once those had been destroyed, the monks had one option: pack up and leave. The church was soon deconsecrated.

This could have been the end of Lo Spasimo's story as a church but really it was the beginning of a new life. Over the subsequent five centuries it has been a public theatre, a grain store, a hospice for the poor, a hospital during the plague of 1624 and a garden for the hospital proper. It has also been storage for snow collected from the mountains (which went into making the city's indulgent gelato) and, after the Second World War, a collection point for all the artistic treasures saved from the city's bombarded houses. By this time Lo Spasimo had also suffered – and withstood – both earthquakes and fires. It was looking particularly dilapidated, which is a lot to say for a church that was already missing its roof.

But then came restoration and, with it, the latest chapter of Lo Spasimo's story. Today the austere, lanky structure is the seat of a jazz school and a venue for atmospheric gigs beneath the stars. Like the city that it inhabits, it's a mishmash of architectural styles, and bears the scars of inadequacies, compromises and mistakes of the past. But it wears them with pride: they are, after all, part of its charm.

"It's not just the art that attracts the crowds – it's the chance to see and be seen, to participate in life's busy parade. And Armenians have mastered this to perfection"

5.

The Cascade
Yerevan

. . . .

If you want to see Armenian life in all its glory, simply go to the Cascade, the scene of protests, meetings and mismanagement.

. . . .

The Armenian capital of Yerevan sits high above sea level, surrounded by even higher land and mountains. But there are heights within the city too.

The Cascade is a gigantic marble-and-stone staircase, designed by modernist architects in the 1930s, that rises some 120 metres. It offers a giddy view of Yerevan from the top and on clear evenings you can see the snow-capped peak of Mount Ararat, the sacred mountain of Armenian culture (though it now sits across the Turkish border). Lining the steps are neatly trimmed hedges and the occasional fountain, while down below there's a sculpture park dotted with works by Fernando Botero and Jaume Plensa.

Because of its location in the centre of Yerevan, the Cascade has long been the natural meeting place for all manner of dissidents and protesters. In the summer of 2015, when the government announced plans to sharply increase electricity prices, tens of thousands occupied the nearby Baghramyan Avenue.

Protesters also often gather in one of the Cascade's numerous cafés to deplore Armenia's staggering inequality; about a third of the population lives below the poverty line. Indeed, the Cascade itself is a case study in mismanagement and chronic underfunding, something that has characterised big projects in Armenia, both in Soviet times and following its independence in 1991.

Construction on the project began in 1971 but it was not finished until the 2000s, when the government handed over the complex to businessman and philanthropist Gerard Cafesjian. In 2009, the New York-born Cafesjian concluded this process by inaugurating a contemporary-art centre inside the Cascade.

It's not just the art that attracts the crowds – it's the chance to see and be seen, to participate in life's busy parade. And Armenians have mastered this to perfection. The Cascade is the focal point for Yerevan's social life, a panorama of every pocket of society. Bored youths loiter with no intent, middle-aged men sit deep in thought and wise old women rest in the shade. There are giggling children, girls in fine dresses, businessmen drinking coffee and Armenians speaking English. All are here to breathe new life into this very, very old city.

"The statues were unveiled in 2013. Had they been created just a decade earlier, there may have been riots in the streets. But not today. Sensitivities have softened"

6.
The Pug and the Poodle
Montréal
....

The tension between Québec's Anglophones and Francophones is depicted in two Montréal statues. But look closer and you'll find a different meaning.
....

On 30 October 1995, voters in Québec turned out in record numbers to vote on the province's independence from Canada. The referendum was the culmination of more than a decade of growing separatist sentiment in the province and the atmosphere across the country leading up to the poll was febrile. The anti-independence vote won by a whisker. Québec would remain a part of Canada.

What legacy did the knife-edge referendum and the years of separatist sentiment leave on the province and its major city, Montréal? The answer, perhaps, lies in two of the newer additions to Montréal's fine collection of public art: a pair of bronze statues, which stand in the heart of the city's historic old quarter, called "The English Pug and The French Poodle".

The statues are of a man and a woman, facing away from one another at either end of a plinth below the imposing tower of the Banque Nationale building in the Place d'Armes square. The woman stares at the grand neoclassical edifice of the original national bank building, often seen as a symbol of the Anglophone presence in Québec. The man, meanwhile, looks to the Notre-Dame Basilica, the most potent symbol of Catholicism in Québéc and, therefore, of French life in the city.

He embodies Québec's Francophone community, she the province's Anglophones. Both have their long noses pointed haughtily in the air, expressing a clear and palpable distaste for the other.

But then there are the little creatures in their arms: the woman carries a French poodle, while in the arms of the man is an English pug. As their owners turn away in contempt, the pooches stare longingly at each other, as if wanting to meet and play.

The statues by Montréal-born Marc-André J Fortier were unveiled in 2013. Had they been created a decade earlier, there may have been riots in the streets. But not today. Sensitivities between Montréal's two halves have softened since 1995 and a sense of optimism has followed. The city's economy is blossoming and its technology sector is the envy of Canada.

The pointed noses on the faces of the statues are strapped on, perhaps to suggest that our prejudices and dislikes are never permanent and that we can remove them if we have the will to do so. Today the story of Montréal's Anglophones and Francophones is one of enthusiastic curiosity in the promise of a city shared rather than divided.

7.
Sint-Annatunnel
Antwerp

. . . .

One of the best views in Antwerp can be gleaned not by crossing a bridge but rather by ducking underground.

. . . .

Antwerp, Belgium's second-largest city, is internationally renowned for its fashion scene, its diamond market and its port. Unlike other major cities, there are no fine old bridges over the river, nor controversial new ones by famous contemporary architects. In fact, there are no bridges at all. The reason? Any proposals for anything that might obstruct ships passing through the Scheldt, the lifeblood of the city, have always been met with a definite *neen*.

However, there is a place where Antwerp is a little bit special – and that's beneath the surface. The only way to get to the Linkeroever (the Left Bank) by foot is the Sint-Annatunnel, a pedestrian tunnel that runs under the Scheldt and brings residents from the Left Bank to the city centre on the Right Bank.

Tunnels can be mysterious in an oddly pleasant way but they are often dim and

"Unlike the traffic-clogged subterranean arteries of London and New York, the Sint-Annatunnel is a peaceful haven – a simple, majestic underwater thoroughfare"

industrial. Who wouldn't prefer to admire the view from the Brooklyn Bridge or the Pont Neuf? But unusually, and unlike the traffic-clogged subterranean arteries of London and New York, the Sint-Annatunnel is a peaceful haven – a simple, majestic underwater thoroughfare.

The tunnel opened in 1933 and still exists almost completely in its original state, from the switches and safety signs to the ceramic tiles and wooden stairs. The two yellow-brick buildings, through which you enter and emerge, were designed by architect Emiel Van Averbeke in the style of new pragmatism, a Dutch period of modernist architecture that started in the 1920s and was characterised by angular shapes.

From the Right Bank at Sint-Jansvliet, as you leave behind the Sunday antiques market and furniture shops, you descend on what is indisputably the highlight: the original, rattling wooden escalator. There is no "standing on the right" in Antwerp. People and their bikes – the Belgians are almost as fanatical about cycling as the Dutch – are more often than not blocking the way. But why would you want to rush past? The escalator is all about the experience: wondering at how this relic is still operating, admiring its beauty and reflecting on a time gone by as you vanish 31 metres below the ground.

Once down, you gaze into a 572-metre-long tunnel that is slightly too brightly lit, with white-tiled walls and a paved floor worn smooth by the passing of bicycles and pedestrians. On foot the journey takes 10 minutes

– voices echoing, seemingly unaware of the amount of water pressing down from above – while cyclists whiz by.

Once on the other side you emerge onto the Left Bank, where residents return to their homes and folk from the city centre come and find a bench on the embankment for the best view of the Antwerp skyline (or a spot of wild swimming). It's far from perfect – Antwerp's old waterfront is facing a much-needed makeover, from a car park to a leafy pedestrian walkway – but, for now at least, the locals are content with occasionally, quietly disappearing beneath the surface of the city.

. . . .

8.
Le Jardin Secret
Marrakech

. . . .

The gardens of Marrakech are symbols of human ingenuity – and none more so than Le Jardin Secret.

. . . .

Seen from the flat rooftops of Marrakech, the Atlas mountains are like a mirage. With their snowy peaks, they seem to belong to continents far away from the baking heat of the Medina. Yet there they stand, close enough to provide more than just an escape from the unbearable heat. Because for a millennium the range has also given Marrakech water – and that's why today the city teems with plants and flowers that defy the dry terrain, in gardens that define the city as much as its buildings.

The first *khettara* (a network of tunnels and wells) was built in 1107 by the imperial Almoravid dynasty to transport water from the aquifer beneath the mountains all the way to the city's then only garden. The system eventually grew to feed mosques, hamams and fountains but for centuries having water flow into the grounds of a private home was a privilege of the wealthy. Only Marrakech's richest were able to afford it, including the families who would inhabit the grand palace on Rue Mouassine in the 19th century.

One of the biggest in the Medina, this riad had two courtyards and a magnificent garden. But its owner, Kaid al-Hajj Abd-Allah U-Bihi, didn't get to enjoy it for long. Suspected of political intrigue, he was poisoned and his home passed from ruler to ruler until, in 1934, it stopped being looked after at all. By 2008 only a few stubborn date plants grew amid the ruins.

Yet life did not stop flowing in these gardens. In 2013, British landscape architect Tom Stuart-Smith was called in to restore them. In 2016 the house reopened its doors under a new name: Le Jardin Secret. It features the so-called Exotic Garden, hosting plants sourced from everywhere from Mexico to Madagascar, and a traditional Islamic garden that presents Morocco's floral bounty. Lavender, rosemary, figs,

olives and orange trees were chosen for the latter.

Even if the narrow channels running through these manicured patches no longer carry water flowing in from the Atlas mountains, the system between these basins is still the ancient original. If you look hard enough in some of the riad's nooks and crannies, you'll spot the pipes and reservoirs that still ensure these plants can survive in Marrakech's sweltering summers.

· ·

9.
Estadio Centenario
Montevideo

· ·

One of the world's most famous football stadiums, Estadio Centenario may have seen better days but it's still where Uruguay's hopes and dreams play out.

· ·

Montevideo's Estadio Centenario is one of the most fabled football stadiums in the world. It was built in 1930 for the inaugural World Cup, which the host, Uruguay, would go on to win.

When it opened, the sleek art deco architecture, rendered largely in brick, was a modern marvel. The architects Juan Antonio Scasso and José Domato were challenged with creating a design that could be built within a year. The centrepiece is an attractive art deco tower that has

become something of an oversized compass point for residents in this part of the city.

The design of the stadium is simple. The circular sweep of the 65,000-capacity arena opens up to the sky. If you looked down at the structure from above it would look like a gaping, wide-open mouth, shouting perhaps – appropriate, given that the former home team Peñarol's supporters are notoriously among the noisiest and rowdiest in the country.

The charm of the Estadio Centenario today is that it's been tampered with very little since the days of the 1930 World Cup. The stadium has been remodelled and now has a smaller capacity but its fabric remains the same – very few renovations have taken place.

Yes, it may have a rather tired feeling, its edges frayed by decades of sporting storytelling. But it's the football that does the talking here. The stadium's faded grandeur is a blank canvas on which triumphs, tragedies and stalemates have been written for the best part of a century.

The Estadio Centenario was named to commemorate the centenary of Uruguay's constitution and its birth as an independent nation. Ever since it has served as a teller of tales, of the trials and tribulations of the city, and of the entire country. From the days of dictatorship to Uruguay's role as one of Latin America's quiet economic powerhouses, Uruguay's sense of itself has, in many ways, been fostered in this stadium.

"The football does the talking here. The stadium is a blank canvas on which triumphs, tragedies and stalemates have been written for the best part of a century"

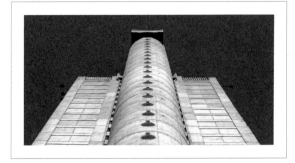

10.
Genex Tower
Belgrade

. . . .

Built to inspire awe and envy in the hearts of western visitors, Genex Tower is now more likely to inspire bafflement.

. . . .

It may be one of the icons of the city but Belgrade's Western Gate is not quite all it should be. Also known as the Genex Tower, this concrete landmark is the first significant structure that many visitors will notice on their way into Serbia's capital. However, this twin-towered relic of the communist Tito era has fallen into a sorry state.

You would never call it beautiful but the Genex Tower certainly qualifies as striking. Its unorthodox design has a hint of Paris's La Défense and the round structure on top recalls London's BT Tower.

When it was built in 1980, it was both a statement of intent and perhaps the last gasp of Tito's Yugoslavia. Yet its location seems unpromising. It stands in an area that suits the description "concrete jungle" better than New Belgrade and the constant roar from the adjacent E70 motorway makes double glazing a necessity.

This was all part of a utopian plan that seemed to make perfect sense in the 1970s when the socialist ideals of the western Balkans were alive and well. Back then, the E70 was known as the "Brotherhood and Unity Highway" running through four of Yugoslavia's six republics. Genex was designed to represent the western gate of the capital Belgrade and to be a symbol of socialist progress. The idea was that international visitors would gaze up in awe as they travelled on the highway to and from the airport.

Now they are more likely to wonder how a local bank got permission to cover the entire expanse of one of the towers with an enormous and unlovely advert. Close up, it doesn't get much better. The forecourt has been covered with bricks, tiles and a non-functioning fountain, and is littered with weeds. One tower appears to be semi-derelict. In fact, it houses a skeleton staff who work for what's left of the state-owned Genex company.

The other block, though, is residential and in reasonable condition. In fact, the panoramic views from a 28th-floor apartment are spectacular: you can follow the Danube and the Sava rivers for miles, or gaze across the ancient city of Zemun and Belgrade's Old Town. There's even a long-closed revolving restaurant on the 35th floor, a dining experience just begging to be revived. Many Belgraders are now fond, or even proud, of the Genex Tower but the authorities have other priorities, notably the controversial Belgrade Waterfront redevelopment, which is angering and alienating many of the city's inhabitants. If just a fraction of that project's cash could be diverted to restoring Genex, it could win a lot of goodwill and Belgrade would regain the gateway it deserves.

. . . .

11.
Elbstrand
Hamburg

. . . .

How Germany's busiest port gained a neighbour in the form of one of Hamburg's most popular sunbathing spots.

. . . .

"Then the cranes crank into motion, lifting shipping containers off the laden vessels. Viewed from the Elbstrand, the scene is mesmerising, a piece of silent, slow-motion entertainment"

Cities regularly offer moments of staggering juxtaposition, whether it's the well-heeled elite living cheek-by-jowl with people on the breadline or the globally recognisable landmark nestled next to the local staple. In some cities you stumble across the old and the new thrown thoughtlessly together or a precious pocket where nature flourishes in the middle of a concrete jungle.

However, few places present as stark a contrast as the Elbstrand in Hamburg. This urban beach on the north bank of the Elbe River, just to the west of the city centre, looks like any other beach: an inviting stretch of yellow sand, hordes of sun-worshipping city-dwellers getting their kit off, and glittering water lapping at the shore. In summer, it's picture-perfect. Except, that is, for what lies directly opposite on the southern bank.

You see, the Elbe is the main artery feeding Hamburg's economy, dating back to the days when it was one of the Hanseatic cities that dominated trade on the North and Baltic Seas. Hamburg is still one of Europe's busiest port cities, an entry point into Europe for ships from North America and Asia and a gateway to the world for Germany's exporters. That port sits on the southern bank of the Elbe, opposite the Elbstrand.

So about 500 metres across the water from where the summer revellers lounge on the sand is a battalion of enormous cranes, painted in striking red-and-blue uniforms, standing to attention on the opposite bank. Vast container ships regularly drift past on their way to the ocean or pull into port. Then the cranes crank into motion, lifting shipping containers off the laden vessels. Viewed from the Elbstrand, the scene is mesmerising, a piece of silent, slow-motion entertainment.

The juxtapositions are extreme: you have the imposing scale of the cranes and the smallness of the bodies laid out on the sand; the natural world against the most man-made of landscapes; and then the human relaxation of a Saturday afternoon against the churn of global commerce. If contrasts are what make cities surprising, fascinating places to live, then the Elbstrand boasts some of the starkest.

12.
Waikiki War Memorial
Honolulu
. . . .

Honolulu memorialised its war victims in a unique way – with a giant swimming pool.
. . . .

On 24 August 1927, thousands turned out for the opening of one of Honolulu's grandest and, frankly, strangest civic buildings. The Waikiki Natatorium War Memorial was an imaginative take on the cenotaph, commissioned to commemorate the 101 Hawaiian service personnel who died in the First World War and the 10,000 or so more who contributed to the war effort. But from its inception this building was also intended to be a celebration of life and living.

The Natatorium is an Olympic-sized swimming pool built directly into the warm blue waters of the Pacific. Originally it boasted bleacher seats for 7,000 spectators, a high-dive board and perfect views of the crystal ocean beyond. The entrance to the pool, a grand beaux arts archway topped with twin stone sculptures of the American eagle, instantly became a city landmark.

"The pool included a sophisticated system of filters. Folklore has it that shoals of tropical fish would wiggle their way through the pipes and join swimmers in the lap lanes"

Designed and built by the US architect Lewis Parsons Hobart, the Natatorium was a feat of engineering. It included a sophisticated system of filters that allowed the sea water to flow in and out of the pool. Folklore has it that shoals of tropical fish would wiggle their way through the pipes and join swimmers in the lap lanes.

The year it opened – 30 years or so after the Hawaiian monarchy was overthrown and the islands were annexed by the US – would prove to be a turning point for Honolulu. The iconic bright-pink edifice of the Royal Hawaiian Hotel opened, heralding the arrival of visitors who would come – first by boat, then by plane – in their millions to the city and the surrounding islands.

But by the 1930s the Natatorium was already showing signs of decay and the wrangle over who should pay for its upkeep would continue over the decade to come. Then, on 7 December 1941, the Japanese airforce attacked Pearl Harbor military base, 22km away. Soon after, the army took control of the Natatorium as a training base for conscripts.

Some years after Hawaii became the 50th state in the union, a huge renovation of the Natatorium was undertaken. But even that couldn't halt the erosion of the ever-lapping tides. In 1979 it closed – and that's how it remains today.

The debate around the Natatorium's fate is a perennial fixture on the agenda of Honolulu politicians. Some have supported tearing it down, while others have fought hard to keep it standing. It was built as a living part of the city. Maybe one day it will be again.

13.
Haydarpasa Station
Istanbul

. . . .

A gift from Germany to the Ottoman Empire, the iconic Istanbul station has survived everything from wars to questionable restoration jobs.

. . . .

"Haydarpasa Station. Spring 1941, 3pm. On the steps, sun, fatigue and confusion. A man stops on the steps, thinking about something." That's how Turkish modernist Nazim Hikmet begins his epic poem *Human Landscapes from My Country*, a book about his people from whom he'd been cut off for a decade as a political prisoner. The steps of Haydarpasa were a fitting place for him to once again get to grips with the mind of the modern Turk because this old railway station is a real junction in Turkey's modern history.

Take a ferry from Istanbul's European side to Kadikoy on the Asian shore and, as you round the headland, Haydarpasa Station seems to rise out of the Bosphorus like a Teutonic castle. There's good reason that Haydarpasa, which was built on wooden piles, looks as though it were cherry-picked out of Mitteleuropa. It was a gift from Germany's Kaiser Wilhelm II to the Ottoman sultan at the height of the alliance between the two empires. Built in 1908 by two German architects, Otto Ritter and Helmut Conu, it has stained-glass windows, turrets and a grandiosity typical of the neo-renaissance that was in vogue in Germany at the time. Haydarpasa was where passengers clambered aboard for services to Baghdad and Damascus.

Germany had helped the Ottoman Empire get its books in order at the turn of the century and, in return for the gift of Haydarpasa, Germany got a rail route direct to the East. But the Ottoman Turks would get dragged into a German war that would cost the sultans their empire.

Haydarpasa itself was troubled from the start. On opening night a fire ripped through the building. During the First World War it was used as an armoury until an act of sabotage caused it to blow up, and it lay as rubble until it was rebuilt in the 1930s after Turkey had become a republic.

Haydarpasa stayed in service even after a Romanian oil tanker exploded offshore in 1979, a major roof fire in 2010 and several botched restoration jobs. But it couldn't keep up with the march of progress. When work commenced on improving the Marmaray commuter rail line in 2014, the clattering cabin doors in the station fell silent.

Occasionally, news of its rain-sodden roof being restored back to life are welcomed but proposals to turn it into a hotel or a shopping centre are met with much resistance. Turks are attached to the idea that Haydarpasa, as a genteel slice of Germania on the Bosphorus, should remain the public, non-commercialised space it always was.

. . . .

14.
RKO Studios
Los Angeles

. . . .

All that's left of what was once a world-famous film studio is a faded symbol of a globe – a reminder of Hollywood's starring role in the American dream.

. . . .

"The building on the corner of Gower and Melrose was once the jewel in the crown of one of the world's finest film production studios. The home of 'King Kong' and 'Citizen Kane'"

The pavement outside 5555 Melrose Avenue in Los Angeles isn't the most picturesque of locations. There's no shade from the scorching Californian sun and there's the constant hum of traffic speeding by. But this spot is of great historical importance to the city: the building on the corner of Gower and Melrose was once the jewel in the crown of one of the world's finest film production studios. The home of *King Kong*, *Citizen Kane*, Fred Astaire and Ginger Rogers. There's one major clue remaining and to find it, you need to look up.

At the intersection of the two tall studio walls joining at this corner sits a large blue globe. It's one of the few remnants left behind by RKO Pictures, the once mighty Hollywood studio that occupied this site for decades. If we were to walk this corner during Hollywood's golden age, the walls would be adorned with rows of posters advertising the studio's films, beneath a set of giant art deco letters spelling "RKO". And rising high above the globe would be the familiar radio tower. That flashing beacon was once as familiar to filmgoers as MGM's roaring lion.

Today the globe remains but the RKO tower is gone. Yet if you take a few steps down Melrose Avenue, you'll find another famed production house. As the RKO era faded, the studio's neighbour Paramount Pictures purchased its backlot and tore down the dividing wall.

Passing through Paramount's famous archway is to literally step inside US cinematic history. It was here that Norma Desmond paid an unexpected visit to Cecil B DeMille in the classic film *Sunset Boulevard*. The soundstage where much of that film was shot is signposted in tribute.

Paramount's backlot is still a thriving production house. Prop couriers carefully transport all manner of weird and wonderful objects. Small cars whiz past, ferrying production staff from one set to the next. And it's not uncommon to bump into screen stars hard at work on their next top-secret project.

Much of what made Hollywood the home of the American dream is little more than a faded symbol and people will often tell you that this city only exists on the screen. But when you're standing on this street corner, the myth of the films feels within an arm's reach.

"London Zoo has a tradition of commissioning great architects to make animal homes that fail to meet their clients' needs"

15.
Casson Pavilion
London

. . . .

The elephant and rhino house at London Zoo is a great example of brutalist mid-century architecture. It's a shame no one told the elephants.

. . . .

It's a handsome London home where no one has lived – and it was never intended that anyone would ever live here. It's a home, you see, that was built for elephants and their friends, the rhinos.

The elephant and rhino house in London Zoo was designed by Sir Hugh Casson and put in situ between 1962 and 1965. And, just as postwar architects were experimenting with brutalist creations for people (some more successfully than others), so Casson decided that elephants might rather enjoy a pen made in the same bold, austere style.

If you want to see the pavilion you don't even need to pay the entrance fee. Like much of the zoo, it's visible to anyone strolling in neighbouring Regent's Park. And this sneaky peak is highly recommended, not as a money-saving tip but because it's one of those urban moments that give you a frisson of excitement in the midst of a mundane day. There you are, out for a run or walking the dog, and out of the corner of your eye you suddenly see a tiger flash past burning bright or a macaw flying into view.

Now, while the architecture says much about the postwar era's passion for modernity, it says much less about Casson's understanding of an elephant's needs and their lack of interest in being given cool homes to live in. He encased the building in rough, rippled concrete – reminiscent of an elephant's skin – but this didn't impress the giant animals that found themselves trapped in the rather tiny and unsuitable lair. Luckily, zoo managers came to realise this and the elephants and rhinos have long since been moved to the greener pastures of a sister zoo outside London.

Indeed, London Zoo has a tradition of commissioning great architects to make animal homes that fail to meet their clients' needs. The original Penguin Pool, for example, was designed in the 1930s by Berthold Lubetkin and, while it has been celebrated in design circles, it turned out that its ribbons of swirling concrete promenades hurt the penguins' feet. They have now waddled to a less sleek but more pleasurable home within the complex called Penguin Beach.

But as you look at the elephant house (AKA the Casson Pavilion) it's clear that it deserves celebrating; even as a sculptural folly it's rather beautiful. Casson's design, with its cluster of concrete cylinders or towers, is meant to conjure up an image of elephants at a watering hole, with their trunks represented by green lanterns that sit on top of the structure.

In fact, it's so handsome that it would make a rather nice human home – if you could cope with a whiffy camel as your neighbour.

16.
Maat
Lisbon
. . . .

Some buildings have the power to transform not just the way a place looks but the way it sees itself. Maat has done just that.
. . . .

In the past 20 years, two projects have arguably done more to popularise the appeal of urban renewal than any other. They're two projects that have been aspired to, emulated and plagiarised by city-planners the world over.

We are, of course, talking about the Guggenheim Bilbao and the High Line. These two structures have become benchmarks for how to turn a place around. Their names are regularly combined with the word "effect" to describe a desired outcome, as in "our building will have the Guggenheim effect". But there's another project that's doing rather well too. Maat – the Museum of Art, Architecture and Technology – on the banks of the Tagus river in Lisbon.

Opened in October 2016, it's the work of the British architect Amanda Levete, whose style is more of the sinuous, shimmering and organic variety than modernist right-angles. And that's what she gave Lisbon, a building that stretches like a sunbather (or maybe a breaking wave or a ship) along the river bank.

Covered in thousands of angular white tiles, it looks different in every light. It's a building for the Instagram age and many of the people who flock here pose for a snap on its steps and then leave in search of a *pastel de nata*, never even making it to the giftshop.

Maat has become a city emblem, a reflection of Lisbon's transformation into a place embracing modernity by being the home of all things tech. The building has also inspired pride. Every taxi driver or local will ask what you think of it – and tell you how great it is.

This stretch of river in Belém has other monuments to certain eras, including the Padrão dos Descobrimentos (or Monument to the Discoveries). When it was built in the 1960s by the dictator Salazar, this structure was also an attempt to instil pride and revitalise the area. But it's a less brazen piece of architecture that has won the day – and planners the world over may well soon be talking about the "Maat effect".

17.
Daily News Building
New York
. . . .

The Daily News Building in New York harks back to the golden age of newspaper journalism (and superheroes).
. . . .

It's an evening like any other outside 220 East 42nd Street in midtown Manhattan. A young, mild-mannered journalist is leaving the office for the day, through the *Daily News* building's shimmering bronze revolving door.

As he strolls along the busy sidewalk, he notices some commotion. Everyone's eyes appear to be gazing up at the sky, fixed upon – not a bird and not a plane either.

The young reporter glances up at the peak of the News building to find a helicopter dangerously perched at the roof's edge with a young woman dangling precariously from her seat belt. He makes a swift dash for the revolving door and, in a flash and a blur, transforms himself into the Man of Steel. Superman.

Before it was immortalised in 1978's *Superman* as the headquarters of Clark Kent's fictional newspaper, the *Daily Planet,* New York's Daily News Building had stood proudly for nearly 50 years as one of the city's most spectacular monuments to the craft of journalism. When plans for the building

"Back then, this section of Manhattan was unpopular and few ambitious architects would have seen a prime opportunity to develop a skyscraper"

were put in place in the late 1920s, architect Raymond Hood had already won acclaim for his 1924 design of Chicago's Tribune Tower. That same year he began work on New York's American Radiator Building with a design that was, ironically, based upon Eliel Saarinen's unsuccessful bid for the Tribune Tower.

Back then, this section of Manhattan was fairly unpopular and few ambitious architects would have seen a prime opportunity to develop a skyscraper. But the *Daily News* had just surpassed one million in circulation and needed somewhere to house all those printing presses.

The *Daily News* is no longer based here but the short walk from Grand Central Terminal, the Chrysler Building and the UN Headquarters hasn't changed much. The News building's revolving door is a reminder of the grand, optimistic age of newspaper journalism. Look up and you'll see a bas-relief depicting a skyscraper reaching for the heavens on top of the words, "He made so many of them", part of a quote attributed to Abraham Lincoln. Look higher and you'll spot the windows affixed with dark, contrasting panels below a series of art deco details.

But gazing all the way up the building might at first provoke confusion. It does appear suspiciously shorter than in the 1978 film. That's because, through the alchemy of optical effects, the height of the building was doubled in the film, adding extra drama to Superman's first reveal during that famous helicopter sequence. Interior scenes of the *Daily Planet*'s lobby were actually shot here too.

The world's largest indoor globe still moves in its eternal rotation, hovering above a series of glass panels depicting the distance between the Earth, sun and stars.

Raymond Hood's later project took him higher still with the Rockefeller Center, though he died before its completion. But his legacy? Well, that still lingers throughout the streets of New York. You need only look up.

18.
Pavements
Global

It's not just about grand buildings, skyscrapers and monuments. Next time you're out, watch your feet.

If you look down at your feet while you're out and about, you'll see some powerful city branding: pavements.

On the Greek island of Mykonos, one of the most handsome distractions is the main town with its labyrinth of narrow alleyways lined with bars, boutiques and restaurants. But, as on other islands, one of the other elements that lets you know you're in Greece is the pavement. Locals paint a series of white lines and swirls like a layer of lace over the stones. The reason seems to be some sort of territorial claim – this space belongs to my house, our alley – so the patterns morph and change, if ever so subtly, to demarcate and divide. But whatever the origins, it's one of the small pieces of urban branding that delivers a real sense of place.

It's the same in the Lusophone world. Whether you're in Rio de Janeiro, Lisbon or the Azores, you'll see something that unites the Portuguese as much as a *pastel de nata*. Calçada Portuguesa consists of small squares of grey and white stones that form patterns and pictures. The late celebrated Brazilian landscape designer Roberto Burle Marx used it to decorate the promenade along Copacabana beach in a wavy pattern. One glimpse of that ripple and you know you're in Rio.

Even in London it pays to take notice of your tootsies. The pavements may not be made of gold but the large flagstones, often made from Purbeck stone, are things of beauty. Many have been in situ for hundreds of years and it's been known for thieves to do away with the finer examples. Of course, cheap concrete has come into play but still in the old slab style. Elsewhere you can see granite cobblestones, known as setts.

You'll have to look a little harder to find another flooring material that was once common in the UK capital: wooden blocks. But no matter. It's those big stone slabs glistening with rain that let you know you're in the London of Mary Poppins.

So wherever you are in the world, remember to look down. There's a whole world at your feet.

19.
Oslo City Hall
Oslo

. . . .

Austere on the outside, garish on the inside, Oslo's eccentric city hall is nonetheless much-loved. But it hasn't always been so popular.

. . . .

"Today it's one of the city's most popular landmarks and even known affectionately in these parts as the 'brunost', or brown cheese (a delicacy, apparently)"

Imagine you're zipping across the waters of Oslofjord on a morning ferry. If you cast your eyes towards the Norwegian capital you'll see a peculiar sight. Rising skywards between the medieval Akershus Fortress and the shiny Tjuvholmen peninsula are two brown towers, like upended Jenga blocks. That's Oslo's Radhuset, or city hall.

If the sun is shining the building looks a russet red but the prevailing clouds here mean that it usually takes on a darker, earthier shade of brown. Draw closer and you may hear the carillon bells chiming from the east tower.

Oslo's blocky, brick-built city hall may host the annual Nobel Peace Prize ceremony each December but its own history is one of conflict and acrimony. First mooted in 1931, the construction was delayed by war until 1950, when it finally opened to coincide with the city's 900th birthday. Many were dismissive, others unsure and some openly appalled by the structure they found themselves lumped with.

As you approach the ornate wooden doors of its entrance the building's rectangular simplicity gives way to a mishmash of imagery, art and sculpture, from fountains and bas-reliefs to wooden carvings and a grandiose, gold-trimmed astrological clock. A series of wooden carvings on the edifice depict Norway's history in images of medieval knights and pastoral scenes, bellicose Norse gods vanquishing wolves or duelling with dragons.

Next to a bay window on the building's east side is a sculpture of a well-dressed man and woman standing side by side. As you turn the corner, however, you see that the woman is holding hands with another, decidedly less swish-looking lover. It's a playful nod to the plot of the novel *Albertine* by Christian Krohg that was published and banned in the 1880s. It's a wry, charming and revealing piece that shows there was humour and wit in the building's construction, and it's one aspect of this initially despised gem that began winning Oslovians over.

Inside the hulking brown building, the main hall is decked out with garish murals depicting scenes intended to galvanise an image of Norwegian nationhood. The eastern wall tells the story of the Norwegian resistance during the Second World War, while the back panel hosts Henrik Sørensen's

vivid depiction of various defining moments from Norway's past. The picture is arresting, action-packed and bold (its title, "Work, Administration and Celebration", is less exciting).

The peculiar building is a beguiling place to explore. At once bold and modern, its design and decoration are a statement of Oslo's struggles to forge its postwar identity – Oslo was under Swedish rule until 1905 and still called Kristiania until 1925.

Although initially decried and denigrated, the boldness of the structure has finally come good. Today it's one of the city's most popular landmarks and even known affectionately in these parts as the *brunost*, or brown cheese (a delicacy, apparently). The city hall has become an unlikely symbol of civic pride.

Oslo is a very different place from when its Radhuset was inaugurated in 1950, and even more different from when it was dreamed up in the early 1930s. Today the fjord city is one of Europe's fastest-growing hubs and its coffers have been swollen by the discovery of offshore oil in 1979.

As the sun dips and your ferry chugs away from Pipervika harbour, in the shadow of this remarkable building, it's strange to think that it has never been more relevant and central to the identity of the city that had to learn to love it.

20.
Pirelli Tower
Milan
. . . .

Despite a number of recent pretenders, the Pirelli Tower remains Milan's leading lady.
. . . .

Compared with Rome and Venice, Milan is no showy good-looker. The city often gets knocked for being a bit drab and its allure is decidedly more subtle. Yet locals do know a thing or two about beauty – after all, the country's fashion and design industries are based here. Residents are also known for pushing the creative envelope. One of the city's proudest sons was Gio Ponti, the architect who bequeathed Milan with a building that has become almost as well known as the city's dazzling Duomo.

Affectionately called Il Pirellone (The Big Pirelli), the 127-metre-high tower was Italy's tallest building when it was finished in 1958. It also broke with local tradition by surpassing in height the statue of the Virgin Mary that perches atop the highest spire of the Duomo.

The Pirelli Tower, which greets travellers who emerge from the city's main train station, was commissioned by the Pirelli family (of tyre-making fame) and work on it commenced in the 1950s. Alberto Pirelli commissioned Ponti to design a US-style skyscraper that would be a symbol of corporate success and a catalyst for the economic prosperity that was taking root in Italy.

Ponti's design shunned the standard block-form and instead opted for a bold, structural skeleton that's visible from the outside. As slender as a supermodel, its width is a mere 18.5 metres. It boasts a smooth curtain wall façade and tapered sides like the bow of a ship. Given its svelte shape, Ponti envisioned that the structure would be susceptible to winds and so turned to one of the foremost structural engineers, Pier Luigi Nervi, an expert in reinforced concrete.

On the inside, the tower is as functional as it is beautiful. With its centrally located corridors and lifts, it lends itself perfectly to busy corporate life. Ponti even added moveable partitions on every floor to accommodate more staff over time.

The designer referred to his work in the feminine: "She is so beautiful that I'd love to marry her." And he wasn't the building's only admirer. It appeared in the opening credits of Michelangelo Antonioni's 1961 film *La Notte*. In Manhattan, architects of the soon-to-be-built Pan Am building took inspiration from her form.

In recent years a flurry of awkward tall buildings have sprouted in Milan. But none can steal the spotlight from this graceful skyscraper that remains the locals' favourite.

21.
Sydney Opera House
Sydney
. . . .

Preposterously beautiful and instantly recognisable, the Sydney Opera House's struggle to come into being against all the odds is a true inspiration.
. . . .

"It's hard to say whether the Opera House has been architecturally influential. Just as nothing looked like it before, nothing has looked like it since"

Sydney's most recognisable trademark could easily not have happened. Or it could have looked entirely different – and entirely less beautiful.

The design, by Danish architect Jørn Utzon, was the winner of an international competition in 1957 and building began in 1959. The years between then and its opening in 1973 were a nightmare of budget blowouts, engineering difficulties, public scepticism and the bitter resignation of Utzon in 1966.

It's hard to say whether the Opera House has been architecturally influential. Just as nothing looked like it before, nothing has looked like it since. Even Utzon himself, one of only two architects to have seen their work awarded Unesco World Heritage status in their own lifetimes, never conjured anything quite so astonishing again. Either way, the Opera House is arguably unique as an arts venue in that its outward appearance may be more culturally influential, and inspirational, than any event it has ever staged.

CITIES ARE GOOD FOR YOU

Acknowledgements

CHAPTER EDITING:

Cities in focus
Andrew Tuck

Essays and comments
Marie-Sophie Schwarzer

Leisure and pleasure
Chiara Rimella

On the move
Matt Alagiah
Melkon Charchoglyan

Urban heroes
Mikaela Aitken
Megan Gibson

How to live
Jamie Waters

Where we work
Andrew Tuck

City rules
Nolan Giles

Culture capitals
Marie-Sophie Schwarzer
Robert Bound

Shop, eat, stay
Josh Fehnert

Tall stories
Carlota Rebelo
Andrew Tuck

The Monocle Guide to Building Better Cities
EDITOR
Andrew Tuck

DESIGNERS
Kate McInerney
Loi Xuan Ly
Maria Hamer
Giulia Tugnoli

PHOTO EDITORS
Matthew Beaman
Shin Miura
Victoria Cagol

Monocle
EDITOR IN CHIEF
& CHAIRMAN
Tyler Brûlé

EDITOR
Andrew Tuck

CREATIVE DIRECTOR
Richard Spencer Powell

BOOKS EDITOR
Joe Pickard

ASSOCIATE EDITOR
Chloë Ashby

WRITER
Melkon Charchoglyan

DESIGNERS
Kate McInerney
Loi Xuan Ly
Maria Hamer
Giulia Tugnoli

PHOTO EDITORS
Matthew Beaman
Shin Miura
Victoria Cagol

PRODUCTION
Jacqueline Deacon
Dan Poole
Rachel Kurzfield
Sean McGeady
Sonia Zhuravlyova

Writers:
Mikaela Aitken
Matt Alagiah
Liam Aldous
Elna Nykänen Andersson
Gal Barnea
Julian Bohne
Michael Booth
Kimberly Bradley
Jessica Bridger
Tyler Brûlé
Petri Burtsov
Ivan Carvalho
James Chambers
Melkon Charchoglyan
Guy De Launey
Clare Dowdy
Zach Dundas
Lucinda Elliott
Josh Fehnert
Peter Firth
Megan Gibson
Nolan Giles
Joleen Goffin
Sophie Grove
Kenji Hall
Daphné Hézard
Morten Hjortshøj
Daphne Karnezis
Imogen Kimber
Will Kitchens
Alexei Korolyov
Kati Krause
Bill Leuty
Tomos Lewis
Kurt Lin
Christopher Lord
Trish Lorenz
Alan Maskin
Tristan McConnell
Charles McFarlane
Blaine Merker
Ricardo Moreno
Tom Morris
Debbie Papyn
Anna Frances Pearson
David Plaisant
Lizzie Porter
Venetia Rainey
Carlota Rebelo
Chiara Rimella
Gwen Robinson
Ben Rylan
Laura Rysman

Jack Sallabank
Clarissa Sebag-Montefiore
Marie-Sophie Schwarzer
Ed Stocker
Jason Strother
Junichi Toyofuku
Andrew Tuck
Clair Urbahn
Jamie Waters
Julia Wick
Fiona Wilson
Joshua Yaffa
Zayana Zulkiflee

Photographers:
Cedric Arnold
Alex Atack
Simon Bajada
Chris Baker
Fritz Beck
Peter Bohler
Jamie Bowering
Lorne Bridgman
Felix Brüggemann
Rodrigo Cardoso
François Cavalier
Jesse Chehak
Terence Chin
Alexander Coggin
Silvia Conde
Dustin Condren
Alex Cretey Systermans
Ana Cuba
Daniel Dorsa
Evelyn Dragan
Ike Edeani
Thomas Ekström
David Engelhardt
Luigi Fiano
Stephanie Fuessenich
Stefan Fürtbauer
Gianfranco Gallucci
Víctor Garrido
Daniel Gebhart De Koekkoek
Julia Grassi
Luca Grottoli
Lindsay Lauckner Gundlock
Tan Hai Han
Tina Hillier
Alexi Hobbs
Monika Höfler
James Horan
Thomas Humery
Evgeniy Ivanov

Lara Jacinto
Rachel Kara
Lek Kiatsirikajorn
Jörg Koopmann
Juho Kuva
Romain Laprade
Jason Larkin
Åke E:son Lindman
Lit Ma
Ana Mello
Thomas Meyer
Conny Mirbach
Shin Miura
Ye Rin Mok
Manuel Nieberle
Anna Nielsen
Felix Odell
Krzysztof Pacholak
Fran Parente
Jun Michael Park
Nathan Perkel
Maciek Pozoga
Jussi Puikkonen
Ben Quinton
Tuca Reinés
Faye Sakura Rentoule
Pilar Rubí
Claudio Sabatino
Gesi Schilling
Jens Schwarz
Gareth Sobey
Mark Sommerfeld
Jan Søndergaard
Ryan Stone
Kohei Take
Marc Tan
Luis Tato
Taro Terasawa
Polly Tootal
Brad Torchia
Albert Vecerka
David de Vleeschauwer
Francesca Volpi
Jake Walters
Graham Walzer
Weston Wells
Adam Wilson
Marcel Wogram
Andrea Wyner
Keita Yamamoto
Vasantha Yogananthan
Marvin Zilm

Images:
Alamy
Kenta Hasegawa
Getty Images
K Kopter
Tom Mannion
Eric Pamies
Rex/Shutterstock
Siebe Swart
Joshua White
Ketsiree Wongwan

Illustrators:
Ryo Kaneyasu
Motiejus Vaura

Research
Dan Einav
Audrey Fiodorenko
Will Kitchens
Paige Reynolds
Jonathan Whitfield

Special thanks
Mikaela Aitken
Louise Banbury
Pete Kempshall
Carlota Rebelo
Amy Richardson
Rachel Sampson

Index

About Monocle

In 2007, MONOCLE was launched as a monthly magazine briefing on global affairs, business, design and more. Today we have a thriving print business, a radio station, shops, cafés, books, films and events. At our core is the simple belief that there will always be a place for a brand that is committed to telling fresh stories, delivering good journalism and being on the ground, around the world.

We're London-based and have bureaux in Hong Kong, Tokyo, Zürich and Toronto, with Bangkok and LA on the horizon. Over the years our editors and correspondents have come to understand what makes a great city – and what stops one hitting its stride. This knowledge is unpacked in this book and throughout our reporting on Monocle 24, in film at *monocle.com* and, of course, across all our print products.

1
Monocle magazine
MONOCLE magazine is published 10 times a year, including two bumper double issues (July/August and December/January). We also have three annual specials: THE FORECAST, THE ESCAPIST and THE MONOCLE DRINKING & DINING DIRECTORY. Look out for our seasonal weekly newspapers too, which cover everything from politics to fashion.

Quality of life
Every summer Monocle publishes a Quality of Life Survey that names the best cities in the world to call home. Join the debate.

2
Monocle 24 radio
Monocle 24 is our round-the-clock internet radio station that was launched in 2011. It delivers global news and shows covering foreign affairs, urbanism, business, culture, food and drink, design and print media. You can listen live at *monocle.com/radio* or download via iTunes, SoundCloud or from our own site.

The Urbanist
The Urbanist is a show presented by MONOCLE's Andrew Tuck about all the elements that make – or break – a city. Featuring everything from debates on high-rise living to how restaurants shape neighbourhoods.

3
Monocle Café and Kioskafé
We don't just write about hospitality and great service. We also have cafés in Tokyo, London and Zürich serving excellent coffee, breakfasts and lunches. And if you're passing through London's Paddington, be sure to visit our pioneering newsstand and coffee shop: Kioskafé.

4
Books
Since 2013, MONOCLE has been publishing a series of large-format books – like the one you are reading now – together with Gestalten. Across the editions you can find out how to build a business that flourishes, what makes a nation tick, how to get yourself a cosy home and which hotels are our favourites in the world.

5
Travel guides
There are now more than 30 guide books to take you from Sydney and Los Angeles to London and Kyoto. Each will, of course, recommend where to stay, eat and drink but these guides also take time to reveal how each city works and the urban details that make it special. They will tell you about a city's architecture, the elements that make up its branding and its top urbanist projects; these themes are also picked up in the essays chapter. Discover how to both let loose and get the deep-dive on each metropolis too.

6
Monocle shop
MONOCLE has a series of permanent shops that act as mini-embassies – you can find the retail team behind the counter in Tokyo, Toronto, London, Merano and Hong Kong – and we also run a series of seasonal shops. As well as all the books, you'll find products made by brands we like and inspiring manufacturers. Drop by and say hello (for the full line-up, and our online shop, head to *monocle.com*).

Join us

There are lots of ways to be part of the ever-expanding MONOCLE world, whether in print, online or on the radio. We'd love to have you on board.

1.
Read the magazine
You can buy MONOCLE at newsstands in more than 60 countries around the world – or get an annual subscription at *monocle.com/subscribe*.

2.
Listen to Monocle 24
You can tune into Monocle 24 radio live via our free app, at *monocle.com* or on any internet-enabled radio. You can also download our shows as podcasts from iTunes or SoundCloud to stay informed as you travel from nation to nation.

3.
Subscribe to the Monocle Minute
Sign up today at *monocle.com* to receive the Monocle Minute, our free daily news-and-views email. Our website is also where you will find a world of free films, our online shop and regular updates about everything we're up to.

Thank you